DATE DUE

Accountancy in Transition

Edited by Richard P. Brief, NEW YORK UNIVERSITY

A GARLAND SERIES

Accounting in England and Scotland: 1543–1800

B. S. Yamey
H. C. Edey
Hugh W. Thomson

Garland Publishing, Inc.
New York & London   1982

Library of Congress Cataloging in Publication Data

Yamey, Basil S.
  Accounting in England and Scotland, 1543-1800.

  (Accountancy in transition)
  Reprint. Originally published: London : Sweet & Maxwell,
1963.
  Bibliography: p.
  Includes index.
  1. Accounting—England—History—Addresses, essays,
lectures. 2. Accounting—Scotland—History—Addresses,
essays, lectures. I. Edey, Harold C. II. Thomson,
Hugh W. III. Title. IV. Series.
HF5616.G7Y35 1982   657'.0941   82-48374
ISBN 0-8240-5332-X

The volumes in the series are printed on acid-free,
250-year-life paper.

Printed in the United States of America

Accounting in England
and Scotland: 1543–1800

AUSTRALIA

The Law Book Co. of Australasia Pty Ltd.
Sydney : Melbourne : Brisbane

INDIA

N. M. Tripathi Private Ltd.
Bombay

ISRAEL

Steimatzky's Agency Ltd.
Tel Aviv

NEW ZEALAND

Sweet & Maxwell (N.Z.) Ltd.
Wellington

PAKISTAN

Pakistan Law House
Karachi

Accounting in England and Scotland: 1543–1800

Double Entry in Exposition and Practice

BY

B. S. YAMEY, B.Com.,

Professor of Economics,
London School of Economics and Political Science,
University of London

H. C. EDEY, B.Com., F.C.A.,

Professor of Accounting,
London School of Economics and Political Science,
University of London

HUGH W. THOMSON

Librarian, Institute of Chartered Accountants
in England and Wales

LONDON

SWEET & MAXWELL

1963

Published in 1963 by
Sweet & Maxwell Limited of
11 New Fetter Lane London
and printed in Great Britain
by The Eastern Press Limited
of London and Reading

Foreword

WITHIN a few years of the grant of the Royal Charter in 1880, the Institute of Chartered Accountants in England and Wales began to collect early books on accounting, both in English and in other languages. Many of the books from which extracts appear, or which are otherwise referred to, in the following pages, were listed in the catalogues published in 1903 and 1913. In December 1913 the Kheil collection of over 1,600 books was purchased; of these books only about 200 are in the British Museum. Important subsequent additions have been the Dutch edition of Ympyn of 1543 (purchased in 1933), Carpenter's *Most Excellent Instruction*, 1632, and Dafforne's *Apprentices Time Entertainer*, 1640 (both purchased in 1957).

More recently two further purchases have brought into the Institute's collection all the works of Luca Pacioli, whose encyclopedia of mathematics, *Summa de Arithmetica*, published in 1494, included the first exposition of double entry bookkeeping to be printed. One of these purchases was his *De Divina Proportione* in which he propounded the theory that there is a divine proportion in all things, particularly in art, architecture and typography. The other was his translation of Euclid, also published in 1509.

As a past chairman of the Institute's Library Committee, I acquired some familiarity with, and a great admiration and affection for, this matchless collection of early books on accounting. It therefore gives me particular pleasure, as President of the Institute, to have the opportunity of welcoming this work of scholarship and research.

PERCY F. CARPENTER, F.C.A.
President, the Institute of Chartered
Accountants in England and Wales.

Moorgate Place,
London, E.C.2.

April, 1963.

Preface

THE first book in English on double-entry bookkeeping was published over 400 years ago. It was succeeded by a flow of publications; and what began as a small and intermittent trickle became, by the eighteenth century, a steady and widening stream. The main purpose of this book is to present a selection of extracts from this flow. Part One contains over a hundred extracts from thirty-one books on accounting up to the year 1800 together with one from 1818. The sample is so constituted that it contains, in patch-work as it were, something on each of the different subjects to be found in the modal treatise of the period, as well as something on the more interesting of the less frequently considered topics. We believe that our selection should enable the reader to form a reasonably clear view of what the early authors thought about accounting, and how they described the manner of keeping business accounts. About one-third of the authors included in the selection were engaged in the practice of keeping accounts or in business; the rest were teachers, though some of them were no doubt called upon to help with the keeping or the adjustment of books. It would be difficult on the basis of the extracts alone to distinguish the contributions of the two groups.

In Part One the authors of the treatises speak for themselves. In Part Two we take over. First, there is a survey, by Yamey, of the books in English up to 1800. The accents here are on the main foreign influences on the earliest books, on the subsequent development of home-bred books, and on the misguided attempt of Edward Thomas Jones to replace Italian double entry by a so-called English system. This survey should help the reader to place in context the principal authors represented by extracts in Part One. In the second essay, also by Yamey, eight sets of extant account-books, dating from the seventeenth and eighteenth century, are described in order to throw light on the practice of double entry in that period. This examination suggests that the early treatises are a reliable mirror of contemporary practice, and serves to underline the major differences between the early practice of accounting and that of the present day. Third, we present a bibliography of books in English on accounting up to 1800, prepared by Thomson. The holdings of the libraries of the Institute of Chartered Accountants in England and Wales and of the Institute of Chartered Accountants of Scotland are separately distinguished. The bibliography does not pretend to be complete, especially in the entries after 1700. But we believe that it is more complete than any previous listing; and we hope that it may serve as a solid foundation for further work.

In preparing this book we enjoyed the good fortune of having access to the incomparable resources of the Library of the Institute of Chartered Accountants in England and Wales. We also wish to acknowledge the generous co-operation of Miss Dunlop, Librarian of the Institute of Chartered Accountants of Scotland.

We acknowledge the courtesy of the following in granting us permission to include photographic reproductions of illustrative materials: Blairs College, Aberdeen, for Plates II and III; The Trustees of the British Museum, for Plates IV and V; The Essex Record Office, for Plates XII, XIII, XIV, XV and XVI; The Librarian, Guildhall Library, Corporation of London, for Plates VIII, IX and XI; The Council of the Institute of Chartered Accountants in England and Wales, for Plates I and VI; The Earl of Aylesford and the Kent County Council, for Plate X; and The Goldsmiths' Librarian, University of London, for Plate VII.

We are also indebted to the Editors of *Accountancy* and *The Accounting Review* for permission to use material published in their respective journals (see p. 180, n. 1).

Contents

Contents

List of Plates

Part One

EXTRACTS FROM BOOKS ON ACCOUNTING

THE extracts are grouped into fifteen sections on the basis of their main themes. It will be apparent that several of the extracts would fit equally well into more than one section.

Titles of books are given in abbreviated form, the date indicating the edition which has been used. More detailed titles are given in the Bibliography (pp. 202 *et seq.*).

Spelling and punctuation are reproduced as in the originals, except that, for the earliest books, where appropriate the letters 'i' and 'j', and 'u' and 'v', have been distinguished as in modern usage, and constructions like 'writtō' printed as 'writton'; and obvious printing errors in the later books have been corrected.

Page or chapter references are given, except where neither is in the original. Chapters or self-contained parts of chapters are given in full, except where the contrary is indicated (by starting or finishing the extract with '. . .').

All footnotes are editorial.

The following short glossary may be helpful:

quaterne great book lidger, leger, leager	}	=	ledger
kalendar alphabet, A.B.C.	}	=	index (to ledger)
stock(e)		=	capital
parcel, percell		=	entry, item
company		=	partnership
rest		=	balance, remainder
to sald		=	to balance, make even.

Sources of Extracts

	Extract Numbers
Booth, *Complete System*, 1789	59
Carpenter, *Most Excellent Instruction*, 1632	23, 51, 65, 66
Colinson, *Idea Rationaria*, 1683	3, 30, 76
Cronhelm, *Double Entry by Single*, 1818	111
Dafforne, *Apprentices Time-Entertainer*, 1640	67, 72
Dafforne, *Merchants Mirrour*, 1660	7, 29, 43, 60, 94
Dodson, *Accountant*, 1750	24, 57
Donn, *Accountant*, 1775	48, 55
Dowling, *Complete System*, 1770	39, 47, 85, 89
Fulton, *British-Indian Book-keeping*, 1800	8, 110
Gordon, *Universal Accountant*, 1787	4, 17, 21, 63, 79, 88, 101
Hamilton, *Introduction to Merchandise*, 1788	10, 11, 61, 75, 81, 90, 95, 102, 105, 107

3

The Utility of Accounting

1

(North, *Gentleman Accomptant*, 1715, pp. 1-3.)

The Books of Merchants Accompts are kept in a certain Method, that from the Stile and Form of the Entries, is called *Debitor* and *Creditor*; which Method is so comprehensive and perfect, as makes it worthy to be put among the Sciences, and to be understood by all Virtuosi, whether they ever intend to make use of it or no, even for pure Speculation, Curiosity, or rather Admiration; as happens, when with some Pains we have attained the Knowledge of any Art or Skill, tho' less complex than this; which, thro' the Invention of past Ages, universal Practice, and in Matters of Interest, (the fiercest Engagement of Human Wit and Stratagem) is reduced, as this is, to the strictest Compendium, and (respecting the Intention and Use of it) to a consummate Perfection. I do not know, that any Art practised among Men, is come up to a positive *ne plus ultra*, but that of Accompting. Common Tale, or Reckoning either by Memory, or its faithful Friend the Pen, is no less vulgar, than speaking, or walking; and these two are improved into those difficult Arts of Oratory and Dancing, (captivating Arts indeed, one of Men, and the other of Women) in which those who practise them, outrun one another, and no Limit of Invention is known, thro' which they may be improved; and so of other Arts, which I do not stay to particularize. But the Art of Regular Accompting, or Book-keeping, altho' Useful beyond any, and of infinite Variety, and of which not a few, able enough in other Things, are utterly incapable; yet in Rule and Method is so contracted and circumscribed, that without a Fault, nothing can be rescinded from, or added to it.

If any one shall say, That Regular Accompting is but a judicious Application of Arithmetick to common Business; I answer, That Arithmetick is indeed necessary, and a Dexterity in the Use of it is to be made a *Postulatum* here, as being presupposed: But in Practice, Accompting is an Art of it self distinct; and Arithmetick to Book-keeping, is as Language to Oratory, or as setting one Foot

5

before another, to the Skill of a Dancing-Master. It hath been observed, that some able Merchants, not to seek in the common Practice of Arithmetick, yet have not been able to keep their own Books; but have hired some professed Accomptants to do it for them: And I dare say, a good Geometrician, who by Profession is most capable of knowing the Rules, with the Tendency or Reason of them; yet being put to keep a Set of Books of a diffused Trade, would soon find himself envelop'd in Darkness and Confusion, and that nothing but Trials and Failings, or (in a word) Practice, could adapt him to the Work, which in its Nature is rather Pragmatick, than Analytick.

To justify this Character of Regular Accompting, I need only say, That the Method comprehends all other Methods, which particular Persons have occasionally Instituted, for their own private Concerns; and that all those Methods, whatsoever they are, were, or can be invented, for the Use of any Accompts, are Parts of, and, as it were, taken out of the *Dr.* and *Cr.*; and so much as they want of that, however in private Concerns serviceable enough, just so much want they of desirable Perfection: For the *Dr.* and *Cr.* is pure and perfect right Reason, and contains the whole Material Truth and Justice of all the Dealing, and nothing else; and this not only between the Accompter, and his Traffickers, but also between all the several Traffickers one with another, so far as they have inter-mixed in the Subject-Matter of the Accompts; and not only so, but also of the Incidents, Circumstances, and Consequences of the Traffick, such as Estimates, Losses, or Advantages thereby. And all this in a perpetual State; so as every Question that can be proposed concerning any Dealing, is answered almost as readily as demanded; and no Person can be injured, who takes his Accompt upon the stating of the Books, so far as it runs: And in all Times, even in After-Ages, the Transactions thus duly accompted, will be understood as well, as if the same had been inquisited at the very Instant of the Writing.

2

(Ympyn, *Notable . . . Woorke*, 1547, ch. 29.)

Although that some persones will saie that it should bee to painfull and busy to kepe a reconyng after suche maner as before we have declared because thei are ignorant and understand it not, or els negligent and slouthful and will not learne, and as the old proverbe is, the ignorante hateth learnyng and knowledge for that thei have no felyng nor savor therein : Yet will we declare unto you how many incomodities and displeasures maie come unto hym that diligently and perfightly kepeth not his boke. First it causeth trouble in mynde and disquietnes of body with hinderaunce in substaunce, and causeth the party to freate and fume at his dooynges, and putteth hym self to more pain, in that his reconynges be not just and perfight as his desire is, then that it should have been unto hym ordrely and perfightly to have kept his boke. Secondarely, it is great shame and dishonesty to hym that kepeth not his boke exactly. Thirdely the evill kepyng thereof, so vexeth the body, that it bredeth fevers & deseases : Fourthly it causeth losse, & last of al cometh deth whiche leveth to the worlde all thynges rawly and unperfightly, and causeth some in the place of (God have mercie on his solle) to saie the devill gnawe the bones of hym, and a vengeance on suche a keper of a boke with many other inconveniences. Then the executors deny debtes, and claime more then was dewe : Then crieth out the wife for her parte : The children muste to lawe, and before thei can attain thei muste spende more then their part shall come unto, because it shalbe valued and used at the pleasure of the executors, for that nothyng was plainly kepte nor diligently written : And finally, this onely negligence of kepyng of bokes hath caused more striefe in lawe and variance of children and frendes then any one thyng in the world : Servantes and factors have undone their Masters, riche men hath sodenly become beggers & could not tell how it should come to passe, wranglers and perjured persones have laughed, when the poore and desolate hath wept and cried out, to the perill and daunger of their solles, and hurt and hinderance of them that wer defrauded of their right by their negligence. Now forasmuche as so many daungers and discomodities commeth of the negligent kepyng of reconynges, any reasonable man (consideryng thesame) me thynketh should not judge this maner of reconyng that we have taught to be painfull, but should for the manifolde comodities that it bryngeth be desirous & studious of thesame, for it is the glasse of a mannes state, wherin all men maie se clerely in what case thei stande, and other persones after theim maie perceive in what state thei wer in duryng their lifes, and how thei left all thynges at the houre of death. . . .

3

(Colinson, *Idea Rationaria*, 1683, p. 1.)

Book-keeping hath certainly been practised many ages ago: for wee read of it amongst the Ancient *Romans* in J. Cæsars time; but it is not to be supposed, that it ever arriv'd to the perfection, as now it is. The *Italians* were the first Merchants, wee read of in *Europe*, and first invented this exact way of keeping Accompts, now in use amongst all Nations; which method hath encouraged them to venture their Stocks in Merchandising, and hath brought them to be so potent as many of them are. *Amsterdam* hath been a great nurserie of this Science, since it was brought there: I have known some Merchants in that City, who have payed 4 or 500. Crowns yearly to their Book-keeper. There are several Authors that write upon this subject, every one applying it to the maner of his Nations Trade, and I have done the like to bring it the easier to the comprehension of all my Countrey-men. It is a Science absolutely necessare for all Accomptants, but especially for Merchants, whether their Trade be great or small. And its beyond all peradventure, that an accurate Methode and exact Form hath alwayes been the principal cause of the rise, progresse and Advance of Trade in every Kingdom and State, where it hath been observed and Encouraged. And its obvious to all Considering persons that this honourable and profitable Science of Book-keeping is the only help, that encourages many to joyn their small stocks together, and by so doing, often from a small foundation Erects a most admirable Trade. For the Hollanders *motto* sayes very well, *Concordiâ, res parvæ crescunt.* Certainly Company-accompts are most necessar amongst us, and this is the difficultest part to learn of all the Book-keeping; but what is 2 or 3 Moneths Study for a Merchant of ordinare Capacity, to learn it wholly, or who would want the satisfaction it gives to men of trade, that in ane Instant can see (as he doeth his Person in a mirror) his whole estate and in what posture it is in at the time? If he be fortunate and acquire much, it directs him the way to Imploy it to the best advantage, if he be unfortunate it satisfies the world of his just dealing, and is the fairest and best Apologie of his Innocence and honesty to the World, and Contributes exceedingly to the satisfaction of all his friends and well-wishers, and to the Confutation and silencing of all his malevolent and detracting Enemies, and often proves the great cause to bring him to a most favourable Composition with his Creditors: whereas these that are ignorant of it, in such a Condition are censured by all, when they have nothing to show but bare words to vindicate themselves. It is a laudable custome they have in *Amsterdam* and *Antwerpe* when a Merchant comes to faile, the Magistrats appoint knowing men to search their books, and by them finding they have been direct and just in their dealings, they advise their Creditors to a favourable composition, which the most part consenting to, the rest must follow, by this meanes many recover again and pay their whole debt.

There are two things which are supposed to be the product of this Countrey, the Manufactories and the fishing trade; which are not to be done with one mans stock, but by many: so men are oblidged to joyn in Partnership, which often blowes up with great discord, if they have not a true form to satisfie the Concerned what is become of their stocks; that let their success be what it will, one may not be wronged more then another. Both these trades have been mightily encouraged by the Kings Lawes and his money too, so it is a pitty that want of form should discourage us, which I believe is not the least cause. Mr. *Roberts* sayes in his Map of Commerce,[1] that he who knowes not true Book-keeping and the necessare Arithmetick, let him not assume the name of a Merchant; and how many are there that know little or nothing of it, yet will be compted good Merchants. . . .

4

(Gordon, *Universal Accountant*, 1787, vol. 2, pp. 17–18.)

. . . Whoever considers the business of a merchant, with respect to its variety, extent, or importance, must see, that a faithful register of all his transactions, disposed and arranged in that order, and adjusted with that precision, by which a real state of the whole, or any particular branch, may be at once discovered and laid open, for his own satisfaction or that of others, is absolutely necessary, not only to the welfare and prosperity, but to the very being of his trade.

In the earlier ages of the world, when all accounts were settled by barter on the spot, there was little occasion for accountantship; but by degrees, as intention grew upon experience, conveniencies of

---

[1] Lewes Roberts, *The Merchants Mappe of Commerce*, 1638.

life formerly unknown were produced, and mankind, emulous to excel, gave genius and industry full scope; thus was the use of money, weights, measures, navigation, arts, manufactures, laws, government, credit, correspondence, banks, bills of exchange, &c. introduced and established, and consequently the use of accountantship became obvious and indispensible. It was not, however, carried to its greatest perfection at once; without doubt, as commerce flourished, and credit became more extensive, the method of arranging and adjusting accounts, became likewise by degrees more regular and uniform.

Were we to trace this important science back to its original, we would be naturally led to ascribe the first invention to the first considerable merchants; and there are none who have a fairer claim to precedency in point of time than those of Arabia. The Egyptians, who for many ages made a glorious appearance in the commercial world, derived their first notions of trade from their intercourse with these ingenious people; and, of consequence, from them likewise they must have received their first form of accountantship, which, in the natural way of trade, was communicated to all the cities on the Mediterranean. When the western empire had been over-run by the Barbarians, and all the countries of which it had been composed, took that opportunity of asserting their own independency, commerce fled quickly after liberty; and immediately Italy, which had formerly been the court of the universe, became the seat of trade; to which the ruin of the eastern empire by the Turks, into whose genius or constitution the arts of commerce never entered, did not a little contribute. The business of exchange, by which the Lombards connected all the trading cities of Europe, likewise introduced their method of keeping accounts, by double entry; whence, at this day, it gets the name of *Italian Book-keeping*.

Thus was the knowledge of accountantship diffused, not only throughout Europe, but by degrees through all the trading countries in the world; by which means a happy regularity and uniformity in accounts every where prevailed, public and private credit were extended, correspondence was enlarged, and property ascertained, not only among merchants, but all other ranks and degrees of men, from the public revenue to the meanest private business; for such is the peculiar excellency of this art, that the accounts of nations can be as easily adjusted thereby, as those of a merchant, it being as readily applied to millions, as hundreds of pounds. . . .

5

(Quin, *Rudiments of Book-keeping*, 1779, p. 153.)

. . . I shall conclude with observing, that it is a *proverb* among the Dutch, " That none can be poor who keep their books correctly." By this they understand, that if the necessary regularity in keeping accounts is observed; as a man can tell at one view whether his manner of living is suited to his fortune, he will consequently be enabled to form a proper medium for adjusting his expenses to his income, by which means he may be guarded against extravagance, and the evil consequences of intemperance; from which flow so many vices, destructive of domestic tranquility. By attending to this salutary maxim, there is no doubt but those who adopt it will reap the fruits of their labour, and find themselves well rewarded for the care they have taken to walk in the paths of *moral rectitude*.

Double Entry and Other Systems of Accounting

6

(Monteage, *Debtor and Creditor*, 1675, preface.)

. . . Now to commend the Way [2] it self to him who is wholly Ignorant; consider, that it gives thee a View of the Increase or Decay of thy Stock: And at all times, if thou keepest thy *Leidger* duely entred, it sets before thee the true state of every Mans Account with thee, and thy Account with them. It will be here objected, That we need not have recourse to this Way, to come to the knowledge of every Mans 'Account, in regard that every Person who keeps Accounts, hath that in his Intention. To this I answer: I confess there are Account-books kept by most Traders, either in Whole-sale, or Retail, and they frame Accounts of *Debtor and Creditor* in them, such as they be: I have observed several of them thus; they have their Book of Goods bought, another of Goods sold, a third of Mens Accounts upon Trust, a fourth a *Cash-book*, besides others according to every mans particular Fancy; which Books have little dependance each one to th'other, as a Merchants *Wast-book*, *Journal* and *Leidger* have; save that, perhaps their *Cash-book* is posted, placed or divided to every one of these in its several branches, *viz.* Part of the Receipts of *Cash* to the Book of Sales; the residue of their Receipts perhaps (in that it concerns nothing of their Shop-Trade, but of Rents, or Moneys borrowed, or left in their hands;) all this they keep no account of, neither is it posted any where. Then for the payments of *Cash*, they are in part posted to the Book of Goods bought; the residue being Repayments of Money lent them, or Money expended, they take no notice of, so as to carry it or place it to any Account: And so when they have payd any man in full, they cross that Account; and when they are payd by any of their Chapmen, they cross this Account also. And this is their track, whereby the Beauty of their Books is turned to Deformity; and then what *balance* can they bring these Books to?

---

[2] The " Way " is double entry.

None at all. Perhaps at the Years end they will cast up their Shop, together with their Books of Buying and Selling, putting the one against the other, and so make an Estimate of their Stock: Perhaps they have omitted one or more Debts on either side, or they have not duly estimated the unposted part of their Receipts or Payments; and so in their Minds or Apprehensions, they find a difference in their *balance* from their Expectation; for they find but so much Profit, and they made account of this and that, which makes them go over and over again with their Worke, every time producing perhaps a different View; for the Ground-work being laid uncertain, the Superstructure must also needs prove confused: They reckon this gained on such a Commodity, and that profited by another, which is not so: And thus by reason they keep not a particular Account of *Profit and Loss*, they distract and confound themselves, and vainly spend their precious Time and Thoughts, when they think to make a *Balance*.

But to the next Benefit: This Way of accounting which we Treat of, carries with it its own proof: And here lies the supreme Excellency and Usefulness of this mystery: For as in the foregoing Section I gave a hint of Shop-keepers and unlearned Accountants Confusion and Uncertainty, so on the contrary, they that put in a due practice this way (commonly called *Italian Book-keeping*) are or may be ever at a certainty, which the other are not, nor cannot attain to. For I may speak it without *Hyperbole*, that it is impossible for us, in this Way to erre so, as not with an ordinary Labour and Capacity to set all to rights again; upon this Maxim, That the Art carries its own Proof; in regard we have all our Concernments lie before us, the one to check the other. Whereas in the several wayes vulgarly used, all is broken, undigested, and without Foundation.

Again, another Utility is this, That as the Method we speak of, is the best of all others, and consequently that which should be altogether in use; There is this in it, That thy Books being duly entred and kept, and thy Transactions or Commerce, be it greater or less, daily posted: Then, after thy decease, thy Heirs and Successors will know how to prove and find out thy Estate with much Facility: Whereas, take the generality of Accountants, First, they all differ in their Forms; The best of them are confused, the others so blotted and blurr'd, so cross'd and raced,[3] that neither Head nor Tail can be discovered: And how many of these, distrusting or

---

[3] Razed, *i.e.*, altered by erasures.

disregarding their own Books, leave them imperfect even in their own spurious wayes, and trust for the most part to their mortal Memories, or loose Papers. Yea many have I known, Persons of great Dealing, taken away by the hand of Death, that questionless (living) had good Estates; being dead, their Widow and Family are turn'd out of all, and outwitted by the crafty surviving *Debtors* or pretended *Creditors*. It is therefore a good Course they take in *Holland*, where if the Husband be the Merchant, the Wife is the Book-keeper. It is incredible, what manifold mischiefs this Irregularity and Ignorance in Accounts hath brought into the World: I have known extreme great errors proceed from this Ignorance; as that a man for keeping no formal Accounts, hath so mistaken the matter, as to sue his Neighbour for considerable summes, and at last the business referr'd to Accountants, he is found considerably indebted to the other: Whereupon it may well be concluded, that he who trusts to his Memory, or scattered Notes, or undistinct Accounts, reckons without his Host. I have likewise heard of some that in policy keep no Books of Accounts, that they may the better make large reckonings to their Correspondents: And here give me leave to tell you, that the Regular Accountant knows not the way of over-reaching, as the wilful ignorant doth; that is, he cannot so likely do it, in regard his Books are his Voucher, and readily manifest how he comes by his Estate, and remain to Posterity to be scanned, to his Praise or Dispraise.

But why do I thus please my self, to entertain my wearied Guests in the Porch, words are but wind, they are effects which the Trading Merchant looks for: The reason of the Art is best seen in the Operation of it. I might inlarge in Arguments taken from the Delightfulness there is in this Method, it bringeth both Ends together (as one may say) and shews a perfect reason of the Increase and Decrease of ones Estate: Also excellent use might accrue by this consideration, that he who daily sees his Accounts fairly and duely kept, knows how to steer the Fly-boat of his Expences, to hoyse or lower his Sails of outgoing, according to Wisdom: Whereas the ungrounded young Merchant reckons at random, goes on and sees not the labyrinth he runs himself into, but at hap-hazard spends prodigally, according to his vain surmize on the one side, of Profit where little or none is; on the other side, of small Expences where they are thick and threefold; and how many are there of these

14

every where (not to speak of such who run on greedily into destruction, by taking more care how to spend and get in debt, than others how to spare and get out of debt,) that by not seeing, are not willing to see and set before them the state of their Affairs, go on in secret decaying of themselves, to the utter undoing of their poor Families? . . .

7

(Dafforne, *Merchants Mirrour*, 1660, p. 4.)

Of needlesse books

This reproveth the keeping of a mans Estate in many Books: as in a Book of Buying, another of Selling, another of Receipts, another of Shipping, and what not? All these Books cannot shew a mans Estate, nor Case of standing with any man, or in any Commodity, untill all matters are drawn to a head upon a paper in form of a Leager; so that they have every way as much trouble in writing their imperfect form, as we in making our work compleat at once: but the generality want capacity to apprehend the manner, and rectifie their own defects: therefore they affect this form but with small affection.

8

(Fulton, *British-Indian Book-keeping*, 1800, pp. 3–5.)

. . . The art of book-keeping has been understood to consist of two branches, or, as they are called, methods; the one denominated *double*, and the other *single entry*. The former method, known also by the name of the *Italian System*, is distinguished by a concise ingenious mode, of rendering one entry in the books equivalent to the purposes of two or more entries by the latter; and as it is founded more immediately on universal principles, and more directly leads to the main design of the art itself than the method by single entry, it is therefore well entitled to the preference it has decidedly obtained; for its supposed intricacy is the only existing bar to its regular and universal adoption: even for accounts of the most limited and simple nature.

The method by single entry (which may truly be defined an imperfect plan, or one that embraces but a part of the accounts of a concern, leaving the remainder to chance) is often, but erroneously, supposed to be the plainest and most concise of the two. At the offset indeed it holds out an alluring appearance to the indolent and uninformed; but the confusion and errors admissible by it, finally teach its votaries to perceive the insufficiency of its principles for the settlement of the crude memorandums (hardly to be called accounts) it has led them to huddle together: and in short, that the effectual principles of double entry, whether known as such or not, must at length be called in to unravel the intricacy of their once favourite, but ultimately acknowledged, prolix and imperfect plan.

Indeed, from the universality of the principles of double entry, it is a difficult matter to form any idea of an account, of whatever nature, unconnected with them; and therefore the distinction here made between the method of double entry, as exclusively applying to the Italian system, and that of single entry, as founded on distinct principles, is rather in deference to custom than in compliance with truth: the author knows not that any plan of single entry exists, adequate of itself to the adjustment of any set of accounts whatsoever. Every man who attempts to keep his books by single entry, and wishes to form a correct account of the state of his affairs, must, as has been above observed, at length resort to the principles of double entry to complete it; that is to say, he must collect all his debits or property, and all his credits or debts payable, and strike the balance between the two; which will shew, as the case may be, either his net stock or net deficiency. The method by double entry does the same, but by a more methodical, and of course more correct process,—all accounts of whatever nature being exhibited by it; whilst every plan of single entry inevitably leaves the collection of a number of accounts to the frailty of memory, or at best to an uncertain estimate: and in this their only essential difference consists. But the method by double entry has another advantage over that of single entry, hitherto perhaps unobserved: it is capable of constantly exhibiting the correct general balance under every alteration the fluctuation of affairs may impose on it; and this too, not only without impediment to the proper progression of the books, but even with greater certainty than heretofore of their progressive exactness. This discovery it will be the chief design of the following work to unfold and explain. . . . [4]

---

[4] Fulton recommended that the journal should contain additional analytical columns, from the entries in which the profit to date and the net assets could at any time be ascertained without difficulty.

9

(Jones, *English System*, 1796, p. 12.)

. . . But, of the two Systems, the method by Single Entry claims, in a certain sense, a preference; as that by Double Entry, being more complex and obscure, admits of greater secrecy in case of fraud, and is more capable of being converted into a cloak, for the vilest statements that designing ingenuity can fabricate.—A man may defraud his partner, or a Book-keeper his employer, if they be so disposed, without ever being detected : or else, how comes it that we often see such opposite changes in the circumstances of men, belonging to the same Concern? The rich man becomes *poor*, and the poor man becomes *rich* !—Co-partners in a Concern become insolvent—The one, whose fortune had originally supported the trade, is reduced almost to want; while the other, who was originally poor, and, being insolvent, ought still to be so, makes a *pompous appearance* in the world, immediately *enters into Trade* again, and finds a *Capital sufficient to answer* every new demand ! ! It is possible to account for this in a favorable way; but a change so extraordinary wears a very *suspicious appearance*. . . .

10

(Hamilton, *Introduction to Merchandise*, 1788, p. 467.)

In the former Part, we have explained that form of book-keeping which is most agreeable to strict method, or general practice. However, as some of the rules we have laid down are arbitrary, and may be varied without inconvenience, so it must happen, that different accomptants will not adhere precisely to the same plan; and the nature of the business may render such variations proper. The form of the principal books may sometimes be rendered simpler and shorter; sometimes fewer may be necessary, or others substituted in their place; sometimes they may be thrown into a different order, better suited to the matter they contain. It is obvious that no treatise can comprehend all the variety of methods which different kinds of business may require, or which different merchants or others may chuse to follow. It will be useful, however, to explain a few, for the learner's instruction; and, if these be understood, he will acquire a readiness in selecting or inventing proper ones, suited to every circumstance. A full knowledge of the regular method is absolutely necessary for understanding some of the following ones, and highly useful for them all.

11

(Hamilton, *Introduction to Merchandise*, 1788, p. 479.)

Shop-keepers, whose business consists chiefly in retail, have occasion for a more concise form of book-keeping than the regular Italian method. As the articles sold are often very numerous, and very small, they cannot bestow the labour of entering each in a variety of places, and have been led to invent other methods, more or less perfect, as their leisure or their skill admitted. Among the least perfect methods we may reckon those where none but personal accompts are kept in the ledger, and where there is no other way of computing their stock, but by collecting the articles due to them from the ledger, and adding thereto the value of goods on hand, from an inventory; and subtracting from that amount the debts they owe. Next to these, are methods where some general accompts are kept in the ledger, to exhibit the extent of the sales, and the gain upon the whole goods sold, although not on each particular kind: And it is a farther improvement, if there be a regular check on the quantity of goods, or, at least, an opportunity of checking them, as often as the owner chooses, by comparing the purchases with the sales. The most perfect methods are those which exhibit the gain or loss on each particular kind of goods. . . .

The Principal Account-Books

12

(North, *Gentleman Accomptant*, 1715, p. 20.)

I may distinguish all the Books any Merchant, or Man of Business, requiring Accompts, can pretend to keep, into the Principal and Subsidiary. The Principal are Three; no more, nor fewer; and those may contain the whole Material, without the others, which are used more for Convenience than Necessity; and may be more, or fewer, as Affairs, or Fancy and Discretion may demand: But of the Three Principal, no one can be spar'd; and those are, 1. The Waste-Book, or (as some term it) the foul Journal. 2. The Journal. 3. The Ledger. The others with Merchants may be these; 1. Cash-book. 2. Accompts Currant. 3. Petty Charges. 4. House-keeping.

13

(Peele, *Maner and Fourme*, 1553, ch. 2.)

Upon the toppe of the firste leafe or Page,[5] saie thus. Anno. M.D. liii. the. xxv. daie of Maie. As in your example. Then write the title of your Inventorie, saiyng: The Inventorie or estate of all suche gooddes, as unto me Fraunces Bonde of London Grocer, dooeth appertain: and also what I owe or ought to answere unto, at this present: the particulars wherof, dooeth more at large ensue. Then proceade to the writyng of your parcelles, wherof the first must bee money, as in your example.[6] Item in Angelles remainyng, to the nombre of. 270. valued at ten shillynges the Angell, amounteth to the somme of one C. xxxv. li. I saie —— 135. li. and the rest of your Inventorie, eche parcell with sommes written at length in suche ordre as you se in the Inventorie of this my

---

[5] This chapter concerns the "inventorie or estate, whiche ought to bee written in the first parte of the Jornall." Though it is not a separate book, it is treated as if it were one, for later Peele transcribes the entries in the inventory into the journal (in his illustrative set of account-books).

The early authors did not regard the inventory as one of the principal books, but as something which preceded them, much as we now regard an opening trial balance.

[6] For the first page of the illustrative inventory, see Plate I.

Booke, wherin you maie not forget your totall somme, whiche muste be written under eche severall particulers, as in the example. Note that all menne have not so large an Inventorie, as I have hereunto made: Though some have muche more, and other some nothyng at all: wherefore, that matier is to be deferred to suche necessitie, as their accompt serveth. For he that can make this Inventorie, can make a larger, or a lesse, as occasion shal serve but he that hath no gooddes (but suche as at his beginnyng, he taketh on credite) nedeth no Inventorie, but maie begin with his Jornall. After all thynges due to the owner, thus entred into the Inventorie, you must cast all those sommes, so beyng written and gathered by the particulars, into one totall Somme: writyng it with a greate penne, faire in sighte, beneth the parcelles, as therein is dooen: then write the parcelles, that the owner dooeth owe, as in the Inventorie of my saied booke is doen, wherin Flaunders accompt is first, at thende therof make in like maner a somme total, whiche somme by thowner due to other, you must subtraie from the other Totall, and the remain is the substaunce of the owner, whiche remain muste in one totall somme, with expresse woordes be set out at large, as in the ende of the Inventorie, dooeth well appere.[7] Thus the Inventorie beyng well understande and knowen, it foloweth consequently, that we should intreate of the other three bookes, nedefull, and necessary for a Marchaunte, and of the face, order, spaces, lines, and markes to them belongyng.

14

(Peele, *Pathewaye to Perfectnes*, 1569.)

Scholemaster. First I begin with an Inventorie for trafique, contayninge dyvers perticulers committed to the order of a servaunte to be employed in trafique of marchaundies.

Scholler. Is it nedefull that all men make an Inventorie when they begin these accomptes?

---

[7] The last entry in the specimen inventory is:

Summe net, of my whole substaunce, al my Creditours being deducted, a-mounteth to —— { 1569. *l.* 17. *s.* 8. *d.* ¼.

Scholemaster. Yea surelie, except they begin without anye thinge, and so proceade uppon creadite, or elles with a stocke onlie in readie monie, otherwyse, if they have anye remaynders, as readie monie, debtes, goodes, and creaditours, they must have an Inventorie. Presuppose that the owner, or master, of this imagined accompte, hath here to fore used trafique, and never before this tyme kepte his accomptes by thorder of debitour, and creaditour, and nowe is minded for thexcellencie thereof, to frequent and use the same; therfore his originall enteringe into this order of accomptes, is (supposed to be) by an inventorie as before. But do you understande what an Inventorie for trafique is: to what end it serveth and the nature and propertie therof?

Scholler. I thinke so.

Scholemaster. Then let me heare your judgement.

Scholler. An Inventorie for trafique, is a note to be taken in writinge of all thinges founde and remayninge in the house apperteyninge to trade of marchaundise, thereby to knowe a mans estate, and doth consist in ij. kindes: the one whereof, is that which a man hathe or ought to have in possession, to saye in readie monie, debtes, and goodes: and thother kinde, is that which he oweth to other men being his creaditours, and by comparinge of the totall somme of the readye monie, debtes, and goodes, with the totall somme of the creaditours, the estate of that accompte is presentlye perceyved (that is to saye) so muche as the monye, debtes and goodes sormounte the creditoures, so much apperteyneth to thowner of that accompte for his proper stocke or capitall in trafique. Although I knowe thus muche, yet, what shall firste be written and what is to be observed in thenteringe of the same nedefull to thorder of debitour and creaditour and where all thinges shalbe perfectlye placed, as yet I knowe not.

Scholemaster. Herein you have sayde verie well: and touchinge your doubtes expressed for writinge, orderinge, and placinge of all thinges nedefull, I will satisfie you. First I thinke good to declare what bookes must be prepared to prosecute the same, and speciallye of the Inventorie booke, and thother iij principall bookes, to saye, the Memoriall, Journall, and Leager, although there be other bookes necessarie, as the booke for copies of letters, and envoyces of goods shipped from your handes, and the booke of acquittaunces taken for money paid out daylye. The Inventorie booke must be of suche bignes, as maye suffice to contayne the whole perticulers of the remaynders, and the leaves thereof to be nombred presentlye. The memoriall booke must be asmuche in quantitie, as the Journall, and a fourthe parte more at the least. And the leager or greate booke of accomptes two tymes as bigge as the Journall. Which memoriall, for that it is the originall and first entrance of all matters in trafique, it requireth therfore a large declaration, beinge also subject to divers writers, by reason it is a common booke, aswell for the master and his accompte keper, as also for anye other of the servauntes wherein to write, and havinge great doyinges for want of leasure, it can not be so fayre and close written, and therefore requireth to be so large as before. It maye chaunce also that some of the percelles in the memoriall shall never be borne into the Journall, that is to saye, money, and wares borowed or lent for a daye ij. or iij, and beinge receaved or delivered agayne, is there uppon to be discharged presentlie without anye farther travaile, savinge to crosse the percell and mencion the tyme of receipt at delivery thereof in the margent.

15

(Ympyn, *Notable . . . Woorke*, 1547, ch. 4.)

Of the maner of the memorial boke, and what maie be written therin.

In this Memoriall boke maie bee written all maner of thynges that daily doth happen, ether by biynges, sellynges, paymentes, receptes, deliverances of billes, assignacions, wages, laborers, cariage, fraight and so furth, and all that belongeth or toucheth to marchandise. But first it is requisite that ye make the title of your boke in the first leafe therof in maner as it is shewed in the exemple of the Inventory, Jornall and greate boke: And then maie ye write clerely all thynges that shall happen, not forgettyng the daie, yere, when, and of whom, or what, and how muche, as in like maner muste bee written in the Inventory: And ye must entre all condicions made, aswell in biyng as sellyng: And also what broker or persone was presente. There are some that write in the beginnyng of this boke of Memoriall the Inventory, whiche I cannot praise, forasmuche as this boke commeth daily into the handes of every persone, and so is it not mete that the Inventory should. And in this boke of Memoriall, maie write the marchant, his wife or servauntes, the one ever when the other is absent: And al thynges to be written directly one folowyng another as thei happen daily, in like maner as ye shall se in the exemple of the Jornall, untill suche tyme as the Marchant hymself or some other apoyncted shall remove the parcelles of his Memoriall boke into the Jornall, & from thence into the greate boke. And in this boke it is not materiall whether ye observe the writyng of any one sorte of money or no, but at your pleasure ye maie write starlyng money, Flemish money as stuivers, guildrens, poundes Flemishe or Brabans or what other money soever be currant in that place wher the boke shalbe kept. But in the other twoo bokes must be written l.s.d. of some certain coyne, as ether sterlyng Flemishe or other as herafter shalbee shewed, and as in the preface of the aucthoure it is declared. And this Memoriall boke is very necessary to all suche as are troubled with greate affaires, and hath more to dooe then maie well be overcome, as in a compaignie or felowship, thone shall dooe one thyng here, and another there, and at home the factoure or wife, and without the master, and so by this Memoriall boke shall it be seen what every one did daie by daie. And a right Marchant of Italy will not faile to write at after none all thynges that he did in the forenone. And so diligent and painfull must all thei be that truly and perfightly will kepe their reconynges. For men have not Angels wittes, but maie forget. And now these bokes beyng redy to write in, that is to saie all these three bokes aforesaid with their A.B.C.[8] or at the least these two last bokes incace men desire not to occupy the first, ye shall cause the outside to be marked with + and likewise at the ende of your boke, and at the beginnyng of every leffe of your boke, that ye maie knowe therby on the out side one boke from another. And as these bokes shalbe filled and newe made, then shall you marke the seconde boke with the letter A. And the third with the letter B. And so continue to tho ende of the A.B.C. And it is very resonable as we have said afore in the second Chapiter that like as children begin their first boke with the + the whiche is the triumphant signe of our salvacion: That even so every good Christen man do begin with the same signe. It is also necessary to write in the said bokes the nombre of the leaves on the corner, that is to saie in the firste boke on the one side of the boke: But in the greate boke on bothe sides, as shalbe shewed in the exemplary, and that for the verifiyng and conductyng of the boke, because that the

---

[8] Alphabet, *i.e.*, index to the ledger.

fewer fraudes and wronges maie be wrought therin, albeit that it is not requisite to doo so in the twoo first bokes, forasmuche as thei depend wholy upon the folowyng of daies monethes and yeres, wherby all fraudes that might bee committed in bokes are avoyded.

16

(Weddington, *Breffe Instruction*, 1567.)

The memorial, or wast boke, what it is and howe it ought to be usid.

This boke namid the memoriall, or a wast boke, is a boke wherin all marchantis, ought daily to write in all suche businis, as is don by them, or ther servantis, in ther feattis of marchandize, as recevinge payinge of mony, takinge, and deliveringe of mony by exchange, acceptinge of billis by exchange, byinge and sellinge, invoizes of marchandize recevid and set awaie withe other as in this boke more at large maie apere.——

The wiche for example I have made here in to severall partis for [9] bokis, be cause marchantis of great dowingis ought to have many servantes to helpe them to write. And when all thingis of ther dowingis, shalbe clered here and agreid apon, betwine party, and party, in this wast boke or bokes, then the same ought incontenent to be faire writton out of the same into the great or principall boke, named the great Boke or lidger, at large perticulerly in Debitor or Creditor, notinge here in this boke or bokes, under the percell in what leaff or folio, it is put ther.——And by this manner, you shall have all your businis in the great boke only, without beinge subjecte to any Jornall or wast boke as some men are accostomid—wiche they to this Boke maie yeat use yf it please them to take somiche pains. And when this boke or partis shalbe fullwritton you mai lai it or them up, in some place, to be kept yf nede be, and make newe, apon the wiche you most alwais make your marke withe a nombre, to saie upon the fyrst wast bokis No. 1. the seconda No. 2. &c. and the leves ought to be nombrid to thende that you maie spedelli torne unto the partis therin contained, yf nede be but in small dowingis you maie make all these partis or bokes to gether in one wast Boke, or memorial accept receving and

[9] Presumably misprint for "or."

paying of mony copies of accomptis recordes and copies of leteris as herin you may perseave by that I have don, and at the beginninge of every part, to glewe on a peace of parchement and to writ apon the same what it dothe containe, But and yf you have great dowingis, as divers marchantis of Itally and other have then, you most make the saide partis into severall bokis coverid withe parchement markid withe your marke and nombred as a fore saide to saie all the fyrst bokis No. 1. they being full writton the seconde newe bokis No. 2 writtinge apon them the name of the businis that they do serve for, and by this manner everi one of ther clarkis or servantis shall have, a boke to write in suche businis as the master shall gyve hym charge of so that in this boke for the feattis of marchandize par example I have comprisid 12. principall matters most nedefull, of the wiche here in this Boke of everi one severalli, I will shewe sufficent examples.——

17

(Gordon, *Universal Accountant*, 1787, vol. 2, p. 20.)

. . . In the hurry, and during the time of business, it would scarcely be practicable, to clothe transactions in that dress, to arrange the accounts in that order, or adjust them with that precision, which the importance of accuracy, order, and regularity in this particular, would seem to require; it hath therefore been judged expedient, to have one common place book, in which, as a general register, transactions are immediately recorded as they occur, which is called the *Waste-book*; and thence, at times proper for the purpose, they are again entered in, or carried to another book called the *Journal*, where the particular *Debtors* and *Creditors* in each transaction are pointed out and ascertained, and the whole narrative expressed in those laconic terms, which are peculiar to accountantship [10]: lastly, from this book, which is only intended as a leading step towards the completion of the whole, the several transactions are collected and carried to the principal book of accounts, called the *Leger*, and so disposed and arranged in their particular spaces and folios, at proper periods, perhaps monthly or weekly, that a true state of the whole, or any part, may be easily and distinctly known, which is the end, use, and design of *Book-keeping*.

[10] See note on next page.

18

(Mellis, *Briefe Instruction*, 1588, ch. 9.)

Of the second booke principall called the journall. Howe it ought to be disposed and ordered.

This Journall ought to bee signed and marked with the same marke or letter as is the Memoriall aforesayde. And also the leaves numbred, setting alwayes in the head of every leafe, the date of our Lorde, and the day of the moneth. And that done, yee shall in good order set the parcels of the Inventorie into ye Journall. And for as much as this Journall is a secrete booke, therefore yee may therein shew write and expresse al your goods moveable and immoveable, rehearsing every parcel unto that leafe wherein it is found, and also recorde thereof where it may bee founde, be it in chist, boxe or bundell, as more largely afterwarde in the chapiter of keeping of letters and other writinges shal bee shewed. But ye shal understande, that the parcels of the Journall ought to bee written, ordered and indited in shorter sentence, without super-fluous words, than be the parcels in ye Inventory or Memorial as hereafter you shal by divers examples have information: but first it is to be noted, that yee knowe the two termes used in the saide Journall after the maner as is used in the same, which as the order of this account requireth, is expressed by two denominations: to wit, by Debitor, and Creditor, whereof the first is the name of the Debitor, receiver or borrower: and the other of the Creditor, deliverer, or lender. To the furtherance whereof there is a Rule,

---

[10] The laconic nature of entries in the journal may be seen in the following waste-book and journal entries for the same transaction (Gordon, *ibid.*, pp. 64 and 70):

18th.

The master of the *Nancy*, has brought in his account of outfit for London, *viz.* freight of goods and passage outwards — — L.207 10		
Stores and a month's wages advanced 37 10		
Balance received nett	170	

18th.

1/2	Cash Dr. to ship *Nancy*, 170*l.*	
	Received balance of outfit for London —	170

(What appears to be the fraction ½ comprises the folio references of the two ledger accounts respectively debited and credited.)

which beeing well understood, will aide you greatly: which Rule is to bee learned as well by rote, as by reason, which is thus.

All thinges received, or the receiver must owe to all thinges delivered, or to the deliverer.

Whereby is meant, that the goods bought, or the money receaved of any person, must in all parcels bee made Debitor, (that is to say) to owe unto the parties of whom it is received. As for example: imagine you have bought clothes of Thomas Long, then to observe the Rule, you must enter the parcel into the Journall, saying: Clothes oweth to Thomas Long &c. If you receive money of any man: according to the same Rule you must say, money oweth to William Hall, &c. And hereby appeareth that part, how the same Rule is observed. Contrariwise, if you sell goods, or pay money to any: Then to the observing of the same rule, you shal say: Henry Par, &c. oweth to clothes. Or, James Welch oweth to mony &c.

Touching the ruling of your Journall, observe these fewe notes. Betweene the two lines next your left hand is the place to set the directions which directeth the parcels that are to be entered from that booke into the Leager or great booke of accompts; betweene ye which two lines before every parcel in the Journal must be drawen a line overthwart, and must have a figure or figures made both above and under the same. The which figures or numbers standing above, doth direct to the leafe of the Debitor parcel, whether the same is born into the Leager: and the other being underneath the line, directeth to the leafe of the Creditor thereof. The lines on the same side of the Journall towardes the right hand, serveth to place the money, as li. s. d. And the large space within and betweene the place of the directions, and the place of li. s. d. serveth to write the parcels of the Journall. You must orderly keepe the yeare of our Lord, and the day of the Moneth, on the toppe of everie page, &c. aforesaide.

19

(Weddington, *Breffe Instruction*, 1567.)

The great boke or lidger what it is, and how it ought for to be usid in the feattes of marchandize.

This Boke ought to containe, 200. or 300. leavez of paper reall or more accordinge unto your dowingis in the feattis of marchandize, and at the upper ende it ought to be signid withe the leters

of the crose rowe,[11] that is to sai your fyrst great Boke withe the
letere A. the seconde new boke withe B. the thride new Boke withe
C. &c. And the leavez of the saide Boks most be nombrid, apon
the right side, and apon the left side, withe one manner of nomber,
to saie the fyrst tow leavez or faces, of the saide Boke is to be
nombred withe the nomber of one, the seconde withe No. 2. the
thride withe No. 3. &c. and in this order you most go throughe the
whole Boke wherof the side next unto the left hand is for your
Debitors, or those that owith unto you, and the side next unto the
right hande, is for your Creditors, or those that you owe unto, and
it most be rulid after the order of marchantis Boks withe spaces, to
saie the folio, pondis, shillingis, pens, for these perties or accordinge
unto the mony of the countries wher as you shalbe resident, So that
the spaces or lynes next afore the L. s. d. is for to put the folio in
to declare wher all suche accomptis dothe stande, to answere unto
the accomptis Debitors and Creditors, in the accomptis throughe
out the whole Boke, and at the upper ende, or hed of everi leaff
in the same Boke, you most write the date of Christ to saie An. 1567.
and so following a longe throughe the whole Boke, and yf the yere
or date of Christ, do change apon ani accompt beinge halff full
writton &c. Then maie you note the same in the margent against
the percell.——And more you most have unto this Boke a Callender,
or A.B.C. &c. for to finde spedelly all the accomptis withe the
Debitors and Creditors containinge in the same, for this Boke dothe
containe all your other boks, as Memoriall, Jornall, or Boke of the
Borse, perticulerly at large, or breaffly accordinge to your dowingis
in ballans, or order of accomptis, Debitor and Creditor, wherby you
maie se spedely what you do owe unto all men. And what all other
men dothe owe unto you &c. And this boke ought to be verri faire
writton, without ani blottinge or eror, and withe one manner of
hande, for to avoide varriance, that might come, yf you do occapie
in compani &c. But and yf your dowingis be great in bijnge, and
sellinge then you mai kepe the perticulers of the same faire in a
Boke apart, only unto the same apertaininge and out of the same
from time, to time, to write it into your saide great Boke netli, and
after the same manner, you maie do for the recevinge and payinge
of moni withe assignations, kepinge also for the same a severall
boke, namid in Itallian the boke of the Borse, or assignations,
because your great Boke shall nat be empached withe the petty

---

[11] Cross-row = alphabet.

paimentis and receattis of moni, or ellis you most make, your great Boke or lidger somiche the greatter, the wiche is the best manner, in smale dowingis, for by this order you shall have all your bussinis or dowingis perticulerli in your great Boke onli, all the wiche ought to be don in so good order and perfection, as though it ware your last will or testament, that all thingis mai therin plainli apere, to answere unto all matters requisid, accordinge to the trewthe, and when thei are full writton, you most kepe them faire in chestis or other, as good presidentis unto your selff, or lerningis unto those that shall come after you. . . .

20

(Peele, *Maner and Fourme*, 1553, ch. 5.)

You shall understande, that every one parcell in the Jornall, ought to bee twoo in the Quaterne, and the cause is, that every of theim dooeth include or contain twoo properties, wherof thone is a debitour, or borower, and the other is a Creditour or lender. The borower, or the thyng borowed, is become Debitour, by reason that it dooeth retain and possesse: and the lender, or the thyng lent, is the Creditour, by reason that it is dispossessed. And the maner how to dispers and devide them, orderly into the saied Quaterne: Is first to write the Debitour into some one side, next your left hande, in a severall place, where under shalbe written any parcell that belongeth to thesame, and in suche ordre, as I have practised in my saied Quaterne. Then shall you on the contrary side, in some other severall place, write the Creditour: where under in like maner shalbe written any parcell of like name: and in such ordre as I have practised in my saied booke. And for an example, I have plainly herafter shewed the maner, of bearyng the first parcell out of the Journall, bothe to the debitour and creditours sides. The waie therunto is, to take your Quaterne, or great boke of accompts in hand, laiyng your Journal before you: & in thenext voide place after the Kalen[dar] write the debitour, the date of our Lorde, and in the place of parcelles, set the same figure that your parcell is of in the Journall, & in the greate space next to it, the name of the monethe, and next therunto, the numbre of the daie. Then write thesame first parcell out of the Journall, into the Debitour side of your Quaterne, that beyng dooen, make over the direccion of accomptes, in your Journall, the numbre of the lefe, wherin that parcell so entered into the quaterne, is debitour, whiche is in Folio. 1. so shall there be lefte in the quaterne booke, upon the same debitours side, the space betwene the parcell so written at large, and the place of money, wheron folio is written, a voide rome without any figure: wherin must stande the figure of the Folio: where you shall chaunce to make that parcell creditour. Then tourne over the lefe of the greate booke, to Folio 2. and upon the creditours side, set the date, parcell, moneth, and daie, agreable to the place whence you came, beginnyng the same creditor, with the worde that proceded of the parcell in the Journall, saiyng: Stocke belongyng to me Fraunces Bonde, is Creditour, by money, and is for 270. Angelles, at tenne shillynges the Angell: Somme —— 135. li. this dooen, write there on Creditours side, in the voide place of accomptes, betwene the parcell written at large, wheron Folio is written, and the place of money, the figure 1. in whiche Folio, that parcell was made debitour, and on the debitours side, from whence you came, in the place of accomptes, whiche' before you lefte voide, sette the figure. 2. in whiche Folio, thesame parcell is Creditoure, and under the direccion of your Journall, make a figure of 2. where in the parcell is Creditour. If you write any parcell at large in the Debitour, you maie make it shorte in Creditour, and contrariwise, if it bee shorte in Debitour, it muste be at lengthe in Creditour. Then go to your Kalendar, to the letter M. and there entre money, saiyng: Money is in Folio.——1. Then for the creditour, go to the letter S. and there entre stocke, as foloweth. Stock is in folio. 2. Thus have you thoroughly done, that one parcel in al poinctes. And so enter not only such as are apropriate unto ye owner, but also any other, either procedyng of the Inventorie, or otherwise chaunced in your Journall, for the tyme of your occupiyng: and in suche like sorte you shall entre all thinges ordrely in their kindes, but in severall accomptes, whereof you maie make twoo or three in one Folio, as the thyng requireth, and is also practised in the Quaterne. And as touchyng bearying the reste of your parcelles, out of the Journall, into the Quaterne or greate booke of accomptes, there is none other thyng to be observed, then hath been before taught, in cariying that first parcell of money: but that the names of thynges are altered. Be sure to observe your rules, in bearyng of ye rest, as before is taught you, in bearyng that first parcell, & you shall quickly learne, puttyng therunto your good will. You shal not nede in your greate booke in any accompte, after the firste parcell on the Debitour side, to begin as that first parcell is begonne, but at the worde To, and on the Creditour side, after the first parcell written, to beginne at the worde (By) as you maie well perceive, if you vewe the booke, but onely in the first accompt, where money standeth.

21

(Gordon, *Universal Accountant*, 1787, vol. 2, pp. 25–6.)

. . . The *Leger* is the principal book of accounts, formed from the *Journal*, as the *Journal* was founded on the *Waste-book*, wherein the articles that compose any account whatever, are so disposed and arranged, that the true state thereof is immediately known. In the *Leger*, the different parts of a transaction, which in the *Journal* were distinguished as *Debtors* or *Creditors*, stand collected, in spaces allotted for them, and placed according to their distinctions of *Debtor* and *Creditor*, on opposite sides of the same folio. Thus, for instance, all the money received in the course of a year's transactions, or whatever other period the merchant fixes for balancing, appears at one view on the *Debtor* side of the cash account, and all the money paid away on the *Creditor* side of the same account; the difference betwixt the one and the other must certainly show what money remains in his chest. In like manner, in a personal account, every sum chargeable on that person stands at his debit, as all the payments he hath made stand at his credit; and the difference of the sides shows at once the state of the account. Again, in an account of goods, the prime cost and charges stand on the *Debtor* side, and the sales on the *Creditor* side; hence the loss or gain upon that article is discoverable at once. Upon the whole, such is the order, arrangement, and disposition of things in the *Leger*, that all the accounts may be adjusted with the utmost precision at any period, so as a true state of the whole, or any part of a merchant's affairs, may be fairly exhibited; which is the end, design, and use of accountantship.

Every folio in the *Leger* is divided into spaces, into which the articles of the *Journal* are inserted, according to their distinctions, and order of succession. On the head of each folio are inscribed the number, place, and year, both on the *Debtor* and *Creditor* sides. At the top of each space stands the title of the account, in large text, marked *Dr.* on the left-hand page, and *Cr.* on the right [12]; below which are inserted the articles, to which the article *To* is prefixed on the *Debtor* side, and *By* on the *Creditor* side. Upon the margin are recorded the dates of the articles in a column appropriated for them, and in the money column the sums; immediately before which stands a folio column, containing the number of the folio wherein the correspondent entry is made. In accounts of goods, or any other accounts, where number, weight, or measure or distinction of coins is considered, there are likewise inner columns, wherein these are particularly inserted. For the more ready dispatch in finding accounts in the *Leger*, it hath an alphabet, or index, wherein are written all the titles of the accounts, with the number of the folio where they stand. In this alphabet, the title of every account is entered under its proper initial letter; only persons names, according to the initial letter of their surname. . . .

22

(Mair, *Book-Keeping Methodiz'd*, 1741, pp. 3–4.)

. . . The Way the ingenious Authors went to Work, was, not by neglecting the Use of the *Waste-book*, which is a Book still necessary; but, continuing to use it as formerly, they took the Materials or Things contained in it, and, by digesting them into another Form, they compiled and made up a new Book out of them, in which the various Transactions and Dealings are disposed, not according to the scattered Order of their Dates, as in the *Waste-book*, but so as that the particular Branches and Articles of every Accompt are placed together; and, that the State of each particular Accompt may easily and distinctly appear, their opposite Parts are separately placed, so as to front one another on opposite Pages of the same Folio, under the Title of *Debtor* on the Left-hand Page and *Creditor* on the Right. Thus, the Purchase of Goods is set upon the Left-hand Page, and the several Sales of the same placed upon the Right. In like manner, the several Articles of Money received

---

[12] The explanation refers here to the common practice of having several different ledger accounts on one folio; for an example, see Plates VIII and IX. (See also extract 39.)

go to the Left-hand Page, and the several Debursements are set fronting them upon the Right. Again, the Debts any Person contracts, are written upon the Left, and the Payments he makes, are inserted on the Right.

This Book they call the *Ledger*, which differs from the *Waste-book* only in Form, not in Matter. The *Ledger* is the *Waste-book* taken to Pieces, and put together in another Order: The Transactions contained in both are the same, but recorded in a different Manner. The *Waste-book* narrates Things in a plain, simple, natural Way, according to the Order of Time in which they were transacted; the *Ledger* contains the very same Things, but artificially disposed, so as Things of the same kind are classed together, and all the particular *Items* and *Articles* belonging to the same Subject are collected and united. In short, the *Waste-book* may be compared to the Pack-sheet in a Fair, wherein Goods are put up as they come to hand; and the *Ledger* to the Shelves and Boxes in a Shop, where the same Goods are sorted and put in order for Sale. Hence it is evident, that the great Business of this Art is, to teach the easiest and best Method of digesting the *Waste-book* into the *Ledger Form*, and reducing Things from the confused and scattered Order of the former, to the Regularity and Distinctness of the latter.

And in regard, transporting immediately from the *Waste-book* to the *Ledger* is attended with great Hazard of Mistakes, as being a complex Task, that requires a good Degree of Attention to consider what is *Debtor* and *Creditor* in every Transaction, that is, what should go to the Right, and what to the Left-hand Page in the *Ledger*; and, at the same Time, employs both Head and Hands in making the Entry itself: Merchants therefore, to render the Matter easy, and to prevent, as much as possible, Errors creeping into the *Ledger*, and also upon some other Considerations, have found it convenient to keep a third Book; wherein every Case of the *Waste-book* is again briefly narrated, and the proper *Debtors* and *Creditors* ascertained: which being done, they are with great Ease transported from it to the *Ledger*. This Book is called the *Journal*.

The Book-keeper, by going thus to work, divides the Task, and so has a fairer Chance for avoiding Errors, than he who would transport immediately from the *Waste-book* to the *Ledger*, since he does by Steps what the other attempts to do at once. . . .

23

(Carpenter, *Most Excellent Instruction*, 1632, p. 6.)

The journall, and lidger.

In the Journall, and Lidger, no man is to write, but hee that keepeth the Accounts, that they may be the more authentique before a Judge, in case of Controversie. Howbeit, to him that is experienced in Accounts, a *Journall* without a *Memoriall*, or a *Memoriall* without a *Journall*, may suffice, for that those bookes import one and the same thing; the leaves to bee numbred either by pages or parcels.

24

(Dodson, *Accountant*, 1750, preface, p. x.)

. . . Note, Some Persons keep no Journal, but only write in their Waste-Book the Titles of the Accounts which become Debtors and Creditors, as is here done in the two Partnership Accounts; with this Difference, that instead of writing them under the Entry, as here, they allow a large Margin, and write them in that: Others never enter Receipts and Payments in the Journal, but post them from the Cash-Book, as is here done in the Banker's Account. . . .

25

(Roose, *Essay to Make . . . Accomptant*, 1760, p. 17.)

. . . From hence the intelligent Reader may perceive that these subsidiary Books, together with a Journal and Ledger, are sufficient for an acute Accomptant, without the Waste-Book, as it has been before noticed that a Waste-Book, Journal and Ledger, are sufficient without these; nay, even that these subsidiary Books may be all dropt, and a Journal and Ledger be made to supply the Place of all of them, as has been before noticed in regard to the Waste-Book: And this, in a Manner, is evinced by real Business, since the Waste-Book and Journal, in this, differ only in their Size, the latter being an Abridgment of the former, as the Debtor and Creditor are expressed alike in both. But for Instruction's Sake, it is absolutely necessary to make Use of a Waste-Book, Journal, and Ledger, or of the subsidiary Books, together with a Journal and Ledger. . . .

Secrecy in Accounting

26

(Peele, *Maner and Fourme*, 1553, ch. 11.)

What is to be done of suche as will have their substaunce kepte in secrete, and of circumspect hede to be taken, that eche parcel of the jornall be truly cast before it be borne into the quaterne.

Such as are disposed to kepe the quaterne in their owne custodie (be it either a master him selfe, or one that is appointed over other in the house, whereby the substaunce may be kept secrete, except unto the saied maister or keper of the accomptes, as for divers considerations some men have good cause no lesse then so to do). They maye binde their inventorye and the parcels therof whiche are borne into the Jornall, in the formost ende of their quaterne before the kalender, and beare the same parcels orderly bothe debitors & creditors into the same quaterne. And all thinges chaunced in occupiyng from the daye of the date in the Inventory (which in no wise must be devided into mo daies then one) that by suche servauntes as can bothe legeably write, and also enter parcels perfectly, be entred in a common Jornal boke, causing the fyrst parcell therof to be made one more in numbre then was the last that came of the Inventorie.[13] And the parcels therof thus finished and orderly borne into the saied Quaterne then may the keper of the saied Quaterne at his time convenient beare the parcels chaunced in the commen Jornall boke orderly both debitors and creditors into the Quaterne. Furthermore it is nedeful to such master or accompt keper, that they oversee either them selves, or appoynte some other, that every parcell in the Jornall be truely cast before they enter them into the quaterne to avoyde makyng of any error in them. The keper of the saied quaterne had not nede to bee muche absent, for that in moost playnest wise the accompt of eche thing, be it either in debt or credite, is described in their bookes.

---

[13] In Peele's journal the entries are numbered consecutively.

27

(Weddington, *Breffe Instruction*, 1567.)

The inventarie.

The inventary is a part or Boke, containinge all suche goodis and marchandize as dothe apertaine unto the principall, hed or master, as well movables as immovables, withe all that he owithe, and all that is owing unto hym, the wiche is most requisid to be made, or begon all upon one daie, and fyrst to begin with thingis of great valleur as mony jewellis, landis and rentis, &c. withe all manner of declarations, or surcumstancis unto the same apertaininge, as by the demonstration therof here against aperethe.——

The wiche Boke the Maister maie holde secreatly unto hym selff yf it please hym, withe a great Boke Debitor and Creditor, only for the same, and by this manner no man shall understande or knowe his estate, but hym selff only, or suche as he shall apoint to kepe the saide Bokes, the wiche is verri requesid amongest marchantis. And all suche mony, marchandize, &c. that he shall put to be occapied in the feattis of marchandize, by hym selff or servantis, that maie your servantis or other knowe and no more.——For the wiche in your secreat great Boke you most make Debitor your great Boke of marchandize, apon accompt, and Creditor the accomptis of those thingis, in your secreat great boke so put into occapyinge, as yf it be mony, make Creditor the accompt of your chest or redi mony, and Debitor the saide accompt of your great boke of marchandize ther &c.[14]——But for breviation I do now put all into one great boke of marchandize, Debitor and Creditor apon ther severall accomptis, wiche maie suffice for example.——And yf at the beginninge, you have no goodis, but suche as you do by, or take apon Credit, ye shall nat nede this boke or part for inventarie, but maie begin apon suche moni, or marchandize, taken, or bought apon Credit, makinge the same Debitor and Creditor in your great boke of marchandize, as you do other thingis, the gains wherof shalbe your Capitall or Stocke, and as you shall do in this inventary for your proper accompt, so in like manner maie you do in all other that maie fortune to come unto you by dethe of frendis marriage, and suche

---

[14] Weddington is explaining how to operate what we should now call a control account in the secret ledger. When an asset is to be transferred to the general ledger (" the great Boke of marchandize "), the asset account is credited and the control account for the general ledger is debited.

like, kepinge the accomptis therof severally here and in your secreat great boke or other, as a fore saide, &c.——

28

(Peele, *Pathewaye to Perfectnes*, 1569.)

Scholemaster. I thinke my selfe well requited in that you have hearein so well proffitted, the rewarde for my travaille hath not so muche benefited me as your knowledge herein attayned hathe dilighted me, but nowe to the declaration of the sayde privat accompte wherein I intende to be verie breffe, for the lyke in effecte (thoughe not in tytell) is practised all readie, for as the originall of thaccompte of employmentes is proceaded of an Inventorie entiteled the Inventorie of employmentes for trafique in marchaundies,[15] so is this private accompte proceaded also of an Inventorie entiteled the Inventorie generall, which contaynethe aswell the net rest of the sayde Inventorie of employmentes, as also all and all manner of other matters touching thinges consiled and kepte secrete to thonlie knowledge of the Master him selfe, that is to saye for the debitour parte, landes in Fesimple, landes holden by lease, Implementes of housholde and for husbandrie, Cattell. Juelles, Plate, detes for anunities, dettes for rentes, readie monie, and the net rest of the state committed to trafique in marchandise. All whiche, are thinges apropriate to the Master beinge thone parte of the sayde Inventorie generall called the debitour parte as before. The creditour parte contayneth what he oweth to other men, aswell for rentes and anunities, as also for wages and fees as may apear. The totall somme of which creditours beinge subtraid from the totall of the debitour parte of the sayde Inventorie, the rest declarethe his stocke generall, which is borne over into the Leager imediatly followinge the saide Inventorie in suche order in all pointes as in the Inventorie for trafique is declared. . . .[16]

---

[15] See extract 14.

[16] In the illustrative set of accounts, there are two ledgers:

  (i) " The Leager or greate Booke of letter A. for thaccomptes in trafique of Marchaundies appertayninge to my Master Frauncis Twyforde Citezen and Mercer of London, kepte and writton by me Anthonie Rice his servaunte. . . ."

  (ii) " The greate boke of accomptes contayninge my Private reconynge writton and kepte in the custodie of me Frauncis Twyford Citezin and Mercer of London contayninge my whole Estate generall as well what I have in Trafique of Marchaundies in thorder of Anthonie Rice my servaunte as also what I have

29

(Dafforne, *Merchants Mirrour*, 1660, pp. 15–17.)

Phil.[17] I have seen your *Dxterity* in the handling of the Inventary-Table, as also in the Booking of a mans known estate; but if a Merchant will not have his estate known, how will you behave your self therein? Ha! I think I have pos'd you now. Now you are stall'd, I trow.

Sch.[18] In such difficult Questions you cannot debarre me, to take the aid of some Renowned Authors: for in the first place of our Dialogue I feared my weaknesse, because I frequented not the daily Examination; but although I frequent not the School, I am yet not ignorant of what the Authors passages are upon this Subject: and therefore I will decide your Question, with the Solution of Master *Henry Waninghen* in the first Chapter, the 17. Questions answer; [19] his words are these: *Cash must be entred in place of Stocke, making all that is due to us Debitor to Cash : contrarily, Cash Debitor to all them that are to have of us.*

With him (in the very same words) agreeth his Disciple *Joannes Buingha*, who now at Amsterdam, after the death of his before-named Master, succeedeth his place in School-mastership.[20] See the 38. page of his Book, printed 1627.

J. Carpenter Gent. in his *Most Excellent Instruction*, printed in London 1632, is a direct *Imitator* of both the former: *See* fol. 20.24. of his Book: and no mervaile; for the greatest part of his published Book, is nothing else but a generall copy of *Henry Waninghens* Book, both in words, and number of the Questions. *J.C.* in his Espistle to the Reader, pretendeth Ignorance, of not knowing the

> reserved to myne owne secrete knowledge as by the severall accomptes therin appearinge at large."

The second ledger has an asset account " Thaccompte of Employmentes for trafique in marchaundies . . . ", while the first has a capital account " Stocke of Employmentes for trafique in Marchaundies . . . ". These two control accounts, equal but opposite in balance, tie the two ledgers together.

[17] Philo-Mathy, the teacher.
[18] School-Partner, the taught.
[19] Hendrik Waninghen wrote his *Tresoor van't Italiaens boeckhouden* . . . early in the seventeenth century. It went into several editions, and was translated into French. The major part of his book consists of series of questions and answers, grouped by topic (see pp. 167–8, below). Waninghen's curious method for concealing the amount of the merchant's capital, expounded and condemned by Dafforne in this passage, seems to have consisted in merging the capital and cash accounts, omitting from the merged account and from the ledger the opening balance of the cash account; to untangle the true balances of the two accounts it was necessary to have information not given in the ledger.
[20] Johannes Buingha, *Corte instructie om boeck tc houden* . . . , 1627, and later editions.

Author, who in the French Language many years agone was easie to be found.[21]

Phil. Shew me some Instances how they would Book their passages.

Sch. In briefe I will: and first,

Of The Wares.

$$\left\{\begin{array}{l}\left.\begin{array}{l}\text{Grograines,}\\ \text{Kersies}\\ \text{Durances,}\end{array}\right\}\;\text{Debitor to Cash.}\\ \qquad\qquad\text{Of the People that owe to us.}\\ \left.\begin{array}{l}\text{Robin Good-fellow,}\\ \text{Herman Hard-head,}\\ \text{John Gentleman,}\end{array}\right\}\;\text{Debitor to Cash.}\\ \qquad\qquad\text{Of the People that we owe unto.}\\ \text{Cash Debitor to}\;\left\{\begin{array}{l}\text{Rowland Red-beard.}\\ \text{Ralph Would-well.}\\ \text{Reynst Reach-farre.}\end{array}\right.\end{array}\right.$$

Phil. Suppose a man at the making of his Inventary hath some mony, how shall he Book that?

Sch. The before-named in the places of their Books mentioned, say, *The Ready-mony is not to be entred, till you disburse the same.*

Phil. Suppose with part of that concealed mony you bought *Wares*, and with other part, paid them unto whom you are indebted: how enter you that?

$$\left.\begin{array}{l}\text{Wares,}\\ \text{People,}\end{array}\right\}\;\text{Debitor to Cash.}$$

Phil. This being thus rehearsed, what will you conclude; have these (think you) digressed?

Sch. Suppose they had, what's that to me? But because you should not flout at me, thinking my capacity to be so stupid, that it is void of distinction, I will in some briefe notes onely touch the same.

First, let me consider whether the Book-owner be more indebted then his Estate is worth; which if he be, then is their entrance good, for his Estates concealment: *for the Debit side of Cash ought to be heaviest, or, having no mony, it must be even, because all is paid*

---

[21] See p. 167, below.

out: but if he have any Estate, then is the *Credit* of his Cash (who standeth in Stocks stead) heaviest: and therefore an *Errour*, being there is more paid, then was received.

Secondly, the commodities that we have at the making of our Inventary, were bought in *former* Books, and there made *Debitors*; and that we now enter them again *Debitors* to *Cash*, is to re-buy them: and consequently, in place of *book-reforming, book-deforming*, and an *undefendable Errour*.

Thirdly, the People whom we now make *Debitors* to *Cash*, are *absolutely* our *Debitors*; and do we *pay* them, who are to *pay* us? many men would desire to be *our* Debitors.

Fourthly, As senselesse is it, to make Cash *Debitor* to People that are to have of us; will they that are to have of us 100. l. for a Bill of Exchange by us accepted, say, *Come my Friend*, you have accepted an Exchange, to pay at time expired, which is now: send your man to my house, and the mony shall incontinently be paid to him? *I think nothing lesse.*

☞ Fifthly, Cash may never be ☞ named. Nota, not named, but when *money* is either truly, and really paid, or, received, as in the 17. place is mentioned. But if these People enter *forged* Imaginaries in the *Fore-front* of their Books: what is not to be expected before the *End*?

Sixthly, The *Stock* which they seek to *conceale*, is manifest in the *difference* of Cash it self. For let them transport their *Cash*, and they shall find (if as before is said, that their Estate stand well) that *Cash* is, and in transporting forward, alwayes remaineth *Creditor*. Ballance that *Cash*, and tell me what shall be done with the *difference*. Carry it to a new account, what then? there it will prove to be *Stock*. Carry it to Profit and Losse, there it will prove to be *Stockes Augmenter*. *Wonder is it*, that these and many other *Forrain bred-defects* must now be *cloathed in English Attire*, and passe for currant amongst us! Surely, our Judgement is weak in the *discerning of this Art*.

Phil. I perceive their passages in Booking of their Matters, doth not digest with you; is there a more plain way? discover that.

Sch. If we were as *Exact Discussors*, as we are *Imitators*; we had not been *so besotted*, as to entertain those Forrain defects, having *better at home*.

Look into *James Peele*, whose well-entrances, through neglecting Age (or disdain of Domestick Writers, and extolling of Forrain) are as strange to us, as though (as the saying is) they were written in Heathen Greek. He sheweth us the fit ground-work, how to conceale a mans Estate, in the Booking of his private accounts, and matters manifested for Merchandizing. . . .[22]

30

(Colinson, *Idea Rationaria*, 1683, p. 5.)

. . . When one intends to keep his Books in form, hee must close up all the accompts in his old Books, and see what the ballance of them is; and so bring it into your new Books, then you will commonly find your stock to be divided in these 4. parts following, *viz.* in money, 2. Goods, 3. Debts owing you, and 4. what debts you are owing to others.

Some will not place their Stock-accompts in their Books, so they charge every thing Debitor to Cash, as the Dutch Authors would have it: but then you cannot place the money which you have in the beginning; so that Mr. *Dafforn* justly condemnes that way, and he would have ane accompt which he calls Private accompt, made use of, in place of the concealed stock. Now I say, a man may have a private stock which he will conceal, and a stock in trade also; but then he must bring none of his private stock into his trading stocks Books, lest he confuse himself. Where in can this private stock consist? it must be in Lands, Houses, Rents, Jewels, and House-furnishing, &c. for which private stock let him keep a Book, which he may easily do apart. But I have in this Book composed ane ordinare stock, which I think any man may bring into his Books. It is true some men begins with none but by the Credit, or may be by being Imployed a Factor for others; so if he fear that others see his Books, then he may fancie of what value he will to make his private accompt Debitor for.

But what if this man should by losses come to faile, then his Creditors, to whom he is obliged to show his Books in such a case, they may see he hath been a great loser; but then they will challenge this private accompt to know what is become of it, and may be, they will then fancie he had such a private stock and so will make no composition with him. So I am for none of those things, let a man place all in his Books as his Condition is: for his Books are not to

---

[22] This presumably refers to Peele's book of 1569; see extract 28.

be seen by any, but whom he pleases, except in such cases as I said before; and then their stocks needs not be seen: which if he feare he may seal up the accompt of it; but such accompts of the Book as concerne the persons who referres their difference to them: I have seen in some of the Dutch Compting-houses two lines written on the wall, in Dutch, *viz.*

Kijck vryelijck om in alle de hoecken,
U hand van de Kas, en d'oogh uyt de Boecken.

Which is to say:

In every corner you may freely look,
Touch ·not the Cash, nor Heed the Merchants Book.

Now let us begin our Books, and place down the Estate wee have; which is our stock, and is like the Trunk of a Tree, it hath many Branches proceeding from one Center. . . .

Subsidiary Account-Books

31

(Hayes, *Gentleman's . . . Book-keeper*, 1741, p. 3.)

AND as the whole Art of the *Italian* Way of keeping Books depends intirely upon the Journal and Leger, I shall not trifle my own, nor the Reader's Time away, in giving unnecessary Descriptions of the several Sorts of Books; that the Journal-Parcels may be derived from, because those may be more or less, according as a Man's Business, or his Fancy may lead him.

FOR the Merchants themselves (who commonly are the most exact in keeping their Books and Accounts of any) differ very much among themselves about the Number of Books, as well as in the Manner of having their Legers ruled; some having them ruled in such a Manner, as they may refer to the Page of almost every Book that a Journal-Parcel arises from, both Debtor and Creditor; and others again have them ruled in such a Manner, as only to reserve a Column to refer to the Folio of the Leger, where the Counterpart of the Debtor or Creditor is entered, and another Column to place the Page of the Journal in, where those Entries are posted from.

32

(Stephens, *Italian Book-keeping*, 1735, pp. 119–20.)

. . . I have intended to give a Definition of *Italian* Book-Keeping in General, and therefore the Principles that have been laid down, are calculated and argu'd upon, in such a Manner, as to make them capable of answering the said Intention, by Reason it is very easy for every Man, of whatsoever Nature or Kind his Affairs are, to render them evident, in all the Circumstances from first to last, as has been propos'd by the Introduction, provided we act up to the Strictness and Extent of the Principles; as, on the other Hand, by omitting some Principles intirely, or not taking them according to such Strictness and Extent, we lose so much Knowledge of our Affairs, or cause it to be more general; however, we cannot help using some of those Principles, as the distinguishing Accounts (with respect to Men) must not only be observ'd in the *Italian* Method, but in all others whatsoever; nor is it possible for any Man to have his Affairs kept clear and intelligible, without observing and being guided by such Reasons as I have, in the treating of Distinctions, most plainly discuss'd; but, notwithstanding, we see the Principles may be apply'd in other Books besides the Journal and Leidger, tho' they at the same Time ought never to be made use of, but when there appears a plain Advantage arising from thence; and this every Man himself is to be the Judge of, as well as of the Form and Method of them, all which I have already taken Notice of.

And thus Company Stewards, Shop-Keepers, Factors, and all other Accounts whatsoever, can only differ in the inferior Books, some using a greater some a lesser Number of them, and of various Natures one from the other, but the Principles are still the same, and must be apply'd in all Cases, as abovesaid; for which Reason it would be of no Advantage to treat of those or any other kind of Accounts, seeing as all that could be said must necessarily relate to the inferior Books, so is it a Thing that is endless, and cannot be demonstrated otherways than what I have attempted above: But, notwithstanding, it will be proper to speak of Company Stewards Accounts, &c. with regard to another Thing, and that is, a Method whereby they are made to be kept in the same Journal and Leidger along with my own proper Accounts; however, in this I shall endeavour to be as brief as possible, because a very little Matter will be sufficient to explain it. . . .

33

(Ympyn, *Notable . . . Woorke*, 1547, ch. 23.)

What maner of bokes are requisite to be had to write in suche thynges as is not mete to be written in the jornall, nor in the greate boke.

Firste it is nedefull to make a litle long boke to write in the charges of houshold as is aforsaid, and therupon write, daily expences of this yere, &c. Another square boke wherin shalbe written the copy of letters and suche other thynges, and therupon shal ye write: The copies of letters, &c. Also another long boke wherin shalbe written all small expences of marchandise, as cariage and so furthe, because the principall boke shall not be troubled nor bloted therwith, the whiche costes shalbe somoned every moneth or every mart and set into the Jornall. And yet a litle long boke wherin the Cassier shall daily write what that he laieth out parcell meale as he paieth it or receiveth it: That is to saie, a some of xx. xxx. or. xl. f. more or lesse, to write in what money he ether received it or paied it, and specially when it is a great some, and that many sortes of money are contaigned in it. And this is very profitable to advoyde errors that might happen. There is requisite also to be kept a Memoriall boke, when ye shall write what thynges ye lend out as hattes, bogettes, males, botes, clokes, woodknives or any other thyng, and what thynges ye have to do for your self, or for any other person and the price that suche a ware is wont to be solde at, and what is mete to be kept, &c. And if it be one that sendeth muche wares into diverse countrees then must he kepe a boke of the contentes of every packe & bale and their Numero and what marke thei are marked withall. And to suche as have great occupiynges is the double A.B.C. very necessarie, but not to other.[23]

34

(Roose, *Essay to Make . . . Accomptant*, 1760, pp. 15–16.)

The cash-book.

The Cash-Book, which is folio'd as the Ledger, is nothing else but keeping a separate Accompt of Cash from it, to which it is posted every Month, by debiting Cash to Sundries, for all your Receipts and Sundries to Cash, for all your Payments, and then posted to the particular Accompts to which it belongs.[24]

It contains, on the Debtor-side, all the Money you have received that Month, and on the Creditor-side, all the Money you have paid. Some state their Cash-Book every Week for their own Satisfaction, and post it to the several Accompts to which it belongs, without

---

23 The double alphabet (index) of the ledger occupies 20 folios of the illustrative set of accounts in the original Dutch treatise (1543) by Ympyn. A double index differs from a single index in that the page for each letter in a double index is sub-divided into spaces for the letters of the alphabet. The entry for, say, " Luca Pacioli ", would be in the space for " P " on the page for " L ". In ch. 10 of the English book it is explained: " And therunto [the ledger] must apperteigne a Kalender, Registre or A.B.C. made of thesame largenesse that the boke is of or litle lesse, entitled in the beginnyng like as the other bokes are, & this maie ye put before or behynde your boke at your pleasure. And moste comonly these Registers be made single, but for suche as kepe greate reconynges and countours, thei use a doble Register or A.B.C. . . . and if the boke [ledger] be five or six hundred lefes, then shal not the syngle A.B.C. do very well: howbeit the doble A.B.C. is used litle of any nacion saving of the Venecians."
24 Plates VIII and IX show an example of a cash account in the ledger, with periodic omnibus entries posted from a cash book.

keeping any Accompt of Cash in the Ledger at all. See it's Form, at the End of the Journal A.

The book of charges of merchandize.

This Book is only paged, and according to *Webster's* Plan,[25] contains an Accompt of all those Charges which have no Accompt opened for them in the Ledger, except that of charges of merchandize; and, consequently, is balanced by Profit and Loss, and such Charges are Shop-Rent, Shop Books, Postage of Letters, Clerks-Wages, and the like. But with others, it contains, besides what is above-mentioned, Charges on all Sorts of Goods and Voyages, as Carriage, Custom, Freight, Wharfage, etc. and consequently is credited by the said Goods or Voyages for their respective Sums. This is nothing else but a petty Cash-Book, since the Total is carried to the Creditor-side of the Cash-Book every Month. See it's Form, at the End of the Waste-Book A.

35

(Malcolm, *Treatise of Book-keeping*, 1731, pp. 62–3.)

Of the invoyce book.

This Book contains an Account (called the *Invoyce*) of all the Goods which I ship off, either for my own Account, or for others in Commission, according to the Bills of Lading; with the whole Charges till on Board; every Invoyce following after another, in Order as they happen. It's nothing but a Copy of what is written in the *Waste-Book* in these Cases: Examples of which you'll find in the following *Waste-Books*; and therefore it's needless to make any particular Example of the Form of it here. I shall only say in general, that after the Date the Narration is to begin thus,—— *Shipped Aboard the Ship —— A. B. Master*; *bound for —— the following Goods*; *consigned to —— for my Account, or by Order, and for the Account of ——*. Or, the Narration may be begun, thus, —— *Invoyce of Goods Shipped Aboard—&c.*

The Design of this Book is for the more ready finding out these *Invoyces*, than can be done in the *Waste-Book*; but, in my Opinion, there is little in this. For the *Index* directs us very readily to the *Account* of the Voyage in the *Leger*, if it's for our own Account, or to the Employer's Account, if it's for another; and these Accounts

---

[25] William Webster, author of a popular *Essay on Book-keeping . . .* , first edition 1719.

will as readily direct us, by the Date, to the *Invoyce*, as it stands
in the *Waste-Book*. Some propose the entering of these *Invoyces*,
both in this separate Book, and also in the Grand Memorial or
Waste-Book; where, they think, every Thing ought to be, to make
a complete Memorial of all our Business together, in Order of Time.
But this Method would be double the Work, to no Purpose; because,
either the *Waste-Book* or *Invoyce-Book* is sufficient. And if it's
thought more convenient to put all *Invoyces* together, you may
chuse a separate Place in the *Waste-Book* for them; though it's of
no Importance whether they are thus placed, or in a Book quite
distinct from the Memorial of all other Transactions.

Again *observe*, That some who use these *Invoyce-Books* have an
equal Space on the opposite Page, against the *Invoyce* of *Goods*
shipped for their own Account; in which they enter all the Advices
from their Factor, concerning the Disposal of those Goods; by which
the whole State of these Affairs is seen at once. But your Factor's
Accounts, in the *Leger*, are sufficient for this.

36

(Malcolm, *Treatise of Book-keeping*, 1731, p. 64.)
There is another subservient Book, which may be very useful to
those who receive or make many Payments, though it makes no
Alteration in the other Books. It is called,

The Month-Book.

It is numbered in Folios like the *Leger*, and divided into Spaces,
on the Top of each of which are the Names of the 12 Months of the
Year; *January*, *February*, &c. allowing a whole Folio, or what you
please, to each Month; and a different Set of 12 Spaces for every
different Year. On the left Page enter the Payments to be made
to you, in that Month: And on the right Page the Payments you
are to make. Make a Column on the left Hand of every Page; in
which, write the Day of Payment. After which, write the Name
of the Debtor or Creditor; and draw the Sum into the Money
Columns: Then, when the Payment is made, either mark it by the
Word *paid*, on the Margin; or, if you make double Money
Columns, enter the Debt in the Inner; and when paid, draw it out
to the outer Columns. In Case of partial Payments, you may shew
it in the *Month-Book*, by some particular Mark; and when the
Whole is paid, draw it out.

Account-Books : Miscellaneous Matters

37

(Weddington, *Breffe Instruction*, 1567.)

Rules verry necessarie to be observid by all marchantis, in the kepinge of ther accomptis or reconningis &c.

Fyrst it is verri nedefull for all marchantis to have understandinge and knowlidge in all manner of marchandize, and to write and rede perfectli, and also promptli to cast ther accomptis, by Arismeticke or countres, and at the beginninge of their writtingis to put fyrst the name of God, makinge the signe of the crosse the wiche is most commonli usid amongest all Christen men.——

More thei ought to be dilligent and verri surcumspect in all ther dowingis and writtingis and to se them selvez well to it, that thei be nat deceavid by to miche trustinge of other.——

The master or principall servant ought to have alwais by hym a breffe ballans, or abstract out of his great Boke, or lidger of all the accomptis Debitors and Creditors, containinge in the same withe the dais of paiment, to thende that he maie se incontenent his estate in all thingis withe his charge and discharge that provision mai be made in tyme yf nede be.——

The counttinge house or place, wher they shall write ought to be quiat or still, and furnisshid withe al thingis necessarie, belonging unto the same, as bokis paper, yncke, standishe pennes, penkniff, wex, seallinge threde, seale &c.——

That all obligations billis of debt, contractes, indentors &c. ought to be bounde in other faier papers, and writton apon what they be, withe the dais of paiment, and soms of moni withe the pertis name or names, that owithe the same, and so to be kept in boxes, or chestis, ther unto apertaininge untill the dais of paiment do comme.——

The leteris that they shall receave from ther partenars, factours or ani otter men, they ought to write apon them the daie of the receat and from whom, and then the daie of the answere, that don laie them up in pressus to them apertaininge, and everi yere ons, to sort out all mens leteris severalli, and to binde them up in papers writtinge apon them the yere of owre lorde, and from whom thei have byn receavid &c. and then to laie them upon shelvez in your countinge hous, or other ther unto apertaininge and as you do this so maie you do withe all other accomptis and writtingis.——

And more when your great Bokis be full writton you most kepe them faire in pressus or coeffers ther unto belonginge, and from time to time make newe the wiche shalbe goodli precedentis, for your childerin or suche as shall come after you.——And now that I have declared my minde in these thingis a fore saide verri nedefull, here next enswinge, I wil gyve further Instructions for the order of marchantis bokis of ther accomptis. . . .

38

(Malynes, *Lex Mercatoria*, 1656, p. 242.)

. . . But in the Journall or Leiger book there may not be any alteration of Cyphers, blotting (nor places left in blanke in the Journal) but one parcel without intermission must follow another, otherwise the books are of no credit in Law, or before any Magistrate; whereas otherwise much credit is given to books well and orderly kept, for the deciding and determination of many controversies which happen between merchants and Merchants, and their Factors, . . .

39

(Dowling, *Complete System*, 1770, pp. 16–17.)

General directions to keep a ledger regularly.

1st, Chuse a Place remote from Noise and the Eyes of Strangers; 2d, write the Titles in a large Text Hand; 3d, write fair, without great Heads or Tails to your Letters, and leisurely, to prevent Mistakes, and draw the Lines by a Rule; 4th, express no more of an Article but what regards that Account on which you write, and what may be contained in one Line, unless the Nature of the Account requires a Distinction of Particulars in several Lines and Sums, as it happens in recording several Bills, Notes and other Paper Effects at one Time; as also in general Accounts [26]; 5th, let the Figures be so placed that Units may exactly correspond to Units,

---

[26] " General " accounts are explained in extract 58.

Tens to Tens, &c. 6th, give to each Account a convenient Space, *viz.* a whole Folio to the Account of Profit and Loss, another to the Account of Bills and Notes, the like to the Accounts of Cash and Charges, unless you bring the respective Articles in Totals from the Cash Book and Book of Charges. To other Accounts you will give so much as you judge they may require, whether it be a whole Folio, or half, a third, &c. 7th, open the Accounts in the *Ledger* one after another, as they occur, leaving no Folio blank, nor turning back to vacant Spaces; 8th, never raze or cross an Article, tho' a Mistake should happen, not only to preserve the Fairness of the Book, but chiefly that every Step and Circumstance of the Affair may distinctly appear, when, on Disputes arising, Recourse may be had to the Books by yourself, your Executors, or others, but mend the Error by a new Post, as will be shewn in the third Part of these Instructions; 9th, when the Space assign'd to any Account is filled, open the Account in a new Place, and to the *Dr.* Side of this new Account carry the Total of the *Dr.* Side of the old Account, and to the *Cr.* Side of the new Account carry the Total of the *Cr.* Side of the old Account, mentioning before each Total of the old Account, transported to Folio (——) and on the new Account, transported from Folio (——) a formal Balance might be used, but this Method is more simple and easy; 10th, when you settle Accounts with your Correspondent, close the Account in your *Ledger* accordingly.

40

(Mellis, *Briefe Instruction*, 1588, ch. 19.)

> In what manner you shall referre or convey the former parcels of the leager when they bee full written, and to what leafe of your leager you ought to bring the rest of such accompt, to the intent there may rise no suspicion in your leager.

It is to bee remembred, when that any accompt by continuance of time used, is full written, whether it be in Creditor or Debitor, so that no more in that accompt may be put; then take the difference betweene the Creditor and Debitor, and make the rest, and which of them remaineth: the rest you shall referre and rescribe it in another leafe of the Leager, there as by course it may be put. And this rescription into a new leafe, ye shal sald the former accompt in that place, and see that you describe the rest in both partes, the one in Creditor of the former accompt, and the other in Debitor, there as yee write the Rest, which Rest yee neede not put in the Journall, like as is touched in the canon of *Lucrum* and *Damnum* [27] : for that were but vaine business.[28]

And for the more declaration I put this example, that Marten hath bought and solde with you long time, by reason whereof his accompt is ful, so yt no more therin may be entered, & this accompt standeth in my leager in fol. 30. now I will report or convey it into a new leafe of my Leager in fol. 60, wher by course I may put in the saide Marten. Now I finde him by a longe accompt Debitor for 580 li. 0s. 0d.

And I finde him Creditor in the same accompt 522 li. 6s. 0d.

The which rest being 57 li. 14s. 0d. I put in creditor opposit. And in salding of the same accompt thus saying: on the debitor side In fol. 60. Marten ought to geve for his rest. as it appeareth in fol. 30 57 li. 14s. which is hether referred: and this in the whole sum saldeth from the accompte in folio 30. And make ye in the new leafe the day & date of our Lord God, and also in the margent of both the leaves, make this signe R. for restes.[29]

41

(Peele, *Maner and Fourme*, 1553, ch. 7.)

The maner howe to examen or peruse your bookes one by the other, wherby to know if the parcels be truly entered out of your jornal, with the use to refourme an erroure chaunced in your quaterne boke.

For the examinacion of your bookes, and triall of your Jornall by your Quaterne, wherby to be out of doubt, that every parcell is truely borne from the one boke into the other, you shal cause one to take your Jornall, and to begin with the first parcell, readynge unto you the tenor therof, & in what folio of your Quaterne that said parcel is made debitor accordyng unto the figure prescribed over a little lyne whiche is overthwart the Jornal, and also in what folio it is Creditor, accordyng unto the other figure under the saied line,

---

27 Profit and loss.
28 The purport of this sentence is discussed on p. 159, below.
29 In the set of accounts which Mellis added to Oldcastle's text (see p. 156, below), there is no account for Marten. There is no example of a balance carried forward from one page to another in the illustrative accounts.

wherunto if bothe your bokes in summes and folios do agree, you may well perceive that parcell to be perfectlye entered bothe in Debitor and Creditor of your Quaterne, then make prickes[30] over and under the figures of your Jornall, and also against the Debitor and creditors parcels in your Quaterne, signifiyng that parcell of your Jornall to be trulye examined, as ye may see practised in the first parcell ofthe Jornall, and so ought you to examen all your Jornall before you make your balaunce. I have not in this practice pricked any mo parcels then the fyrst in the Jornal, and the cause is, that the printer coulde not do it without much trouble. And in this your examinacion of your bokes when you find a parcel in your Quaterne having the letter R. you shal not nede to staie therat, for that it is no part of your Jornall, but as you have learned before, a remayne thether borne.for lacke of roume, which you may in like maner examen as before is saied.[31]

Furthermore, if ye shall chaunce in your examinacion to find any parcel entred out of your Jornall upon debitor in your Quaterne, & should be upon creditor, then remove it to the creditor in the same accompte to requite the erroure, makyng against the other so missed some maner of note, wherby you maye knowe that it was founde an error at your examinacion, and beare the same that was chaunced amisse, to his ryght place. And as touching this examinacion, I thinke it good that it be not deferred wholly to the ende of your accompt, for that it wil not only aske long time, but also be a let and trouble to the proceadynge in your newe accompt, but rather alwayes as your leasure serveth, cease not to practise your examinacion, and so shall you be in the better readines to make your balaunce spedely, and also out of doubt, of any thing before passed from the Jornall.

42

(Macghie, *Principles of Book-keeping*, 1718, p. 14.)

Rule VIII. In Case there be a complex Parcel in the *Waste-Book*, as was observed at *Rule* IV. which makes the *Journal-Post* to contain Two or more *Debitors*, and but one *Creditor*, or *vice versa*, to contain but one *Debitor* and several *Creditors*; then you must

---

[30] The "pricks" are clearly shown in Plates X and XI, reproducing entries in the seventeenth-century journals of Sir John Banks and Sir Charles Peers, respectively.
[31] That is, carry-forwards of balances ("remaynes" or "rests") on accounts are not passed through the journal.

enter, at once, *Sundry Accompts*, Debitors to that one *Person* or *Thing*. Or, on the other Hand, that one *Person* or *Thing*, Debitor to *Sundry Accompts*. After which, follows the 4 last Particulars mentioned in *Rule* III. and [with a *viz.*] we mention the sundry Persons or Things as *Debitors* or *Creditors*, with their several Sums confin'd to an inner Column, as was directed at the said *Rule* IV. All which is done to avoid the making of Two or more *Journal Posts*, when this one may serve the Turn, and answer the Design of this Method more naturally and truly.

Rule IX. But if there happen a complex Parcel, containing both sundry *Debitors* and sundry *Creditors*, as falls out frequently in *Barter*, we may comprehend the whole Matter by making *Sundry Accompts*, Debitors to *Sundry Accompts*; the *Debitors* being above the Line, and the *Creditors* below, and the *Sum* of both, being the same, in the middle, respecting both the *Debitors* and *Creditors*. But it may also be resolved into Two Entries, *viz.* by making *Sundry Accompts* Debitors to the Person with whom we deal; and again, in another *Post*, we enter that *Person*, Debitor to one or *Sundry Accompts*; both which Entries are cleared from the Two Rules immediately preceeding.

Rule X. But if one would shorten his Work in the *Journal*, or the Number of his Accompts in the *Leger*, he must observe, that several Species of Accompts may be denominated by one and the same common Title, whereby he may bring Two or more, as he pleases, under one single Accompt denominated by the said general Title. Thus, *Barley*, *Oats*, *Wheat*, &c. may be designed *Grain*; and so all Sorts of it may be crowded into one Accompt, provided we deal but little in such Kind of Commodities. Again, If we buy up or receive from Abroad sundry Parcels of Merchandize, and not being willing to give each of them a particular Accompt, we may call them all, *Goods brought from*, or *belonging to such a Place*, even altho' these Goods should be of different Kinds, which is mostly used when the Merchant receives Goods from others to sell in Commission as their Factor.

On the other Hand, if one would know more distinctly, what is lost or gain'd upon any particular Accompt, wherein he has much Concern and Trade, he may divide the same into subparticular Accompts, and assign each of these Branches a special Denomination (which frequently we have a Precedent of, but are sometimes oblig'd to invent new Titles) *e.g.* Thus often-times the Accompt of

Profit and *Loss*, ought to be subdivided into it's several *Branches*, such as *Interest-Accompt, Insurance-Accompt, Provision-Accompt, Charges-Accompt, &c.* besides a general Accompt of *Profit* and *Loss*, into which all these at length terminate, together with other Things which cannot be otherwise denominated, than by the general Title of *Profit* and *Loss*. But this shall be more particularly exemplify'd in our practical Set of Books.

43

(Dafforne, *Merchants Mirrour*, 1660, epistle dedicatory.)

. . . Yet *more Rubbes*: The word REPERTITION [32] is not used in my Book, as *James Peele*, and many Merchants do; which would much *abridge* the prolixity of my Journal passages. True it is, I have not used that word *Repertition*, since Art-discerning hath befriended me. Concerning *James Peele*, I peaceably passe him, in respect of the Antiquity of his Work, and long interred Body. As for that word *Repertition*, used at present among Merchants, I say, that an *experienced Merchant* is not confined to the strictnesse of School-rudiments, they being the main Tenor of this Book; as by the Title thereof appeareth in these words:

> *Directions for the perfect Ordering, and*
> *Booking of his Accounts.*

Note, the Title saith not, *For the Abridgment of his Accounts*, because a Merchant must governe his Books as the Circumstances of his Traffick requireth. True it is, the ground-knowledge of Book-keeping is in it self the same: but the words and manner of Entrances are derived from the Trafficks form, though in all, the words *Debitor* and *Creditor* are used. But whosoever endeavoureth to confine Me to use the word *Repertition* in this Book, laboureth to induce me to enter such imaginary Titles in my Journal, that neither

---

[32] In his *Pathewaye to Perfectnes*, 1569, Peele introduced this word, which was subsequently replaced in practice by " Sundries " or " Sundry Accounts " (see extract 42) or " Severalls ". A specimen journal entry of Peele's begins:

" Reperticion appertaining to sundry accounts oweth. . . ."

In this entry several ledger accounts are to be debited, and one account (Money) to be credited.

In the " repertition " entry shown on Plate X there is no collective noun for the numerous personal accounts which are to be credited.

are entered into *Kalendar* nor *Leager*. Look into the *Kalendar* or *Leager* of *James Peele*, and see if in either you find a Title termed *Repertition*: neither can you find any in the Merchants *Kalendar* or *Leager*; therefore is the Title *Repertition* a forged Title. For this is a certainty, that *such Title words as each Journal parcel beareth, such words ought to be entred in the* Kalendar *and* Leager *Titles.* . . .

Debits and Credits

44

(North, *Gentleman Accomptant*, 1715, pp. 8–9.)

The Art of Regular Accompting depends wholly upon this Supposition, viz. That every thing negociated comes out of something, and goes into something, having (as they say of Motion) its *terminus a quo & ad quem*. But this farther, that if there happen any Increase or Decrease of the Whole, or any Part in the Transition, there is a common Receptacle, or Place, which receives or furnisheth exactly the same. So that however spaciously the Books are branched out, there is conserved a perpetual Par, or Balance of the Whole. According to this Notion, all the *Drs.* and *Crs.* are declared; for that Person or Thing which takes is made *Dr.* that is, stands *charged*; and that Person or Thing which delivers, or parts from, is the *Cr.* or *discharged*; and in every Entry of a Negociation, the first thing done is to set down these Terms of it, that is, the *Dr.* and the *Cr.*; and then what the Nature and State of it is. . . .

45

(Peele, *Pathewaye to Perfectnes*, 1569.) [33]

All ye that your accomptes by debt and credite use,
Each Journall percell when you wright: in no wise do refuse
To make eache thinge receaved, or the receaver,
Owe to eache thinge delivered, or the deliverer.
And eke in places twaine, of Lidger loke ye set,
Eache percell that in Journall standes. The first must be the debt.
Which debt shall aunswered be, in creditour alone,
(Reparticonns onlye except, where manie springes from one.[34])
And or [35] ye wright receave, but wright before you paye:
So shall no parte of your accompte in anye wise decaye.

[33] A somewhat similar verse appears in Peele's earlier book.
[34] For " repertition " entries, see extract 43.
[35] Archaic for " ere."

And reckon justlye ofte all variaunce for to cease,
For reckenings even make frendship long, & dailie to encrease.
If ye these rules observe as guides to your accompte,
Your worke shal then be perfect sure, no doubts shal truth surmount.

46

(Hayes, *Gentleman's . . . Book-keeper*, 1741, p. 13.)

The grand general rule.

All Things received, or the Receiver,

or,

The Account upon which the Thing is received,
must always be made Debtor.

And all Things delivered, or the Deliverer,

or,

The Account upon which the Thing is delivered,
must always be the Creditor.

47

(Dowling, *Complete System*, 1770, pp. 23-4.)

General Rules for Dr. *and* Cr.

A real Account that has or is to have a Title in my Ledger·

Is Dr. { When it becomes my Property. When any Charge attends it. } Is Cr. { When it ceases to be my Property. When it brings in any Thing.

A Person or Personal Account.

Is Dr. { When he becomes accountable to me. When I cease to be accountable to him. } Is Cr. { When I become accountable to him. When he ceases to be accountable to me.

An imaginary Account of Gain *or* Loss.

Is Dr. { When I lose and have no real or personal Account to Charge or Debit. } Is Cr. { When I gain and have no real or personal Account to Discharge or Credit.

The same Rules otherwise expressed.
For a real Account, to which I give a Title in my Ledger.

| When it becomes mine, When it costs me any Thing, | } it is Dr. { | For its Cost or Value. For that Cost. |
| When it ceases to be mine, When it brings me in any Thing, | it is Cr. { | For its Price. For the Value it brings. |

For a Person or Personal Account.

| When he gets into my Debt, When I get out of his Debt, | } he is Dr. { | For what he then contracts. For what I pay or cease to owe him. |
| When I get into his Debt, When he gets out of my Debt, | } he is Cr. { | For what I then contract. For what he pays or ceases to owe me. |

For an imaginary Account of Gain and Loss.

| When I lose and have no real or personal Account to Charge or Debit, | } it is Dr. { | For the Loss. |
| When I gain and have no real or personal Account to discharge or Credit, | } it is Cr. { | For the Gain. |

48

(Donn, *Accountant*, 1775, p. 7.)

. . . From what has been said it is evident,

1st, That the *Stock Account* is *Debtor* for all I *owe* by the Inventory; and *Creditor* for what I *have* in my Hands, or is owing to me, mentioned in the Inventory.

2dly, *Cash* is *Debtor* for whatever is *received*, and *Creditor* for what Money is *paid* or *given away*.

3dly, *Profit and Loss* is *Debtor* for all *Losses*, and *Creditor* for all *Gains*.

4thly, *A Person's Account* is *Debtor* for what I pay him, or he owes me; and *Creditor* for what he pays me, or I owe him.

5thly, An *Account of Goods* is *Debtor* for the Value of all received, with the Cost and Charges thereto belonging; and *Creditor* for what any Ways goes out.

And in buying or selling, this Rule is general:

> What I receive
> Or the Person receiving } is Debtor
>
> What I deliver
> Or the Person delivering } is Creditor

49

(Handson, *Analysis of . . . Accompts*, 1669.)

Sales of Wares

For Mony: Dr. Mony: Cr. the Wares sold and delivered (the Mony being received upon the delivery of the Wares sold, which is not usual.)

For Time, or
For part Mony, part time, or
For part Mony, part Wares, part by anothers bill, part time

> Dr. the party that buyeth those Wares: Cr. the Wares sold and delivered for the whole sum.
> And for the Mony received make: Dr. Mony: Cr. the party buyer in the second branch.
> And in the third branch: Dr. the party whose bill you take: Cr. the buyer.

In barter

Wares for Wares simply: Dr. the Wares received: Cr. the Wares delivered both be of equal value, which seldom hapneth.

For part Mony, part Wares:
> Dr. Mony for so much as is received.
> Dr. the Wares received for the value of them.
> Cr. the several Wares delivered for the whole sum.

For part Mony, part Wares, part Time:
For part Mony, part Wares, part anothers bill, part time:
> Dr. the Party or Parties that buy the same.
> Cr. the Wares sold and delivered for the same Sum, as before.

For part Mony, part by anothers bill:
> Dr. Mony for the sum received:
> Dr. the party whose bill is taken for the value thereof:
> Cr. the Wares sold and delivered for the whole sum.

For part Wares, part by anothers bill:
> Dr. the Wares received for the value of them:
> Dr. the Party whose bill is taken for the rest:
> Cr. the Wares sold and delivered for the whole sum.

By advice from your Factor: Dr. that Factor: Cr. the Voyage or Voyages for the Goods sold by him.

The contrary whereof is to be observed in the buying of Wares.

50

(Handson, *Analysis of . . . Accompts*, 1669.)

Payments of Mony

Owing by you by Bill, Bond, Accompt or otherwise: Dr. the Party or Parties to whom the same was due. / For Wares bought for Mony: Dr. the Wares so bought and received. } Cr. Mony.

Lent at Interest by Bond: Dr. the Party or Parties borrowers for the Principal and Interest. { Cr. Mony for the sum paid. / Cr. Profit or Loss, or the Acc. of Interest, for the Interest thereof.

For Interest of Mony formerly taken up (the principal being continued) Dr. Interest, and Profit or Loss: / For Assurance of Goods Shipped: Dr. the Accompt of Assurance of, or Profit and Loss. / Remitted by Exchange: Dr. the Factor or Party to whom the Bills are payable. / By Bills of Exchange charged upon you: Dr. the Factor or Party under-writing those Bills. } Cr. Mony.

For Charges. { Of Wares bought: Dr. those Wares / Of Goods Shipped: Dr. the Voyage / Extraordinary. / Of Household. } Dr. Profit and Loss, or petty expences. } Cr. Mony.

51

(Carpenter, *Most Excellent Instruction*, 1632.)

Charges of goods.

Charges of goods received to sell for anothers account
    The former account of your friend is debtor; and Cash Creditor for the monie paid.
Charges of goods or wares: Account of wares is debtor, Cash is Creditor.
Charges of goods shipped; voyage is debtor, and goods shipped Creditor.

Charges by paiment of monie for wares bought; the wares is debtor; and Cash is creditor.

Charges by payment of monie for goods shipped; Voyage is debtor, and Cash is creditor.

Charges extraordinary, or household expences: Profit and Losse is debtor, and Cash creditor. . . .

52

(Mair, *Book-keeping Methodiz'd*, 1741, pp. 16–17.)

There are some Cases so simple, that they cannot properly be divided into a Dr. Part and Cr. Part, but consist of one of these Parts only: e.g. If a Merchant, by the Death of a Friend gets a Legacy, or any other way receives Goods or Money, as an Addition to his Stock, for which he gives nothing out; it is evident, from the first Remark, that the Thing received, whether Goods or Money, is *Debtor*: But then, in the present Case, neither any Thing, nor any Person, can be made *Creditor*: Not a Thing, because nothing goes out, as an Equivalent for the Thing received; not a Person, because no body has a Right to demand Payment or Restitution. In Cases therefore of this Nature, a fictitious Cr. must be contrived to supply the Want of a real or personal one. That which is commonly used in this, and some other such Cases, is *Profit and Loss*. Supposing then that the Merchant receives the above Legacy in ready Money, the *Journal* Entrance will be, *Cash* Dr. to *Profit and Loss*. For the same Reason, when a Merchant gives away Money or Goods, for which he is to expect no Return, he makes *Profit and Loss* Dr. to the Thing delivered. Thus, when he pays Shop-rent, Ware-house Rent, or other Things of the like Nature, the Entrance is, *Profit and Loss* Dr. to *Cash*. In like manner, when a Merchant sends Goods to Sea, it is plain, by the second Remark, that the Goods, being the Thing disposed of, are to be esteemed Cr. but then there is no Dr. for neither is any thing received in their stead, nor is the Factor to whom they are consigned, as yet chargeable. A fictitious *Debtor* must therefore be had, namely, *Voyage*, which is always made Dr. on this Occasion. As suppose a Merchant ship off Tobacco to *Rotterdam*, the *Journal Entrance* will be, *Voyage to Rotterdam* Dr. to *Tobacco*. And the Voyage is again discharged, by being made Cr. when Advice comes that the Ship is arrived, and the Goods received by the Factor. There are some other fictitious Terms necessary on some other Occasions, which shall be taken notice of afterwards. Before I finish this Remark, I shall obviate the Learner's Surprise, who probably may think it strange, to find such a compound and inconsistent like Term as *Profit and Loss*, and be ready to imagine that it would be better, in the first of the Cases above, to make *Profit* Cr. and in the second, to make *Loss* Dr. But this would occasion two different Accompts in the *Ledger*; the former of which would have the Cr. Side filled up, and nothing on the Dr. Side; the latter would have all its Articles on the Dr. Side, and nothing on the Cr. Side. To prevent this, the two are joined together, and charged Dr. for Losses, and made Cr. for things gained: By which means both are reduced to one *Ledger-accompt*, whose Dr. Side contains all the Articles of Loss, and its Cr. Side the Articles of Gain. It were indeed to be wished that we had some *English* Word of such a general Signification, as to be equally applicable to denote Gain or Loss. Such a Word would be more suitable and convenient for this purpose: But as we have none, the compound Term *Profit and Loss* must be used. *N.B.* The Articles of Profit and Loss are always very numerous, but the *Ledger-accompt* is somewhat eased by other Accompts that are commonly kept; which are nothing else but particular Branches of itself, such as, *Charges of Merchandize*, *House-expences*, &c.

53

(Malcolm, *Treatise of Book-keeping*, 1731, pp. 13–14.)

For *Real Accounts*. *Debtor* and *Creditor* are here applied in an artificial and improper Sense, which is borrowed from Persons: The Foundation of which is this, *viz.* That Money being contrived for a Medium of Commerce, by which all Things are valued, in order to a just and equal Exchange; therefore we must in every other real Account mind not only the Quantity, but the Money Value (the Cash Account we shall consider by it self afterwards.) And as these are really different Things, we may, under this Distinction, very easily apply the Notion of Debt and Credit to such Accounts; so that when any Thing becomes mine, I consider it as a Subject which owes, or is accountable to me for such a Sum of Money as it has cost me, either in Specie, or other Effects, or I owe for it, or which I expect to make out of it (cost what it will;) for, in Effect, 'tis the same Thing to me, as if some Person owed me this Money; and so

I charge it as my Debtor. Again, when it is given away, and some other Thing or Person is accountable to me in place of it; it may easily be conceived to have hereby discharged so much of the former Charge; and therefore we apply the Word *Creditor* to express this, and to distinguish it from the other Side. If the Money Value is greater or lesser than the Charge, it comes under the Notion of *Gain* or *Loss*. And, *Lastly*, Though no *Person* or *Thing* comes in place of it, yet so much being actually gone away, that Subject is no longer *chargeable* for it, because it can never be made out of a Thing that is no more, and must therefore be made Creditor or discharged, to shew the true State of the Account; and for the Cash Account it self, we *charge* and *discharge* it for what's received and given out, the same Way as other real Accounts.

And here it's to be observed, That the Word Cash comes originally from the *Italian* Word, *Cassa*, which signifies a Chest; for the Chest in which the Money is kept was considered by the Inventors as the Debtor and Creditor for what is received and given, to make the Subject charged and discharged different from the Money, as in other real Accounts.

But now, in reality, all this does, in effect, answer no other Purpose, than to shew what I receive and give away separately; in order to know at all Times, by the Comparison, what remains of the Quantity, and what I gain or lose as to the Money Value: The Notion of Debt and Credit being (as already observed) added as an Improvement, for the sake of some Consequences deduced from it, for the further perfecting of the Method; as you'll learn in the following Rules.

On Some Selected Ledger Accounts

54

(Macghie, *Principles of Book-keeping*, 1718, pp. 9–10.)

Def. [inition] VIII. Now having enquired into the principal Parts of Merchandizing, we might, pass to adapt proper Titles to every one of our Accompts, (as was proposed at *Def.* VI.) and so state them *Debitor* and *Creditor*: But this is needless, seeing that all such Titles are materially contain'd in the Instances adduced, and so will need little Art to draw them thence, thereby to stile or denominate any Part of our Business. But to make the Matter plainer, we shall divide Trade and its Accompts another Way, *viz.* by considering them either, as *Personal*, *Real*, or *Nominal*, *i.e. Fictitious*, *Accompts*: Each of which may be defin'd in the Manner following.

1. *Personal Accompts* are such, as have only the bare Names of Persons for their Titles, and arise from my dealing with such Persons as are neutral, or Strangers in a common Way of trading, *viz.* in buying and selling upon Time, or bartering, borrowing, lending, promising, wagering, *etc.* or when they respect me as my Correspondents, (*i.e.* my Imployer or Factor) or Partners in Factorage or Company Accompts, where such Accompts are only meant of such Persons their particular Accompts.

2. *Real Accompts* are such, whereby we denominate *Things* of all Sorts; whether *Money*, *Wares*, *Moveables*, *Houses* and *Possessions* of all Kinds, whether the Wares be in our Hands, or in the Hands of our Factor or Partner.

3. *Fictitious* or *Nominal Accompts*, are such as are contriv'd on Purpose to supply the Defect of a *Debitor* or *Creditor*, in all personal or real Accompts; seeing that no Accompt can alone consist of a *Debitor* without a *Creditor*, or *vice versa*. And therefore, *e.g.* when I receive any Thing, without giving out or delivering (or being in the least obliged to give out or deliver) any Thing in Compensation thereof, as in the Case of a *Gift*, or any Kind of neat Gain; then I say, I must contrive a *Creditor*, to which the Thing received must be made *Debitor*, which in the general must be *Accompt* of *Profit* and *Loss*, or a particular Branch thereof, *viz. Interest-Accompt*,

65

Proper Charges-Accompt, *Accompt* of *Household-Expences*, *Insurance-Accompt*, *Bottomry-Accompt*, *Accompt* of *Wagers*, *Promises*, *Hazard*, *&c.* with more of that Kind, as shall be mentioned in their due Place. The same might have been said as to the Converse hereof, when we give out or deliver any Thing, without receiving or expecting to receive any Thing in Compensation thereof; the Answer to which may be easily deduced from what is already said, without adding one Word more about the Matter.

55

(Donn, *Accountant*, 1775, pp. 6–7.)

Imaginary Accounts are found necessary for preserving the Balance of the Leger; for by the foregoing Rules we know, that each Person in the Inventory must have a distinct Account, in which each respective Person is to be made Debtor for what he owes me, or Creditor for what I owe him; and every Thing, whatever it be, that I have in my Possession must be made Debtor. But then, what must be the correspondent Debtor or Creditor to preserve the Balance? For all that I aim at here, is to shew, that such Subjects belong to me, and that there are such Articles of Debt and Credit betwixt such Persons and me, which are to be entered by proper Expressions. Hence, I must form an imaginary Account, called the *Stock Account*, which I must make Debtor for all I owe by the Inventory; and Creditor for all the Effects that are in my Hand, and Debts owing to me by the Inventory. Hence this Account may be considered as representing myself, who am the Owner of the Books; the Articles on the Creditor Side shewing what I have in my Possession, and what Debts are owing to me; and those on the Debtor Side, what I owe.

The Use of the Profit and Loss Account may be thus shewn. If I sell Goods for more than they cost me, the Excess being so much gained, I enter it on the Creditor Side of the *Profit and Loss Account*; on the contrary, if, through their being damaged, or some other Misfortune, I am obliged to sell them for less than they cost me, it is evident, the Defect is, with Respect to me, so much lost, and therefore, in Contradistinction to Gain, I enter it on the Debtor Side of this Account. Again, when I give away or lose any Thing, as it is to me as a real Loss, I enter it on the Debtor Side of this Account, to shew how much my real Estate is diminished thereby.

Consequently, on the contrary, when I receive any Legacy or Present, it being the same to me as if I had gained so much by Trade, I enter it on the Creditor Side, to shew how much my real Estate is augmented thereby. In a Word, every Thing given away, or received, or Debt contracted, for which there is Nothing exchanged in Return, or Obligation for it on any Person, is to be esteemed as a Gain or Loss, though in strict Propriety of Speech it may not be such. Thus, in particular, *Discounts* or *Rebates* allowed in Payments of Debts, *Interest of Money*, *Expences of House-keeping*, &c. belong to this Account; and the Method of entering these, or any other, must be plain, from what has been already said.

56

(Mellis, *Briefe Instruction*, 1588, ch. 18.)

Of the famous accompt called pofite or losse, or otherwise, lucrum or damnum, and how to order it in the leager.[36]

Item touching the accomptes (of profite and losse) of necessitie it must have one accompt proper in some one place of your Leager, conteyning both a Debitor and Creditor side, as hath any other parcell: and on the Debitor syde therof must bee written all manner of losse sustemed: And on the Creditor side all thinges gained. And this said accompt groweth oft in the Leager in divers parcels of goods whereof the sale happeneth, to profite or losse, which must bee saldid in this accompt of profite and losse, &c.

And when any accompt of goodes in the Leager is all solde, and that the Debitor part remayneth in summe of money more than the Creditor part, than is that goods sold for losse of as much as the rest amounteth unto: wherefore to sald thus, you must thus write on the Debitor side.[37]

Septemb. 00 Profite and losse oweth li. s. d. lost
               by receiving of money before it
               was due. As in Creditor.   00 £ s. d.

And contrarywise if any parcell all solde, remaining upon the Creditor side, more than the part of the Debitor side: then is that good solde for profite or winning.

[36] Plate VI reproduces the first page of this chapter.
[37] It will be seen that an example of another class of transaction was printed in error: an abatement to a debtor. The next example is also out of harmony with the text.

> Profite and losse is due to have
> li. s. d. gained by paiment of
> money made to M.N. as in his
> accompt in Debitor.   00 £ s. d.

And finally to conclude the accompte of this your estate of gaine and losse: Take the difference betweene gaine and losse, and if there be any surplus of gaines, as happily there must, the same is to bee caried to the estate of your accompt, but first the said Rest is to bee written on the Debitor side of this your accompt, to sald or make the same even with an *R.* before it, as thus.

Decemb. 31 *R*, More l. s. d. for the cleer rest of
> this accompt gained, and to
> make it even is borne to my
> stocke in Creditor, folio   1 li. s. d.

And thus you may understand, that all Restes made in the accompt of *Dare*, of the accompt of losse and gaine, commeth of such goods as bee sold for losse. And all Restes made in the side of *Habere*, commeth of such accomptes as be delivered or sold for gaine, &c.

57

(Dodson, *Accountant*, 1750, pp. v–vi.)

To avoid the Inconvenience which would arise from crouding the Account of *Stock* with every Article of *Gain* or *Expence*; it has been found expedient to keep an Account, by the Name of PROFIT AND LOSS, to receive and balance them against each other.

And where some kinds of *Gain and Expence* occur frequently, it has been usual to keep other inferior, or auxiliary Accounts of the same kind, such as *Estate, Interests, Discounts, Premiums, Commissions*, etc. or on the other Side, *Expences of House-keeping, Charges of Merchandize, Taxes*, etc. which serve to collect Articles of the same kind together, from whence they may periodically (i.e. once in a Week, Month, Quarter, etc.) be transferr'd to the Account of *Profit and Loss*.

58

(Malcolm, *Treatise of Book-keeping*, 1731, pp. 44–5.)

Of general accounts.

Accounts of Goods may be more general, or more particular; because, of Goods of the same Name, there may be several Species and Distinctions, each of which may be brought into a separate particular Account, or they may be all put into one Account.

For *Example*, There may be a general Account of *Wine*; or a particular Account of *Red Wines*, and another of *White Wines*; or they may be distinguished by the Country, as, Accounts of *French Wines*, and Accounts of *Spanish Wines*.

Again, *Linen Cloth* has many Species, as *Muslin*, *Cambrick*, and what is particularly called *Linen*; which of the *Dutch* kind we call *Holland*; the *Linen Cloth* of different Countries may also have different Accounts; and, if they have different Species, be also subdivided.

Woollen Cloaths have also a Variety of Species, as what is more particularly called *Cloth*, *Druggets*, *Serges*, *Camblets*, *Crapes*, &c. Here may be formed a general Account for all the Kinds you deal in; or one for each: Or to avoid too general an Account, or too many particular Accounts, class two or more (as you think fit) together; and either name them all in the Title, as Account of *Cloths* and *Druggets*; or *Cloths Druggets* and *Serges*; or distinguish the several Classes by Numbers, and so the Titles of the Accounts will be, *Woollen Cloths* first Class, or second Class. How the Species belonging to each Class are to be distinguished in the Account, you'll see immediately.

These Species are again subdivisible; thus, *Cloths* into *Broad* and *Narrow*, or into *Cloths* of one Colour, and mix'd: Or *Broad* and *Narrow*, may be each distinguished as the Colours are simple or mix'd: Or *Cloth* of simple and mix'd Colours into *Broad* and *Narrow*. Thus you may make a Variety of Accounts particular or general.

Again, the Manufacturers of particular Places may be brought all into one Account, especially such as are made of the same Materials, as *Wooll*, *Flax*, *Iron*. Thus (for *Example*) *Norwich Woollen Manufactures*, *Manchester Linen Manufactures*, &c. and these may be subdivided into Classes, or Assortments, as before mentioned.

The like Distinctions and Subdivisions you may conceive in most other Things. And as to the forming of Accounts for them, I must first say in general, that it depends upon the Circumstances of one's Dealings in these Things, whether it will be most convenient to make the Accounts general or particular, and how many Species to take into one Account; for which he must apply in the most judicious Way he can, this *Maxim*, viz. That too many particular Accounts, or too general Accounts, are equally opposite to that Clearness and Readiness, with which the State of our Affairs ought to appear in our Books.

If you make a general Account for two or more Species; then, that the State of the Account may be distinctly and readily found, by the Comparison of the two Sides, it is necessary to make a Quantity Column for every Species, and set its Name on each Side on the Head of it. And if you also make Subdivisions of these, so must the Columns be subdivided; as in this Specimen, representing either the Debtor or Creditor side of an Account of Wine.

				Hds.	*l.*	*s.*	*d.*
Account of Wine. Here there is no Distinction of Countries or Colours.							
In this Form the Colours are distinguished; and other necessary Distinctions left to the Narration, or to the Journal.		Red Hds.	White Hds.				
Account of French (*or* Spanish) *Wine.* This represents an Account for a particular Country, with a Distinction of Colours.		Red Hds.	White Hds.				
Account of Red (*or* White) *Wine.* This is an Account for a particular Colour; with a Distinction of Countries.		French Hds.	Span. Hds.				
Account of Wine. Here is a general Account in which both the Countries and Colours are distinguished.	*French*		*Spanish*				
	Red	White	Red	White			

From this you'll easily conceive how to make Columns for the Divisions of any other general Account: Thus, where several general Accounts of the same Name are distinguished by Classes, as *Woollen Manufactures* first Class, there must be a Column for every Species of that Class.

59

(Booth, *Complete System*, 1789, p. 28.)

. . . In the set of books now under consideration, I have supposed the proprietor to be a large importer and exporter of various kinds of merchandize, and to be part owner and husband of several ships: for without this, I could not have introduced forms of all such entries as would apply to every occurrence in trade. But it may be remarked that, except the account of Hemp, which is a bulky and distinct article, seldom intermixed with others in buying or selling, I have introduced only one account of Merchandize, to serve in general for the common run of purchases and sales. Even the sales of Cargoes imported from the West Indies, are confined in the Ledger, to one account for each vessel respectively, though they belong to different proprietors: every attempt beyond this, I know from experience, will prove fallacious; and so far from adding to that clearness and perspicuity, which should ever be the principal objects in Book-Keeping, it will create unnecessary trouble and confusion, by multiplying nominal accounts in the Ledger; an error already too common among those who have written on this subject: as if it were possible, for any person in an extensive line of business, to keep distinct accounts in the Ledger for every article he deals in. I am sensible it is proper that he should know the gain or loss upon particular articles, as well as upon the whole of his traffic; but the Ledger is not the proper place for a detail of every *minutiae* of this sort: whoever attempts it upon a large scale of business, will find that he has undertaken an herculean task; and instead of affording him the satisfaction he may have promised himself, it will prove a continual bar to his books being kept up; and if his concerns are very large, can only tend to destroy the patience, and the health of his Book-Keeper. . . .

60

(Dafforne, *Merchants Mirrour*, 1660, epistle dedicatory.)

. . . My intent is not to prescribe these *Principles* as fully sufficient, though for their *Number* approveable: for time at present
doth not yield permission to impart what my Affections desired,
and *Will* determined to divulge; but these are *Allurements onely*,
to stir up the *better experienced* to amend what I (through want of
Art) have not so compleatly handled as I desire, and it deserves,
being an *Art* (saith *Simon Stevin* in his Princely Book-keeping,[38]
fol. 7, & 12.) worthy to be numbred amongst the *Liberall* Sciences.
But I already hear Objections against the *First*, & *Second* Waste-
books; that therein are exercised some accounts, which are altogether
needlesse here in *England*: as is the Banck-Account. I grant it to
be an Account not usefull in our Kingdome; but that the knowledge
thereof should be un-usefull to this Arts-Learners, I deny. True it
is, that by *Birth* we are *Circumferenced with the Ocean*; but the
Great-All hath not so strictly limited us within the bounds thereof,
that we are abridged from the *Conversation* and *Entercourse of
Merchandizing* with forrain Nations, as well by their frequenting
of our *Borders*, as we Commercing with them in the Body of their
Countries. And when our Merchants (Old or Young) trade with
them in their places, *must not they learn to be acquainted with their
phrases* used among them concerning *Commerce*? Of which
BANCK is none of the least in severall places of Europe, unto
which our English Merchants have their Concourse. And must the
advertisement of the *Course* thereof (before we come to the Actuall
exercise) be a *Blemish*, and accounted as a *needlesse thing* in my
Book? *Right Worshipfuls*[39] behold the Rancor of black Envy, that
endeavoureth to have us ignorant of Martiall affairs, untill we come
to the point of Battail. The like Objection is alleaged against my
entring of an Account of *Time* and *Ready-mony*.[40] What if we
have them not in use amongst our selves? Let us cast up our
accounts with other *Nations*, and (to our cost) they will teach us
how to frame an account of *Time* and *Ready-mony*, if our *Factor*,
or *Correspondent* be in disburse for us any quantity of mony, and

---

[38] Simon Stevin's *Vorstelyke Boeckhouden* was published in 1604.
[39] The " epistle dedicatory " is addressed to the governors and fellowships of the Merchant
Adventurers of England and other groups of merchants.
[40] A person's " account current " or " account of ready money " referred to amounts due
or payable on demand or at short term; his " account of time " referred to obligations
dated further ahead. The terms are used in extracts 78 to 80.

for Time worth the reckoning, as experience hath shewed me in many passages. And what then? Must not we seek the aid of some experienced to assist us? because we regarded not the documents of them (at home) that endeavoured to inform us of the *Manner* and *Matter*. What *Amercement* doth not this *Disdain worthy* wilfull Ignorance merit? . . .

61

(Hamilton, *Introduction to Merchandise*, 1788, p. 327.)

If an accompt with a foreigner is to be settled in British money, we have no occasion to compute the value of the articles in foreign money, and the entries are the same as in domestic trade: But, if the accompt is to be settled in foreign money, we must enter the value of each article, reduced to that money, in an inner column. In these accompts, if we are able to receive the money which is due us, at a more advantageous rate of exchange than we expected when the debt was contracted, or pay the money which we owe, at a cheaper rate, there is a gain obtained; on the contrary, a loss is sustained, if the rates of exchange undergo the opposite alterations. . . .

If the sums of the inner columns be equal, there is nothing due by the one party to the other; and then, if the sums of the outer columns be unequal, the difference is gain or loss. But, if the inner columns be unequal, the balance due from one party to the other must be valued at the current rate of exchange; and, after the value is added to the proper side, the difference of the outer columns is the gain or loss.[41]

If we have different transactions with a foreigner, some of which are to be settled in British, and some in foreign money, the articles should be entered in separate accompts. The title for the former is, *A.B. his accompt*, because it generally contains business transacted by us at his desire. The title of the latter is, *A.B. my accompt*, because it generally contains business transacted by him at our desire. The balance of one accompt may be transferred to the other when we settle. . . .

[41] The debit side of an "exchange account" of 1758–59, in William Braund's ledger, is shown on Plate XVI. The inner column, immediately right of the date, shows the amounts in Portuguese currency. The closing balancing shows a profit on exchange of almost £300.

In the treatises the inner columns for the foreign currency entries are usually alongside the main money columns.

62

(Malcolm, *Treatise of Book-keeping*, 1731, p. 47.)

Of houses and ships.

(1.) For *Houses*, which are let out; you may give to each a particular Account; or make a general Account for them all: Debtor for the prime Cost or Value, with all the Expence of *Reparations*, *Taxations*, and *Improvements*: And Creditor for the Rents received or owing for them, and the Price of them when sold.

Observe. The Rents may be entered as they fall due, or not till they be paid; but this is not convenient in case they stand long unpaid; and therefore the first is the better general Rule. And for the *Tenents*, it will be convenient to give them one general Account, which may be called, *Possessors* of *Houses*, naming the Person in every Article, as you enter the Rent due on the Debtor side, or discharge it on the Creditor side. . . .

(2.) For *Ships*; you may either have a general Account of *Ships*, for all that you are concerned in; or a particular Account for each: *Debtor* for the Value it cost you, and *Creditor* for the Price when sold. As for the Charges and Profits arising from it, I shall consider that in two Cases. 1. If you employ her only in Freight, the Account is Debtor for all the Charges of *Reparations* and *Navigation*; and Creditor for the Freights paid or owing. Or after Stating the Account of her *Charges* and *Freight*, enter on the *Ships* Account only the Difference; for most commonly these Accounts are stated and given up by the *Ship-Master*, so that the Owner has no more to do but *Receive* or *Pay* the *Balance*. 2. If you employ your Ship in Trade; then to keep a clear and separate Account of the Gain and Loss by your Ship, and by your Merchandize, charge your Goods (or the *Voyage Account*. See the next Section) with the Freight, as you would pay to a Stranger; and place all the Charges of *Reparations* and *Navigations* to the Debt of the Ships Account and the *Freights* to the Credit.

63

(Gordon, *Universal Accountant*, 1787, vol. 2, p. 57.)

. . . 10. *Accounts of Voyages* [42] contain, upon the debit side, the prime cost and charges of the cargo; and, on the credit side, if any thing at all, the receipt or disposal of the goods by the factor, and perhaps returns made for them. Hence there will be two varieties. 1. If the credit-side be empty, there hath been no advice of the ship's arrival, and therefore the account remains in its original state, by being credited by *Balance* for the charge at the debit. 2. If the credit-side is filled up with the disposal, the account is evened to or by Profit and Loss, for the difference.

11. *Factor my account of goods*, contains the same on both sides, and is closed in the same manner as any other account of goods.

12. *Accounts of stores* contain, on the Dr. side, the cost and charges *per* invoice of all cargoes whereof the receipt hath been acknowledged; and, upon the credit side, if it contains any thing at all, an abstract from the books of the store, ascertaining the money received, the outstanding debts, and the goods yet unsold. In the first case, close by *Balance*, for the charge at the debit, and in the last, to or by *Profit and Loss*, for the difference of its sides.

13. *Factor my account on time* contains, on the debit side, the debts due to the factor on my account; and, on the credit side, the payments made him; so the difference, if there is any, is the debts still outstanding; wherefore the account is closed by *Balance*.

14. *Factor my account current* contains, on the Dr. side, whatever I can justly charge against him; and, on the credit side, whatever I am in reason accountable for to him: so that the difference will be a debt due to or by the factor, and therefore closed with *Balance*; unless some part of the difference hath arisen from the rise or fall of exchange, in which case, such difference must be evened with Profit and Loss, previous to the balance betwixt parties. . . .

---

[42] The accounts described in this extract are referred to in the discussion of factors' accounts, extract 79.

64

(Mellis, *Briefe Instruction*, 1588, ch. 23.)

The manner to know and hold the accompt of a retayling shoppe in your owne hand, or else in the charge of another person.

When you holde a shoppe furnished with servantes, without your house, then in good order do thus: all such goods which daily you put to the retailing shoppe, Make the saide shoppe Debitor thereof in your owne bookes, and Creditor those goods which daily you put into the retailing shoppe: and conject in your owne imagination, that this retailing shoppe were a person Debitor, of al the which you put into the saide shoppe, and doe laye out for it in any wise: and this order observe surely. And the contrariwise of al that you again receive, of that accompte make the shoppe of retaile Creditor, as though it were a Debitor. For all such as it rendreth, yeldeth or conteineth part or portion after portion. And afterwards when you behold this accompt, you may perceive if it be wel guided or not: and there bee many that make the foreman of the shoppe Debitor, notwithstanding it cannot bee justly done without the will and consent of him: and therefore beware that yee never entre any parson in your booke, ether for Debitor or Creditor for your saide shoppe, except the consent of the same person. Also other stuffe and implementes necessary for the said shop, as ballance, weightes, measures, for the use of the same, and of all such make the shoppe Debitor, or him that hath the charge by writing of an Inventory of his owne hande, or by his consent: and this shall bee sufficient when you assigne the governing of your shop to any other man. But if so were that you will keepe the sayde shoppe in your owne handes, then as before is saide, all that you buy, make Creditor them of whom you buy, with the condition if you buy for time: and if for ready money make Creditrice the stocke,[43] and Debitrice the shoppe: and if you sell but litle in retaile not amounting 3 or 4 or 5 li. then such money keepe in a little Chest, by the space of 7 or 8 daies of retailing, and then make the Capsa Debitor, and the shoppe of retail Creditor of al that is sold, saying thus: *Per* capsa of retail for so many dayes, accompted unto this day for divers goods solde, &c. wherfore with a cleere sentence compile your parcels of all your

[43] Error for " cash ".

accompte of retaile, for all this worke is to order and guide every cause by good engine and memory, so that you may know directly to what ende every accompte may come. For in a proverbe it is saide : *Qui exercet mercaturam & non cognoscit pecuniam suam, efficitur musca, &c.* And therefore in eschewing of perilles, provide remedie to set your woorkes, that they may come to light or cleernes.

65

(Carpenter, *Most Excellent Instruction*, 1632, pp. 22–3.)

How to hold the account of a retayling shop.

The manner how to charge your Shop or your Journey-man with Wares, is to make the Receiver your Journy-man (if he take upon him the charge) Debtor to such Wares as you delivered : Or otherwise, if you charge, or make no person Debtor, but the Shop : Then make Retaile Account, Debtor to the Wares so delivered.

And contrariwise, of all that you againe receive, or take out of that Account, make the mony so received Debtor; and Retaile Account Creditor; or else the party who hath taken in charge that Account.

There be many that make the Fore-man of the Shop Debtor; but because it cannot bee justly done without the will and consent of him, therefore beware that you never put any person in your Booke, for Debtour or Creditour for your said Shop, without the consent of the same person.

Also all other Stuffe and Implements necessary for the said Shop, as Ballance, Waights, Measures, for the use of the same, for all such make the Shop, or him that hath the charge Debtor, by writing of an *Inventory* of his owne hand, or by his consent. And this shall be sufficient, when you assigne the government and charge of your Shop to any other man.

The Treatment
of Selected Types of Transaction

66

(Carpenter, *Most Excellent Instruction*, 1632, p. 85.)

Of that which you receive upon mariage, or that which you pay; as also receiving and disbursing hereditary goods.

FOR the summe that you receive, you make *Cash*, or such goods, Debtor; and Capitall Creditor.

And on the contrary, for as much as you pay, hee makes your Capitall, Debtor; and *Cash*, or such goods, Creditor.   *As,*

1 First, if you receive both monie and goods in Mariage; Cash, and such goods owe to your Capitall, or to your name; adding therewithall by whom you have received them.

2 If you give goods and monie to any one in his mariage, Capitall oweth to the *Cash*, and to such goods, therewith adding to whom you gave them.

3 If you receive monie and goods by heritage, *Cash*, and such goods owe to my Capitall.

4 If you disburse monie and goods by heritage; Capitall oweth to the goods, and to *Cash*.

5 If you receive some bill of Rents by heritage; Capitall of Rents oweth to your Capitall.

6 If you receive monie by heritage, and deliver it to some one at Interest; he to whom you so deliver it, oweth to my Capitall, as well for the Capitall, as for the Interest.

67

(Dafforne, *Apprentices Time-Entertainer*, 1640, p. 41.)

Of gratuities given, or received.

Quest. 147. Suppose I GIVE AWAY any thing, upon what *Consideration* soever it be; How shall I enter that?

Answ. Profit and Losse Debitor to the GIVEN MATTER that stood upon my Booke.

Quest. 148. Suppose that it was not entered into my Booke; How?

Answ. What was not entred to your Booke, cannot bee written from thence againe; and there's an end of an old Song.

Quest. 149. Suppose that I RECEIVE any thing, *it being Given mee*, upon what *Consideration* soever; How?

Answ. The RECEIVED MATTER Debitor to Profit and Losse.

68

(Vernon, *Compleat Comptinghouse*, 1734, p. 123.)

Youth. If I receive Money for any Legacy that is left me, how must I Book that same?

Master. You must Debtor Cash, because it receives the Money, and Credit Profit and Loss, because it is so much Profit to you; or you may Credit Stock for the Money, it comes all to one.

69

(Hayes, *Gentleman's . . . Book-keeper*, 1741, p. 34.)

Of legacies, gratuities, marriage fortunes, &c.

FOR all Sums that you shall receive upon any of these Accounts,

| | Ct. Stock, if the Sum be large. |
| Dt. Cash. | Ct. Profit and Loss, if it be but inconsiderable. |

AND for all Sums that goes out by the Way of Portions to Children, &c.

Dt. Stock, or Profit and Loss, and Ct. Cash.

WHEN a Sum of Money is left to you for a Legacy to be paid to you after a certain Time by the Executors of the Deceased,

Dt. the Executors who are to pay the same and Ct. Stock, or Profit and Loss.

BUT if you receive a Legacy out of an Estate wherein you are the Executor,

Dt. the Estate, and Ct. Stock, or Profit and Loss. . . .

70

(Hayes, *Gentleman's . . . Book-keeper*, 1741, p. 24.)

Of monies lent or borrowed upon interest.

I F you lend out Money for a certain Time at Interest,

Dt. the Borrower for   Ct. Cash for the Money lent.
the Principal and   Ct. Profit and Loss, or Interest Account,
Interest.   for the Interest.

W H E N he pays the Principal back again with the Interest,

Dt. Cash for Principal   Ct. the Payer for the same.
and Interest.

I F you borrow Money for a certain Time upon Interest, on your own Account,

Dt. Cash for the Sum borrowed.

Dt. Profit and Loss, or Interest   Ct. the Lender for both sums.
Account, for the Interest.

71

(Malcolm, *Treatise of Book-keeping*, 1731, pp. 50–51.)

Of interest for the loan, or forbearance of money.

When Money is borrowed upon Interest, the Principal goes to the *Borrower* or *Lender's* Account and the Account of Cash, and the Interest to the *Profit* and *Loss* Account. But in stating the Interest there is this Variety, *viz.*

You may charge the *Interest* on the Account of the Borrower or Lender before it falls due; thus, upon your Lending or Borrowing, state the Interest which will be due at the Term of Payment; and after that, state every Term's Interest at the beginning of the Quarter, half Year, or Year, according as it is payable: And if Principal and Interest be paid before the Term to which Interest is charged, there will be so much to be taken out of the Account again, by an opposite Entry. Or,

You may charge the Interest only from Term to Term, as it falls due. Or, *Lastly*, Enter it only as it is paid: And in this Case it needs not be placed to the Person's Account, unless it be to prevent Mistakes, or to let you see by the Account, what Interest is due. For by first placing it to the Account, and then discharging the Payment, it will be understood, that all the Interest, from the Time of last stating of Interest, is due: Remembering, both in this and the Method of the preceding Article, that when the State of that Person's Account is demanded, all the Interest then due, is to be placed to the Account.

If any Thing besides the legal Interest is paid for the Loan of Money, it has nothing to do with the Person's Account.

Observe, That some propose to keep an Account of Interest as a Branch of the *Profit* and *Loss Account*; where your whole Concern in Interest may appear distinctly. But as this Account, unless one deals both in Borrowing and Lending, will be all Debt, or all Credit, it is not convenient.

72

(Dafforne, *Apprentices Time-Entertainer*, 1640, pp. 39–41.)

Receiving mony upon bottommary, ships-keele, or seas-hazzard: that is, to wager upon the adventure of the sea.

Bomary, or Bottommary, by the Dutch termed *Bodemmerije*; a name taken from the *Keele*, or bottome of a Ship. In the *Low-Countries* it is very much in use; so that the Master of a Ship that entendeth a Voyage into Forraine Countrie, is often necessited to take mony upon the Adventure of his Ship, to performe his intended Voyage; which mony so taken, payeth 25, 30, 40 or more *per Cent.* upon the safe ending of the said Voyage, because the so lent mony is transported beyond the Seas; so that if the ship perish, or that the Ship and Goods are all cast away, then the adventured mony is also all lost.

Quest. 135. Suppose that (according to my order) my Factor at Amsterdam hath delivered unto an English Ship-master 1,000. Ricks-Dollers, at a certaine advance for each Doller; ——; provided that the said Master is to saile to East-land, there to buy Commodities, and so to returne to England; ——; at whose first Anchoring upon any English firme land, the time of the Condition is expired; and the Master is liable to pay me Principall and Advance; How?

Answ. $\begin{cases} \text{Ship-master} \\ \textit{Debitor to} \end{cases}$ $\left.\begin{array}{l} \text{Peter} \quad \textit{Pinchback} \text{ at Amsterdam My} \\ \text{accompt-Current for the Principall.} \\ \text{Bomary-reckoning, Sea-hazzard, Sea-wager} \\ \text{(or to Profit and Losse) for the Advance.} \end{array}\right.$

Quest. 136. Suppose that the Master is well arrived; and he payeth me partly with Corne, and the remainer with Rix-Dollers, by which I loose; How?

Answ. This hath three Journall entrances.

First, Corne —— —— $\left.\begin{array}{l} \textit{Debitor to} \\ \text{the Ship-} \\ \text{Master} \end{array}\right.$ For the value.

Secondly, Cash —— For the mony.

Thirdly, Profit and Losse For the losse on Dollers.

Quest. 137. What shall be done with the accompt of Bottommary?

Answ. Either now for this One parcell, or at the yeares end for more parcells, may be entred

Bottommary, Sea-hazzard, or Sea-wager, *Debitor* to Profit and Loss, for what is Now Gained, or shall be Gained at the years end by that accompt.

Quest. 138. Suppose the Ship to be cast away; How?

Answ. $\left.\begin{cases} \text{Bottommary,} \\ \text{OR} \\ \text{Sea-hazzard,} \\ \text{OR} \\ \text{Sea-wager} \\ \text{OR} \\ \text{Profit and Losse} \end{cases}\right.$ Debitor to the Ship-master, for Principall and Advance.

Quest. 139. Suppose that I Wager upon any mans journie from London to Ireland, and backe within a limited time; and I receive the mony presently; How?

Answ. Cash Debitor to Sea-hazzard, or *Adventuring-accompt.*

Quest. 140. Suppose it to be onely Wagered, but not received untill the journies finishing; How?

Answ. The Wagering man Debitor to Sea-hazzard. NOTA, as for the booking of the Gaine, or Losse of the Wager, you may gather that from the 138. and 139. Questions.

Quest. 141. But that will not content some; therefore enter them at large.

Answ. Set downe what you desire to have answered.

Quest. 142. Suppose you winne the Wager, and the Wagering man payeth you with mony; How?

Answ. Cash Debitor to the Wagering man.

Quest. 143. Suppose you lose the Wager, and pay the man; How?

Answ. There must be NOTED, whether hee stood upon my Booke, or not.

Quest. 144. Suppose that he did not; but that he then paid you present monie at the Wager laying, as in the 139. Question.

Answ. Sea-hazzard Debitor to Cash, for the paid Losse.

Quest. 145. Suppose that hee stood upon my Booke, as in the 140. Question.

Answ. This hath two Journall entrances.

First, ——⎰ Sea-hazzard ⎱ The Wagering man, for his Debits discharge.
Secondly, ⎱ Debitor to ⎰ Cash, for the paid Losse.

How to close the accompt of *Sea-hazzard*, may be seen in the 138. and 139. Questions.

73

(Malcolm, *Treatise of Book-keeping*, 1731, pp. 42-3.)

Of money lent upon bottomree.

Bottomree is the lending Money upon the *Bottom* of a Ship, bound to a certain Place; upon Condition that if the Ship is lost, the Debt is discharged: But if she arrives safe in the Terms of the Contract, the Money lent, with the Interest agreed upon, becomes a real Debt, to be paid to me or my Factor, where the Ship arrives; and till the Payment be actually made, it is a Debt upon the Ship.

For the Entry of such Transactions in the *Leger*, we must consider them separately, with Respect to the Borrower or Lender upon *Bottomree*.

1. For the *Lender*. To follow the General Rules; the *Borrower* has a particular Account, in which he is made Debtor for the Money lent, and Interest, and Creditor when it is paid, or the Ship lost. But if you deal much this Way, it will be convenient to bring in all your Business of this Kind, into one General Account,

representing all Persons who borrow from you upon *Bottomree*; which you may Title thus,

> *Account* of *Borrowers* upon *Bottomree*; or simply,
> *Bottomree Account.*

It is to be used the same Way as the *Borrowers* particular Account would be; remembring to name the Person concerned in every Article.

OBSERVE, The Interest needs not be entered till it be paid; though in some respect (as you'll see below) it is better to do it when the Principal is enter'd.

Again, Those who make particular Accounts for the *Borrowers*, make a general Account for the *Interest*, which they call *Bottomree* Account, or *Profit* and *Loss* by *Bottomree*, which is *Debtor* for what is lost, and *Creditor* for what is gain'd; The Design of this is to see all the Gain and Loss by *Bottomree*, separate from other Gains and Losses. But this Purpose is sufficiently answered by the general *Account* for the *Borrowers*, by charging the Interest with the *Principal*; which shews the Method of a general Account to be in all Respects preferable.

2. For the *Borrower*. He must make an Account of *Lenders* upon *Bottomree*; to be made Creditor for Principal borrowed with the Interest, and Debtor for the Payment, or upon the Loss of the Ship.

OBSERVE, Tho' Ship Masters are most commonly the *Borrowers* upon *Bottomree*; yet a Merchant, the Owner of the Ship, may *Borrow* upon *Bottomree*; and if such a Person is concerned both in Lending and Borrowing, he must have two Accounts, one for the *Borrowers*, and one for the *Lenders*; or one general *Account* of *Bottomree*, with double Money Columns; the one for the *Borrowers*, the other for the *Lenders*.

74

(Macghie, *Principles of Book-keeping*, 1718, pp. 21–2.)

To find out the true debitor and creditor in borrowing and lending, which contains the five following cases, viz.

Case 1. $\mathbf{WHEN}$ Money is *borrowed* or *lent*, to be repaid with the usual Interest thereof at a prefix'd Time. The *Borrower* enters.

Sundry Accompts, (*viz. Cash* for the principal Sum borrowed, and *Profit* and *Loss*, or *Interest-Accompt* in particular, according to the 2*d* Part of *Rule* X. for the Interest thereof) Debitors to the *Lender*, for the Principal and Interest of the Money borrowed.

The *Lender* enters.

The *Borrower* Debitor to *Sundry Accompts, viz.* to *Cash* for the principal Sum *lent*, and to *Profit* and *Loss*, or *Interest-Accompt* as above, for the Interest thereof; in all, for the Principal and Interest of the Money lent.

Case 2. When Money is *Lent*, or *Borrowed*, upon *Bottomry*, which differs from the preceeding Case, in that 'tis lent upon *Hazard*, so as never to be repaid again, unless the Ship arrive safely at a certain Port condescended on: Tho' indeed it agrees therewith, in so far as the Money lent, when due, is always to be repaid with *Interest*, at 40 or 50 *per Cent.* which is so great, because of the Risque the Lender runs. Whence the Term *Bottomry* is derived from the Merchant's lending or borrowing Money on the Bottom of the Ship.

The *Borrower* enters.

Sundry Accompts, (*viz. Cash* for the principal Sum borrowed, and *Bottomry-Accompt* for the Interest thereof) Debitors to *Hazard* for the Sum borrowed on Bottomry, both Principal and Interest, payable in Case of the Ship's safe Arrival.

The *Lender* enters.

The *Ship at her safe Arrival*, (or *Hazard* as above) Debitor to *Sundry Accompts, viz.* to *Cash* for the principal Sum lent, and to *Bottomry-Accompt* for the Interest thereof; in all for the whole Sum of Principal and Interest, *Lent* on Bottomry, and payable in case of the Ship's safe Arrival.

Not. 1. *Bottomry-Accompt*, as in the above Solution, is almost of the same Nature with *Interest-Accompt*, tho' I know not how the same is confusedly treated of by Authors, while they dissent about the Manner of stating this Accompt: For the making of *Hazard* or Ship at her Arrival, *Debitor*, or *Creditor*, takes away all the Ambiguity of this Case, which has not been noticed by most Authors.

Not. 2. It will be also needful to solve the Cases of the *Event* or *Issue* hereof, *viz.* when the Ship is safely arrived, so that the Money becomes then due: Or, when the Ship is cast away, whereupon the

Lender has lost all, having nothing to demand of the *Borrower*, as in the Two following Cases, *viz.*

Case 3. Suppose the Ship to be safe arrived at the desired Port.
The *Borrower* enters.

Hazard (which being last made *Creditor*, must be now charged, seeing the *Business* and Issue is out of Peril and determined) Debitor to the *Lender* (or to *Cash*, if the Sum be paid) for the whole Sum of Principal and Interest borrowed, which now becomes due to him.
The *Lender* enters.

The *Borrower* (or *Cash* if he has paid the Sum already) Debitor to *ditto Ship at her safe Arrival* (or to *Hazard*, if before it was made *Debitor*) for the whole Sum of Principal and Interest, that now becomes due by ditto Borrower.

Case 4. Suppose the Ship to be lost at Sea.
The *Borrower* enters.

Hazard Debitor to *Bottomry-Accompt* for the Sum borrowed on Bottomry, both Principal and Interest, whereby it appears, that the Borrower has gain'd the principal Sum borrowed, seeing the Matter formerly in Hazard, is now determined, and that this Accompt of Bottomry at last closes with *Profit* and *Loss.*
The *Lender* enters.

Bottomry-Accompt Debitor to *Hazard* (or to such a *Ship at her Arrival*, if the same was before made *Debitor*) for the whole Sum of Principal and Interest lent on *Bottomry*; whereby it appears, that the said Lender has lost the principal Sum borrowed, seeing the Business formerly in *Hazard* is now determined, &c.

Case 5. When Money is *borrowed*, or *lent*, upon a *Pledge*, which the *Lender* is to restore at the Repayment of the neat Sum borrowed.
The *Borrower* enters.

Cash Debitor to such a *Person* the *Lender* my *Pledge*, &c. which both Things must be named to specifie the Bargain, the Meaning whereof is, to the *Person*, who has my said *Pledge* in his Hand for the neat Sum borrowed.
The *Lender* enters.

The *Borrower* his *Pledge*, as above, Debitor to *Cash* for the neat Sum lent.

Not. 1. Hence may be easily solved the Case of lending upon a Pledge, when Interest also is to be paid with the Principal; for 'tis almost the same with *Case* 1. of this III *Problem.*

Not. 2. Or, if the Case be, when Money is borrowed or lent without a Pledge, and to pay no Interest, 'tis very easily solved by *Rule* V. of the preceeding *Sect.*

75

(Hamilton, *Introduction to Merchandise*, 1788, pp. 471-2.)

In all commercial countries there is a fixed rate of interest, and the merchant's gain should only be estimated by the excess of his gross profits above the interest of his stock. The latter may be obtained with little risk or trouble; the former alone is the reward of his industry, and the compensation for his hazard. And, if the profit of his trade be less than his stock would have yielded at common interest, he may properly account it a losing one.

It is easy to form a general estimation of his profits in this sense, by deducting the interest of his nett stock from the gain which the balance of his books exhibits: But it is a matter of some difficulty to determine the gain or loss on each branch of his business, with allowance of interest for the money employed in it.

The accomptant will readily perceive, that, for this purpose, interest must be computed in the several accompts of goods and voyages on which money has been advanced; and, if this interest be deducted from the gross gain, or added to the loss, the real success of each branch will be exhibited.

The common order of an accompt of goods in the ledger is by no means proper for instituting a computation of interest. The goods are entered on the Dr. when bought, and on the Cr. when sold; and, if interest were computed thereon, it would extend from the time of purchase to the time of sale; whereas it ought to extend from the time of advancing the money till the time of recovering payment. For this purpose, accompts of goods must be kept in an order that exhibits the extent and continuance of the advance; where nothing is entered on the Dr. till the money be laid out, and nothing in the Cr. till the money be recovered. Progressive computations of interest on these accompts, drawn out as directed Part I. § 118.[44] will show what the money employed in each branch of trade would have yielded at common interest, and consequently determine the real gain or loss.

---

[44] This refers to Part 1 of the book, " Arithmetic "; the section explains how interest on current accounts is calculated.

If we buy goods at long credit, and sell them for ready money, or on short credit, we may happen to have the money in our hands for some time; and, as we may lend it out at interest, or employ it in other branches of our business, during the interval, the advantage arising from it, computed as above, should be added to the profits, or deducted from the loss on the accompt which yields it.

Company (i.e. Partnership) Accounts

76

(Colinson, *Idea Rationaria*, 1683, p. 22.)

Of companies-accompts.

WHen one keeps the Book for several Companies, in which he is a Partner, he must take notice to give the true designation of them in his Books, lest he confuse the one with the other. Several distinctions are used by some, either by the several names of such as are concerned, or by Numbering the Companies; and according as one hath Partners, let him write them on the Alphabet, naming particularly every one, as many as they are in their several Companies, *viz.* N^r. 2. 3. 4. And otherwayes he may say, Company *Greenland*, *Lewes-fishing*: or if they deal in Wines, then say, Wine Company, with such and such that are concerned, naming them in the Alphabet and *Leger* Title. It is ordinare, to keep Books apart for such Men in Companies; but when one doeth so, let him observe to place down in his own Books, what his concerns be, and wherein they consist. As if another were to keep the Companies Books; (for in these, his Accompt must be placed, as the other Mens are; but in his own he must say only such men my Accompt with them in Company Debitor.) *viz.*

139. Q. *SUppose another buy goods and make you half concerned in the bargain, you paying him in the value of your share Immediately, in money, goods, or bonds of others?*

A. Such a Man my Accompt with him in Company, Debitor to Cash, if it be money: If it be goods, Debitor to goods; If to any persons, whose bonds I give in for my share, then Debitor to such persons.

140. Q. *If he sell the goods, for both your accompts, to advantage, and pay you in your share both stock and profite?*

A. If he pay me in money, then Cash is Debitor to such a Man my Accompt with him in Company.

141. Q. *What do you then for the profite on the half which belonged to you?*

   A. Such a Man my Accompt with him in Company Debitor to profite and loss.

142. Q. *Suppose there be loss on the goods sold?*

   A. Profite and loss Debitor to such a Man my Accompt with him in Company, for the loss, and Cash Debitor for the money I receive.

143. Q. *If a Man buy goods upon time, with your consent, wherein he makes you for half Partner, only he keeps the accompt, and disposes of them for us both, whats Debitor for your share?*

   A. Seing I pay in nothing as yet, but promise to do it when the time of payment expires; then I make use of Promise-Reckoning Debitor to such a Man my Accompt with him in Company for so much. . . .[45]

77

(Malcolm, *Treatise of Book-keeping*, 1731, pp. 64–9.)

Company accounts.

THERE may be a great Variety here, according to the Nature and Constitution of Companies; and the Conditions upon which Men enter into Partnership. I do not take it for my Business to insist upon every Supposition that might be made; my chief Design, in all this Treatise, being to give a true and universal Notion of the Method of *Debtor* and *Creditor*, by explaining the general Principles, and making as much Application as may sufficiently illustrate them. For the whole Knowledge of *Book-keeping* is comprehended in a few fundamental Rules and Notions; so that the Design or End, and the Method in general, being well considered, and distinctly apprehended, there is no Necessity for a vast Variety of Applications: A few Cases well chosen (especially if you see practical Examples thereof, duly stated in Form, as is done in the following *Waste*, &c. *Books*) will fix the Notion of the Method, and open all the Nature of it, so as to put one who has duly considered the essential Parts, which are few and general, in a Capacity to

[45] The discussion of company accounts ends with question-and-answer number 400.

apply them to any Subject and form such arbitrary Schemes (still within the Limits of the general Rules) as shall exactly answer the End of *Book-keeping :* Therefore I have thought it sufficient, upon the Head of *Company Accounts,* to make the Application in a few Instances of more *private Partnership :* And for the greater Distinctness, I divide them into two Branches, and upon each Branch make two Suppositions, concerning the Constitution of the *Company.*

BRANCH I. When I am concerned in a Company, where the Accounts and chief Management are under the Direction of another Partner.

BRANCH II. When I am Accountant and chief Manager.

Again, As to the Nature of the *Company,* I make these Suppositions:

1. I suppose a very simple Kind of Society, which I call an *Unfix'd Company*; because they have no standing and fixed Stock, but (for Example) buy, from Time to Time, Parcels of this or the other Kind of Goods, to be disposed of in domestick or foreign Trade; and withdraw their Shares of the Value sold, when they please; by which Means their Stocks or Effects in Company, perpetually vary, according to the Value of those different Transactions: And such Partnerships may be enter'd into for one single Parcel of Goods, or Voyage; or they may continue for some Course of Trade.

2. I suppose a fix'd Capital Stock, of which every Partner furnishes his Share; and this to be the subject Matter of all the subsequent Transactions of Trade.

Company Accounts.

Branch I. When another Partner is Accountant and Manager.

Supposition I. When the Company is unfix'd.

In this Case the Manager (*A. B.*) is obliged, at all Times, to exhibit fair and distinct Accounts of the State of Affairs to his Partners: I have no more to do but to keep plain Accounts of what I give, or owe to the Company, and what I receive; which I do under these Titles, *viz.*

1. A. B. *My Account with him,* &c. *in Company* ½ (or ⅔, *containing every Share*) is

Debtor for all that I give out, or owe to the Company, as my Share of the Stock, and Charges; *that is*, of the first Stock, or any subsequent Purchase; and all Charges which I am accountable for a Share of.

Creditor for all that I receive on Account of my Concerns in Company, or allow for the same (See the 2d *Observation* below) and for my Share of Losses.

Observe, 1. The Partners may have Accounts in my Books, as other Men have; and even the Partner *Trustee* may have another Account; because, that described is the Account of a mere Trust; and must be distinguished from the real and absolute Debts betwixt us, upon other particular Dealings: Besides which, there may be absolute Debts betwixt us, relating to the Company's Concerns; as when he pays or stands bound for the whole, or part of my Share and Effects purchased for *Company Account*; or I the like for him; as, if he should draw a Bill on me for Payment of more than my Share. This other Account I call,

A. B. *His proper Account.*

Debtor and *Creditor* for what we mutually owe, and pay upon other particular Dealings, or what he stands bound for, or pays for me, or I for him, of our Shares of the Effects purchased for the Company.

Observe, 2. When *A. B.* advises of Money received for Effects of the Company sold, unless I immediately draw my Share from him, I make his *proper Account* Debtor *to my Account in Company*, for the same, that I may more readily know what Money is in his Hands; but especially, this is useful, when I was owing him a Debt, particularly for *Company Account*, which he now pays himself out of the Money come into his Hands; and if he charges Interest for what he has advanced for me, I give his *proper Account* Credit for the same.

3. When the Partners come to a Reckoning with their *Trustee*, he will charge them with his *Provision* or Allowance as Manager, and other petty Charges, and Interest for Advance of Money, which have not yet been charged to Account, for my Share of all which I make *my Account* in *Company* Debtor to his *proper Account*. And now, for what *A. B.* gives for clearing of his Trust, let it be charged to the Accounts according to their Uses; and then the *Account in Company* will shew what I have gained by the Partnership; and

A. B.'s proper Account will shew what other real Debts are betwixt us. See more concerning this, in *Chapter* III.

Company Accounts.

Branch I. When another is Manager.

Supposition II. Of a fix'd Company.

My Account in Company with A. B. &c.

Debtor for my Share, stocked in, or owing; and this Account I never touch more, till the *Company Accounts* are examined and balanced with the Managers; and then if I withdraw my Stock, this Account is Creditor for it: What Gain or Loss falls to my Share, I state to the Account of *Profit and Loss*; and if the Company think fit either to encrease or diminish their Stocks, I make this Account Creditor for the Part lessened, or Debtor for the Addition.

In this Case I give also the Partners *particular Accounts* in my Books; and for the Partner, who by being chief Manager, gives his Name to the Company, upon his particular Account I place every Thing (except what is already said to belong to the former Account) which I give or receive from him upon *Company Account.*

Company Accounts.

Branch II. When I am Accountant and Manager.

Supposition I. Of an unfix'd Company.

Every Partner keeps *Accounts* for himself by the former Directions; and I am bound to keep Accounts for them all (because their Effects are in my Custody, and under my Management) which I may do either in my own Books, if their Affairs are but simple; or I may do it in separate and distinct Books, if the Value and Circumstances of their Affairs require it. I shall take the most simple Case first, *viz.* That I record the Company's Transactions in my own Books; which is done upon these Accounts.

1. *Account of Goods in Company with* ——

Use this Account the same Way as if the Goods were all your own, *i.e.* make it Debtor for all that's brought in, or purchased for the Company's Account, with all Cost and Charges; and Creditor for what's disposed of out of the same.

Observe, You may use a general *Account*, or a particular one, for every kind of Goods, as you think convenient; also, you may name all the Partners, and their Shares, in the Title; or say only, —— with *A. B.* and *Partners*, if there are any more; or give it any other Distinction you please, whereby it may be known to what Company the Goods belong.

For every Partner there must be an Account, and perhaps two; which are these,

2. A. B. *His Account in Company with* ——

Creditor for his Share of all the Goods (or Stock) of the Company, stocked in at first, or brought into it afterwards; and of all Charges and Expences, and of the neat Gains.

Debtor for what I pay my Partner on Account of his Concerns in Company, or give out of his Effects in my Hands, either in Bills, Goods, or Money given out for his Account, or what else he ought to allow for the same, as his Share of all Losses.

This is an Account of a mere Trust; and therefore the following Account will also be necessary.

3. A. B. *His proper (or particular) Account.*

Debtor and *Creditor* (as any other Person's Account in proper Trade) for what we mutually owe, and pay, upon other particular Dealings; and even Things relative to the Company's Affairs, which fall not within the Use of the former Account: Particularly, it is Debtor to me for what I advance or am bound for, of his share of Goods or Charges that belong to the Company; and Creditor for his Payment of this, or what he advances, or is engaged for of my Share; and when I draw a Bill upon him for more than his own Share, which he accepts for my Account: But if he accepts for the Account of another Partner, I give him Credit for no more than his Part, and give that Other Credit, as if I had drawn on him.

If the Uses of these Accounts be carefully considered, the *Debtors* and *Creditors* in all Transactions of domestick Trade in Company, will be easily discovered: But to make the Application as plain as I can, I shall subjoin a few Cases,[46] which when you have well considered, and compared with the Description of the Accounts, you'll see that this is all that's necessary to be known or remember'd, for these, or any other Cases; provided also we take along with us the general Rules for other Accounts that may be

---

[46] Malcolm discusses twelve "cases"; only three of these are reproduced here.

concerned; which are never to be transgressed; for 'tis plain, every Transaction of Company Trade must be recorded the same way as the like Transactions of proper Trade, (with the bare change of some Titles) the only Thing that's new here, being, the Record I must make for my Partner's Shares due to them, and by them.

Case 1. If my Partners give me *Cash* to be laid out for their Account, in buying Goods, I make *Cash* Debtor to their *Account in Company*, for their Share; or make *Cash Debtor* to my *Partner's proper Account*, for what he gives; and when that is laid out, make this *Account Debtor* to his *Account in Company*. Both Ways are equal upon the Matter; but the first is shortest. When the Goods are bought, they are *Debtor* to *Cash*; but if they stock in Goods, or pay the Money at the Buying, or I draw upon them for their Shares; I make the *Account of Goods Debtor* to their *Account in Company* for their Share, and to what I put in for my Share.

2. If I buy Goods for the Company from a Stranger, or sell them out of my private Effects, either I have Money in my Hands that belongs to the Partners, or not; in both Cases I first charge the *Goods in Company Debtor* to *Partner's Account in Company*, for his Share, and to what I have given, or the Persons to whom I owe my Share; then I make Partner's *Account in Company Debtor* to *Cash*, for so much of his Share as I have laid out at this Time; because this is a real Payment to him of that Money in my Hands; and for what I have advanced or stand engaged for on his Account, I make *his particular Account Debtor* to *Cash*, &c. If the Partners pay in their Shares at the Buying, or stand personally obliged for the same (when bought of a Stranger) or when I draw Bills on them immediately for their Shares; the Seller has Credit for nothing but what I owe him for my Share; and there is no more to be done than what is first said. But if I draw on any Partner for more than his Share, *his proper Account* must be *Creditor* for that. If I pay for those Goods by a Bill on one who owes the Company, the Goods are *Debtor*, as before, to *Partners Account in Company*, to shew their Share; but because it is paid by their Share of this Debt, make their *Account in Company Debtor* (to discharge me) to the Person, on whom the Assignment or Bill is drawn. . . .

5. If by Order, or Consent of the Company, I take Goods for Payment of a Debt owing to the Company —— *Goods in Company* (received) are *Debtors* to the Person who gives them; or if they are

received in *Barter*, they are Debtor to the Goods given out; and for these nothing need be put on the *Creditor-side* of the Partners *Account in Company*; because they are received only in return for other Value of the Company's, which is already on the *Creditor-side* of their Account. But to shew every Step, I may make the Goods received *Debtor* to Partner's *Account in Company* for his Share thereof, and at the same Time make this Account *Debtor* (to discharge my self of what's given out) to the *Account* of Goods given out in the one Case, and to the Person who now pays the Debt in the other Case. And if there is more received than given out, or than the Debt which was due, the Surplus paid or owing, must be considered as a new Purchase, and stated as above, in *Case* II.

OBSERVE *also*, If I take these Goods for my own Account, then I'm become absolutely *Debtor* to the Company for their Shares of the Debt now paid; and if we suppose the *Debtor* would have paid the Debt in Money, then I'm accountable for it as if it were Money paid. . . .

An.M.D.LIII.The.xxv.of May.

The Inuentorie or Estate of all

soche goodes, as vnto me Fraunces Bonde of London Grocer dooeth perteine, and also what I owe, or what I ought to make aunswere vnto, at this present, the particulers wherof, dooeth more at large hereafter ensue.

	li.	s.	d.
Moneie. Item in Aunggelles the numbre of 270 valued at x.shilinges the Aungel, amounteth to the somme of one hundret thirtie and fiue poundes. Somme.	135.	00	00
Item in Rialles, the nōbre of xlviii. valued at fiften shillinges the Riall, amounteth to the summe of xxxvi. poundes. I saie.	036	00	00
Item in double Douckates, the nombre of xxviij. valued at xii. shillings, which amounteth to the sōme of xvi.li.xvi.s	016.	16	00
Item in white monie of diuerse sortes to the somme of one.C. lxxvi.li.xiiii.s.iiii.d.	176.	14	04

Summe.C C C lxiiij.li.x.s.iiij.d.

	li.	s.	d.
Jewelles Item in Ringes of Golde. 3 one of them with my seale, the other twaine with stones, wherof thone is a Diamonde, and the other a Rubie: all thre weighing one ounce, and a halfe, valued after thre poundes the ounce, amounteth to the summe of foure poundes ten shillinges. I saie.	004	10	00
Item in Bracelettes of golde two, weighing. ij. vnces, and one quarter, valued at.lvi.s. the ounce, amounteth to the summe of iij.li.x.s.x.d.	005	10	10
Item one Tablet of Golde enameled, weighing one ounce. and thre quartres, valued after fower poundes, the once amounteth to the summe of seuen poundes. I saie.	007	00	00

Summe.xv.li.x.d.

	li.	s.	d.
Plate. Item in Goblettes of Siluer, & percel Guilt one neste with a couer.iii. in the nest, weighing xxxv.ounces, and a quar. valued after fiue Shillinges, & iiii. pence the Ounce, amounteth to the summe of nine poundes, and eight shillinges: I saie.	009	08	00
Item in Saltsellers two, of siluer, one guilt, and thother percel guilte, weighing thirtie ounces, and one haulfe valued after sixe shilinges the ounce, amounteth to the summe of nine poundes, thre shillinges.	009	03	00
Item in Spones of Siluer, one douzaine, with the Knoppes Guilt, weighing fourtene ounces, valued after fower shillings and sixe pence thounce, amounteth to the summe of thre poundes, and thre shillinges.	003	03	00

Summe.xxi.li.xiiij.s

I. James Peele, *Maner and Fourme*, 1553:
First page of Inventory.

Creditors——

The ballans of my olde great boke for marchandize signid with A owit be to haue the 27 daie of Nouember £ 2313. 8. 4. ß. fls. and is for the net rest and ballans of my Capitall or Stocke in all monys ——————————————————q | £ 2313 ß 8 ß 4

The same daie £ 53. 11. 4. ß. fls. and is for the net ballans of Thomas Martyns accompt in all monys ——————————— 6 | £ 53 ß 11 ß 4

The same daie £ 500.———ß. fls. and is for the net ballans of Paulis Vandallis accompt in all monys —————————————— 6 | £ 500 ß ——ß

The same daie £ 120.——ß. fls. and is for the net ballans of Antonio de Markis accompt in all monys —————————————— 8 | £ 120 ß ——ß

The same daie £ 250. 6. 9. ß. fls. and is for the net ballans of Iois van den Steens accompt in all monys ———————————— 8 | £ 250 ß 6 ß 9

The same daie £ 374. 16. 6. ß. fls. and is for the net ballans of Francis Durant, for his accompt of tyme for sale here in all monys —— 10 | £ 374 ß 16 ß 6

The same daie £ 196. 12. 9. ß. fls. and is for the ballans of Gilles Vermeullens accompt in all monys ——————————————— 10 | £ 196 ß 12 ß 9

The same daie £ 9. 16. 3. ß. fls. and is for the net ballans of Willyã Foster for his accompt corrant here ——————————— 12 | £ 9 ß 16 ß 3

The same daie £ 19. 5.———ß. fls. and is for the net ballans of Petter Collens accompt in all monys —————————————— 12 | £ 19 ß —5 ß

The same daie £ 22. 8. 8. ß. fls. and is for the net rest and ballans of Richard Maye for my accompt corrant withe hym in London, in all monys ————————————————————————— 14 | £ 22 ß 8 ß 8

The same daie £ 30.——ß. fls. and is for the net ballans of Willyã Foster, for his accompt of tyme for sale here in all monys ——— 14 | £ 30 ß ——ß

Somma £ 3890. 5. 7. ß. fls.———

II. John Weddington, *Breffe Instruction*, 1567:
Opening Balance Account, Debit Side.

Debitors ———

T He ballās of my olde great Boke for marchādize signyd wᵗ
the A owithe to gyue the 27 daie of Nouember £ 1610 · 13 · 4 ß
fls and is for the net ballans of the accompt of my cheſt or redy mony ——————————————————————————— 3 £ — 1610 ß, 13 ß — 4

The ſame daie £ 184 · 1 —— ß fls and is for the net reſt and ballans
of my accompts of plate and iewellis ———————————— 4 £ — 184 ß — 1 ß —

The ſame daie £ 540 —— ß fls and is for the net reſt and ballans of
my accompt of landis and rentis —————————————— 4 £ — 540 ß — ß —

The ſame daie £ 48 · 18 · 4 · ß fls and is for the net reſt and ballans of
my accompt of houſholde Stuff — ————————————— 5 £ — 48 ß, 18 ß — 4

The ſame daie £ 393 · 15 —— ß fls and is for the ballans of VVolff
Buſſyners accompt in all monys ————————————— 7 £ — 393 ß, 15 ß —

The ſame daie £ 260 —— ß fls and is for the ballans of ory accompt
of Holmus Fuſtians, in all monys ————————————— 7 £ — 260 ß — ß —

The ſame daie £ 245 · 3 · 4 · ¼ · ß fls and is for the net ballans of Francis Durantis accompt of tyme of byinge here in all monys —— 9 £ — 245 ß — 3 ß — 4 ¼

The ſame daie £ 127 · 8 · 9 · ß fls and is for the net ballans of Iohan
van Dams accompts in all monys ————————————— 9 £ — 127 ß — 8 ß — 9

The ſame daie £ 60 · 14 · 8 · ß fls and is for the net reſt and ballans of
my accompt of peper in all monys ————————————— 11 £ — 60 ß, 14 ß — 8

The ſame daie £ 101 · 16 · 10 · ß ¼ fls and is for the net reſt and ballance of Francis Durāt for my accompt of tyme for ſale withe hym
in London in all monys ——————————————————— 11 £ — 101 ß, 16 ß, 10 ¼

The ſame daie £ 6 · 9 · ß fls and is for the net ballans of Iohan
Edes accompt here corrant in all monys ————————— 13 £ — ß — 6 ß — 9

The ſame daie £ 104 · 13 · ß fls and is the net ballans of Richard
Maye for my accompt of tyme for ſale withe hym in London in all
monys ——————————————————————————— 13 £ — 104 ß — 1 ß — 3

The ſame daie £ 30 —— ß fls and is for the net ballans of Iohan de
Landmetters accompt in all monys ————————————— 15 £ — 30 ß — ß —

The ſame daie £ 85 · 8 · 4 · ß fls and is for the net ballans of Philip-
pus Boldis accompt in all monys ————————————— 15 £ — 85 ß — 8 ß — 4

The ſame daie £ 61 · 13 · ß fls and is for the ballans of Io. an Edis
accompt of tyme for byinge of marchandize here in all monys —— 16 £ — 61 ß — 13 ß — 3

The ſame daie £ 36 · 15 · 8 · ß fls and is for the ballans of VVillyam
Foſter accompt of tyme for byinge ———————————— 16 £ — 36 ß, 15 ß — 8

Somma £ 3890 · 5 · 7 · ß fls ——

III. John Weddington, *Breffe Instruction*, 1567:
Opening Balance Account, Credit Side.

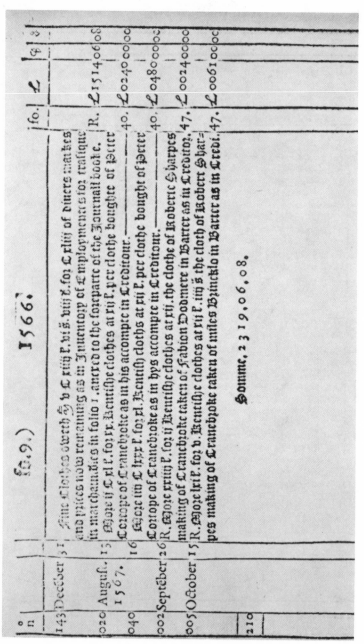

IV. James Peele, *Pathewaye to Perfectnes*, 1569:
Goods Account, Debit Side.

n			fo.	£	s	d
143	Marche. 01	Fine Clothes is dew to haue by L. viij. hūd. lxvj. ffol: for L cliij. of diuers marckes and prices Shipped into Spaine as by the perticulers in Jornall and the accompt of Voyages into Spaine in Debitour.	20.	£ 1514	06	08
020	Septēber 20 1567.	Mores in L rl P. for x x Baewuffis clothes of diuers warez Cottops makinge shipped to Andwarpe as in thaccompt of Voyages in Debitour.	45.	£ 0240	00	00
020	October 11	Mores in xl P. for x x. Beuuffie Clothes of diuers Cottops makinge shipped to Andwarpe as in the accompte of Voyages in Debitour.	45.	£ 0240	00	00
020	Marche. 06	Mores in L rl P. for x x Beuuffie clothes of diuers Cottops makinge deliuered with other percells to fir Edward Bruanftone of Yorke Knighte in	64.	£ 0240	00	00
007	09	R. Morleyy P. for Vij. Kentifh clothes of diuers Sharpe making now remayning whych to make this accōpt euē is beqne to goods remayninge in	65.	£ 0085	00	00
210						

Somme . 2 3 1 9 . 0 6 . 0 8 .

V. James Peele, *Pathewaye to Perfectnes*, 1569:
Goods Account, Credit Side.

Of the famous accompt called *profite or loſſe*, *or otherwiſe*, *Lucrum* or Damnum, and how to order it in the Leager.

The xviij. Chapter.

Item touching the accomptes (of profite, and loſſe) of neceſſitie it muſt haue one arcompt proper in ſome one place of your Leager, conteyning both a Debitor and Creditor ſide, as hath any other parcell: and on the Debitor ſyde therof muſt bee written all manner of loſſe ſuſteined: And on the Creditor ſide all thinges gained. And this ſaid accompt groweth oft in the Leager in diuers parcels of goods whereof the ſale happeneth, to profite or loſſe, which muſt bee ſaldid in this accompt of profite and loſſe, &c.

And when any accompt of goodes in the Leager is all ſolde, and that the Debitor part remayneth in ſumme of money more than the Creditor part, than is that goods ſold for loſſe of as much as the reſt amounteth vnto: wherefore to ſaid thus, you muſt thus write on the Debitor ſide.

Septem-

VII. William Hoskins, Ledger 1655–67:
Factorage Account, Debit and Credit Sides.

London ⸱ Anno 1672

Ballance in my last Bookes N° B, Debr

April 2 To Ballance my last Books N° B as appeareth in fol 204 of y° Leager Lay.
to Sundry Acco.ts ducts to him on such Ball as appr. fol. 2 . . . . 000 | 10021 | 02 | 11

Stock in Land & trade — Debr

1678
July 3 To Henwarz ffrank in portion with my daughter . . . . . . 49£ | 10000 | 00 | 01
Deter 20 To Caleb Banks, for what my Son hath had of me £ 3042: 15: 9d 55£ | 03042 | 15 | 9
June 30 To Ditto Caleb Banks my Son given him & payd severall t imes 86£ | 03581 | 19 | 2
                                                                    £16624 | 14 | 11
                                                              100£ | 136557 | 09 | 3
June 24 To Ballance thy booke . . . . £ 153195 | 04 | 2

Cash — Debr

April 2 To Ball° C¹⁸ Leager N° B. resting in Cash° . . . . . £ | 110117 | 06
April 2 To sundry o Accompts in Leag. fol. 2. from 1° dpr to 12 Aug. Distanced . . . . 000 | 01100 | 00 | 09
Aug.ber 28 To Sundry acc.ts f° 5. him 12 Aug. to 30 sept . . . 00 | 17293 | 00 | 89
Novembr 2 To sundry acc.ts f° 6. from 30 Octobr onto 1st Nober 00 | 9591 | 06 | 05
Deter 12 To Sundry acc.ts f° 9 from 1st Nober onto the 2d Deter 00 | 7948 | 00 | 11
January 15 To Sundry acc.t f° 10 from 2 Deter onto 10 Janu° 00 | 10476 | 09 | 01
Ditto 31 To Sundry acc.ts f° 10 from 10 Janu° onto 22 ffebry 00 | 10491 | 02 | 07
Aprill 30 To Sundry acc.t f° 12 from 22 ffebru° onto 30 aprill 00 | 32343 | 17 | 11
June 10 To Sundry acc.t f° 13 from 30 April onto the 10 June wa 00 | 40923 | 03 | 06
July 21 To Sundry acc.ts f° 15 from 10 June to the 21 July . 00 | 14665 | 18 | 04
Deter 11 To Sundry accompts f° 16. from 21 July onto 11 Deter wa 00 | 22049 | 14 | 08
January 31 To Sundry accompts f° 20. from 11 Deter onto 31 Janu° 73 00 | 13189 | 02 | 07
March 24 To Sundry accompts f° 21 from 31 Janu° to 31 March 74 00 | 40769 | 00 | 04
July 10 To Sundry acct f° 22 from 31 March to 10 July 74 00 | 28189 | 05 | 05
Octobr 2 To Sundry accompts f°23 from 10 July to 2 Octobr 00 | 13694 | 01 | 01
                                                           £ | 332041 | 03 | 09

VIII. Sir John Banks, Ledger 1672–84:
Page of Accounts, Debit Side.

London · Anno 1672

Contra   Cred.r

Aprill	2	By sundry acc.ts as appeareth ⅌ been fol. 1	00 1100212 02 11

Contra   Cred.r

Aprill	2	By Ball.ce of Ledger N.o B. as ther app.d also fol. fo 2	011 1019960 09 106
6 June		By ffitt & Losse upon acc.mpts adiusted & ballanced as appears	736 22450 14 09
			124410 19 03
9 May	3	By ffitt & Losse upon acc.ts adiusted & ballanced fo & ⅌ praglie as appears ⅌ ballance her out	54 8953 10 JL
			133340 18 2
602 Nober	4	By Caleb Banks my Son placed vnto his acc.t ⅌ same fo	004 3042 15 9
			94 168905 10 5
84 June	14	By ffitt & Losse fo6 be prayses £ 16003 10 3	153195 04 2

Contra   Cred.r

Aug.t	2	By Sundry acco.ts for acc.t &c from 1 Apr to 12 Aug	00 1 01209 10 100
Sept.	28	By Sundry acc.ts fo 3 from 12 Aug to 30 Sept 72	00 1 13150. 17. 07
Nouember	2	By Sundry acc.ts fo 5 from 30 Sober vnto 1.st Nouember	00 1 9549. 11. 10
Deter	12	By Sundry acc.ts fo 8 from 1 Nober to 12.th Deter	00 1 5942. 08. 03
January	15	By Sundry acc.ts fo 9 from 12 Deter vnto 15 Janua	00 1 10045. 00. 00
Ditto	31	By Sundry acc.ts fo 10 from 15 January vnto 31 Janua	00 1 19471. 13. 04
73 Aprill	30	By Sundry acc.ts fo 12 from 31 ffeb vnto 30 Aprill	00 1 32345. 13. 01
June	10	By Sundry acc.ts fo 14 from 30 Aprill vnto her 10 June	00 1 40705. 00. 00
July	21	By Sundry acc.ts fo 16 from 10 June to 21 July	00 1 14624. 03. 00
Ster	11	By Sundry acc.ts fo 17 from 21 July vnto 11 ster 1673	00 1 21993. 05. 07
January	31	By Sundry acc.ts fo 20 from 11 Ster vnto 31 Janu. 73	00 1 13150. 02. 10
March	2	By Sundry acc.ts fo 22 from 31 Janu. vnto 31 March 74	00 1 41093. 11. 10
July	10	By Sundry acc.ts fo 24 from 31 March to 10 July 74	00 1 28033. 11. 10
Ster	2	By Sundry acc.ts from 10 July to ⅌ October fo 23	00 1 13627. 11. 1
Ditto		By New acc.t Cash in ballance	321 252. 13. 1
			333041. 05. 09

IX. Sir John Banks, Ledger 1672–84:
Page of Accounts, Credit Side.

X. Sir John Banks, Journal 1672–84:
Entry for doubtful debts.

XI. Sir Charles Peers, Journal 1689–95:
Two entries.

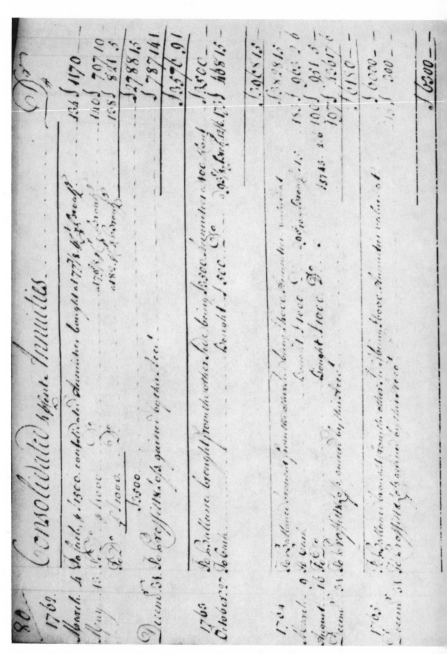

XII. William Braund, Ledger 1758–65:
Investment Account, Debit Side.

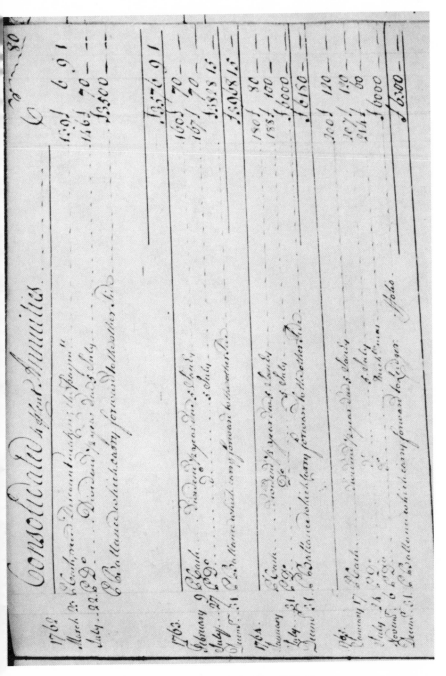

XIII. William Braund, Ledger 1758–65:
Investment Account, Credit Side.

1754

July 2 To Legacy &c. my A/c for Comm.n & Brokerage ... 74 £ .. 1 8

Dec. 31 To Sundry .... 56 .. 4

... To Capital .... 2 .. 533 11 2

£ 589 12 11

1755

Jan. 11 To Rich.d Barnard for the Value of his Coat given him £ 18 ..

25 To Cash p.d ½ a years Window Tax to Mich.s 1754 for M.r
Emdeons living in my house at Braxhall, w.ch he ought to have ... 3 .. 1 ..

Oct. 14 To Tim Carter for his trouble & Expence in coming }
down to London to endeavour to purchase } 50 .. 20 ..
D.r Clarke's Rectory of Great Tey }

Dec. 31 To Sundry, lost by Reduction of the India }
Dividend & fall of West India other Stocks } .. 5244 12 ..

To Sundry for the Expence hither incurred }
by repairing Rebuilding & furnishing my } .. 3550 14 3
house called Braxhead Lodge }

... To Sundry a/c of Journal .... 517 .. 5 5

1756

£ 9336 10 8

Dec. 31 To Sundry for the Expence this year incurred }
by repairing rebuilding & furnishing my house } £ 316 13 7
called Braxhead Lodge }

... To Sundry lost by the fall of Stocks this year .. 1352 10 ..

... To D.o by d.o Adv.d on 2d 22.5 Lottery Ticket £31 19 6 30 .. 4 6

£ 1699 8 1

XIV. Peter Du Cane, Ledger 1754–56:
Profit and Loss Account, Debit Side.

54		
Dec.r 31. Cr Income	6 £	457. 8. 5
Cr Sundry		132. 4. 6
	£ 589. 12. 11

'55		
Jan.r 25. Cr Cash rec.d Mr Cornelisens trad.n Share &c. for to discharge ½ a years Tyth. of the Landing hand at Bradhead d.o from from Mich.s to Lady day &c	13 £	4. 12. 6
Dec.r 31. Cr Income	6	274. 18. 5
Cr East India Comp.s Bonds .... £17. 1. 7 Cr Capital lost this Year by Building - Fall of Stocks &c had 9039. 18. 2 Ditto	}	9056. 19. 9
		9336. 10. 8

56		
Ap.l 6. Cr Bank Direction for the half bought of last Year	115 £	126. 13. —
Dec.r 31. Cr Sundry viz Profit & Loss of Insurance £310. 10. 10 Acco.t of Insurance ...... 17. 2. —	}	327. 12. 10
Cr Income	6	286. 2. 5
Cr Ann.y & Lottery 1756 gained	85	33. 17. —
Cr Capital lost this year by fall of Stocks &c		925. 2. 10
	£ 1699. 8. 1

XV. Peter Du Cane, Ledger 1754–56:
Profit and Loss Account, Credit Side.

XVI. William Braund, Ledger 1758–65:
Exchange Account, Debit Side.

Factorage Accounts

78

(Weddington, *Breffe Instruction*, 1567.)

The manner howe a marchant, ought to take accompt or reconninge of his factour, or servant, and how to gyve accompt or reconninge unto any other marchant &c.

Alwais from time to time, you most gyve order unto your factour or servant to sende you the perticuler accomptis of all suche marchandize, as he or they shall have, by your order, bought or solde for you, withe all the chargis perticulerly, be longinge unto the same, the wiche as you shall receave, from time, to time from hym or them, you most fyrst peruse diligentlie, and se yf in all thingis they be just, and yf it be the accomptis of marchandize bought and sent you, or unto other men for you, fyrst you most see what mony he hathe paid for the same withe all chargis, and how myche ther dothe rest of the same to be paide at time.——

And yf it be the accomptis for marchandize solde for you, fyrst you most see what mony he hathe recevid net, for the same, all chargis deductid, and how miche ther dothe rest for to be recevid at time by obligations. All this beinge well perusid, you most make the same Debitor, or Creditor in your great Boke, apon your accomptis corrant or time in your factours handis in London or ellis wher, to saie yf it be for byinge of marchandize make your factour or servant Creditor, and for selling of marchandize, you most make hym Debitor.——

And all this beinge don demande fyrst of hym, your accompt of time for sale of your marchandize, by the wiche you shall perseave, what he hathe recevid therof in mony, and how miche dothe rest to receave at time, by obligations in his handis for your proper accompt.

Then demande of hym your accompt of time for bijnge of marchandize, by the wich you shall perceave how miche he hathe paid therof in moni, and how miche dothe rest to paie at time, by his obligations for your proper accompt, so that the conclusion of the saide accomptis of time, for sale, and bijnge, as a fore saide, at suche time as ani perte therof, be wholli receavid or paid, thei are brought from the accomptis of tyme, Debitor or Creditor into your accompt corrant or redi moni the wiche accompt corrant or redi moni, you most demande last of all, the wiche is the conclusion of the whole, beinge recevid or paide.——

And by this order you shall se what your factour or servant owithe you en time by obligations for sale, and how miche you owe, unto him in time for bijnge, and last of all bi the accompt corrant, what he owythe you in redi moni, or how miche you do owe unto him in moni, and by this order as you have taken the accompt of your factour or servant a fore saide, in like manner you ought to gyve up your accompt unto all other men, for ther affaires don by you, by commission, withe all accomptis pertable, betwine you and other men etc.

79

(Gordon, *Universal Accountant*, 1787, vol. 2, pp. 39–42.)

Case 8. To journalize the varieties in shipping of goods to a factor.

In all cases of this kind, *Voyage to* —— *per* such a ship is *Dr.*; but the *Crs.* vary according to the circumstances.

1. If the goods have been already entered in your books which you ship on board the *Molly*, for *St. Kitts*, for instance:
   Voyage to St. Kitts, per the *Molly*, Dr. to *Sundries*.
   To *Goods specifically*, for their respective quantity and value.
   To *Cash*, for what charges you pay.
   To *the Creditor*, for any charges due.

2. If the cargo is bought of *Sundries* for cash, *Cash* will be the sole *Cr*.

3. If the cargo is bought of Sundries, part for money, and part on credit, *Cash* and the *Sellers* will be the *Crs*.

4. If the cargo is made up, partly from your own ware-house; partly of goods bought on credit, and partly for ready money, the *Crs*. will be *Goods*, *Sellers*, and *Cash*.

Note 1. Whatever varieties may occur in this case, will be easily made out from the foregoing.

2. Some, instead of voyage, &c. debit the factor immediately,

others the insurance-office where the cargo is insured, but neither of these methods can be with propriety recommended.

> *Case* 9. To journalize the varieties of the first advice from the factor.

In this case, the voyage must always be discharged for the amount with which it was debited, but the manner varies according to the nature of the advice.

1. If the first advice contain an account of sales for ready money, enter, *Factor my account-current* Dr. for nett proceeds at once.
2. If it contains an account of sales on time, enter, *Factor my account on time.*[47]
3. If it contains an account of sales for part money, part time, enter, *Sundries,* viz. *Factor my account-current*; and, *Ditto my account on time.*
4. If it contains an account of sales of only part of the cargo, enter, *Sundries, Factor my account-current,* for the amount, if for ready money;
   Ditto my account on time, if sold on credit; and,
   Ditto my account of goods, for the goods on hand.
5. If it contains only an account of the ship's arrival, and receipt of the cargo, enter, *Factor my account of goods.*

Note 1. When there is but one kind of goods, as linen, checks, &c. the title is, *Factor my account of linen, checks,* &c. instead of *goods.*

2. If the goods are sent to your own store and supercargo, the *store* is debited, instead of *my account of goods.*

> *Case* 10. To journalize the varieties of the second advice.

The entries in this case vary according to the nature of the first advice; for whatever was then charged, must now be discharged.
1. If the factor formerly advised, that the goods were received, but not sold, there will arise three varieties in the second advice.
1. That the goods received are now sold, in whole or in part, for ready money; in which case, *Factor my account-current* is Dr. to *ditto my account of goods.*
2. That the goods are sold for part money, and part on time, in which case, *Sundries,* viz. *Factor my account-current,* and *ditto my account on time,* Drs. to *ditto my account on goods.*
2. If the factor formerly advised, that the goods were sold on time, there will arise two varieties in the second advice.

---

[47] Some of the special accounts referred to in this extract are described in extract 63.

1. That he hath received payment of the debts outstanding, without abatement; in which case, *Factor my account-current* Dr. to *ditto my account on time.*

2. That in recovering payment he was obliged to allow abatement for bad debts, complaints of the goods, &c. in which case, *Factor my account current*, and *Profit and Loss*, must balance the *account on time.*

Case 11. To journalize the varieties when returns are made by the factor.

1. If returns are made in goods directly to yourself, and you receive advice thereof before the ship arrives, enter, *Voyage from* —— Dr. to *Factor*, &c. unless your factor had sent no previous advice of the fate of the voyage outward, when the voyage outward falls now to be discharged.

2. If the arrival of the ship brings the advice with the invoice, *Goods received* may be entered at once Dr. to *Sundries*, viz. to *Factor*, &c. for their cost and charges at the port where they were shipped, and to *Cash*, for freight, duty, and other charges paid here, or to any other person or thing, as corresponds best with the circumstances.

3. If the goods are shipped by your order to your factor, at some other port, something expressive thereof must be included in the title, as *Voyage from Philadelphia to St. Kitts*, &c.

4. If you are remitted directly in bills of exchange, *Cash, Bills receivable*, or *Correspondent* is Dr., according as you convert it immediately, retain it after acceptance till payment, or remit it for acceptance and payment to your correspondent elsewhere.

Note, There is no difference in the *Journal-entry*, whether your factor is possessed of your effects, or your order; only when he ships off goods for your account, *Factor my account-current* is always Cr.

OBSERVATIONS

1. Though in this and the two preceding cases I have minutely described the entries that may be made upon the different advices that may be received from a factor, in consequence of an adventure, to open to the young accountant the different links by which the beginning and end of an account of this kind may be connected, yet I would be far from recommending the method to practice. It is always to be supposed, that letters of advice are carefully

preserved, and these will be good enough vouchers that the goods were duly delivered to your factor, although no entry thereof be made in your books till he transmit the account of sales; when the *account-current*, or *account on time*, is debited at once, or perhaps both, according to circumstances, which will cut off the use of the account of goods, and save a great deal of writing, which in the former method is unavoidable. There are some who even abridge this last method, by omitting every intermediate account, and balancing the voyage by the factor's returns only.

2. Those who consign only to their own stores, generally debit the *Store*, and not *Voyage*, when the goods are shipped off; and as it is impracticable to keep a distinct account of the sales of every cargo by itself, the *supercargo my account-current* gets credit for all remittances made, whether in goods or bills; and when an abstract of the books is transmitted, which is generally once a-year at some particular period, the *Store* is then credited for the money received, and the outstanding debts.

80

(Malcolm, *Treatise of Book-keeping*, 1731, pp. 59–61.)

Accounts for factorage.

WHEN I act in Commission as Factor for another, the Transactions will be comprehended under these general Heads, *viz.* my receiving Effects of his to dispose for his *Account*, with the Account of the Charges and Expences, and Provision thereupon; my disposing thereof; my buying up Goods, and sending them elsewhere by his Order, and for his *Account*; or sending away his consigned *Goods* in my hands; our mutual Draughts and Remittances for his Account. These, and what else concern, or relate to my Management as Factor for another, you'll have orderly and distinctly recorded upon the following Accounts.

We may suppose that a Factor has it in his Commission to make no Sales upon Time, but all for ready Money; or he may sell upon Time; and in this Case, either he is not accountable for those Debts till he receives Payment; or no further than common Justice (according to the known Rules and Laws in such Matters) can oblige him for his Mismanagements; or he is bound by Agreement for Security and Payment of the Debts. I shall explain the Accounts with a View to these Circumstances.

With your Employer keep these Accounts, *viz.*

A. B. of —— *his Account of Goods, ⅌ Ship* —— D. M. *Master.*

Debtor for all the Charges they cost while under my Care, and for the Commission due to me.

Creditor for the Value of the Sales.

OBSERVE, There ought to be a distinct Account for every Consignment, and if there is but one Species, name it.

A. B. of —— *his Account Current.*

Debtor for whatever he owes, or is accountable for to me as his Factor, which does not stand charged on the preceding Account.

Creditor for whatever I owe, or am accountable for to him as his Factor.

OBSERVE, 1. His Account of *Goods* is distinct for every Consignment. If there is but one Kind, let the Title bear it, and make Columns for the Species and Quantities.

2. The Buyers on Time must have particular Accounts; but to make a parallel betwixt these and proper *Foreign Accounts*, you may use this *General Account* for all the Buyers, *viz. A. B.* his *Account of Out-standing Debts*; though the same Reason does not hold here, because the Buyers know only you; and when they have already an Account in your Books, it is more proper to charge it there: Or, if you think this general Account of any good Use, you may use it for all those Buyers; and upon their particular Account, who have such already in the Books, make some Mark whereby to know that they are Debtor on this Account; that nothing be forgot when you clear Accounts with them.

3. You may charge your Provision [48] upon every Sale for the Value, and at every Sale for ready Money, deduct all Charges and Provision owing; and for the Balance of that Money, make *his Account of Goods Debtor to his Account Current.* (See *Article* VI.) And the Debts owing remain upon the Creditor side unbalanced till they are paid; and then do the same; but ordinarily the *Account of Goods* is not balanced till all are disposed of; or, that your Employer demands his Account, and then charge the *Account of Goods,* Debtor to *Cash* and to *Profit,* &c. for all Expences and Provision due to you, and to his *Account Current* for the Balance of ready

---

[48] Commission.

Money received for the Sales of his Goods; your Charges and Provision being paid; and give him up also an Account of his *Outstanding Debts*; but the Account is not to be balanced for those, unless he now takes the Goods out of your Hands; in which Case, make his *Account* of *Goods* Debtor to the Buyers; and assign him to the Debt; and his *Account Current* will shew the true State of Affairs betwixt you, besides what *Goods* remain in your Hands.

4. When Abatement is made to the Buyers at Payment, my Employer is bound to allow it, if it is made for defect in his Goods; or by order for Advancement of Money to answer his Bills; and then his *Account* of *Goods*, or *Account Current*, is made Debtor for the same: In other Cases it may fall upon me as Factor, as when I have taken up his Money upon Abatement before due, to serve my self; or, when having insured the Sales, I make Composition with the Debtors altogether for my own Account, then *Profit* and *Loss* is Debtor for those Abatements.

5. If by Order I send away any of his Goods consigned to me, I make his *Account* of *Goods* Debtor for the Charges; and also put on the Creditor side in the Quantity Column, so much sent away by Order; but without any *Debtor*, because the Hazard of the Voyage is my Employers; and I put the Quantity there only for a *Memorandum* to my self; but nothing in the Money Columns; and so the Balance of the *Leger* is safe.[49] And if there was no Sale of his *Goods*, but the whole were now sent away by his Order, I then balance the *Account* of *Goods*, by marking his *Account Current* Debtor to it for the whole Charge, on the Debtor-side; and with that Sum set down the Quantity on the Creditor-side of the *Account* of *Goods*.

6. If I oblige my self for the Sales on Time, then, when the Goods are all disposed of (or at any Time, when I would make a Balance) I carry the whole Balance of his *Account* of *Goods*, to his *Account Current*; because it is all absolute Debt upon me, only I may distinguish the Articles that are not yet due: Or in this Case,

---

49 Plate VII shows the account entitled " Drapery for the acc°. of Tho. Samways " in the ledger (1655–67) of William Hoskins. It is debited with the general charges paid by Hoskins (" as by the particulars of the booke of Charges ") and the " provissions " (commission) on sales; credited with the sales proceeds; and the balance (" neate provenon ") is carried to Samways' " acc° Currant ". The unsold quantity balance of the cloth is carried down from the credit to the debit side, it having been placed in " Le Gondis hands to sell ". This transfer has no entry in the money columns (as in the text, above). The last entry on the credit side records that the " neate provenon " of the cotton " mentioned on the other side " [the previously unsold balance] was placed to Samways' current account.

because all the Sales are unconditional Debts upon me, I need keep but one Account, *viz.* his *Account Current*, and make it Debtor for whatever he owes me as his Factor, and Creditor for what I owe or am accountable to him for his Account: And this will do well, especially with the Use of a *Factor-Book*; which see described below. If that Agreement for the Sales is made after Part of the Goods are sold, make the *Account* of *Goods* Debtor for the *Præmium* or additional Provision on the Sales already made on Time, and for all that follows; or balance the Account now, and make no more Use of it, but of the *Account Current*.

N. B. Some use such an Account, as *A. B.* his *Account* on *Time*, to which they make the *Account* of *Goods* Debtor for the *Out-standing Debts*; but it is unnecessary, since these may as well stand upon the *Account* of *Goods*, till they are paid, and then the Balance goes to the *Account Current*.

7. When my Employer's Goods are all sold, I make the *Account* of *Goods* Debtor for the Provision due to me, and for what Charges are not already enter'd; and then I balance this *Account* by making it Debtor to his *Account Current* for the Difference, which is the neat Product of his *Account* of *Goods*; and in this State, a Copy of his Accounts is to be sent him. And *observe*, That this is not commonly done till the Out-standing Debts are all paid, unless the Factor take these Debts upon himself.

8. If I return any of my Employer's Goods, by his Order; or send them off to another of his Factors, who is accountable to himself immediately; I have nothing more to do, but to state what is due to me, and balance the Account, as in the last Article.

The Valuation of Assets

81

(Hamilton, *Introduction to Merchandise*, 1788, p. 334.)

Desperate debts.

A merchant should be careful not to overvalue his stock; and therefore, when a debt becomes desperate, it should either be thrown out of the books altogether, or distinguished in such a manner, that it may not mislead him in estimating the amount of his property.

If you choose to throw it out entirely, charge *Profit and Loss Dr. to the Bankrupt*. But if you follow that method, the debt must be entered in a separate book kept for that purpose, as there is always a chance, however small, that it may be recovered, through a change of circumstances. If that happen, enter *Cash Dr. to Profit and Loss*, for the sum received.

If you chuse to reserve it in the books, you must open an accompt, under the title of *Bad debts*, and charge that accompt Dr. to the persons whose debts you despair of recovering. This brings all the bad debts to the same accompt; exhibits the amount of them at one view; and saves the trouble of transferring the particular accompts from ledger to ledger: And although it introduces the amount of these debts as an article of your stock at the general balance, no great inconvenience follows; because the title by which they are distinguished must lead you to make the proper estimate. If you follow this method, when a debt, charged as bad, is recovered, you must enter *Cash Dr. to Bad debts*. If any of these debts become likely, through an alteration of circumstances, to be recovered, we may open the debtor's accompt anew, by charging him Dr. to Bad debts.[50]

---

[50] Plates X and XI reproduce entries in seventeenth-century journals illustrating the two different accounting treatments of bad and/or doubtful debts.

82

(Stephens, *Italian Book-keeping*, 1735, pp. 37–8.)

. . . Admit the State of my Affairs stood thus:

First Account. John Jones D^r.	*l.*	*s.*	*d.*	First Account. Per Contra C^r.	*l.*	*s.*	*d.*
Security to me - - - -	100	0	0				

Second Account. Jacob Tonson D^r.	*l.*	*s.*	*d.*	Second Account. Per Contra C^r.	*l.*	*s.*	*d.*
Security to me - - - -	63	0	0				

Third Account. Isaac Newton D^r.	*l.*	*s.*	*d.*	Third Account. Per Contra C^r.	*l.*	*s.*	*d.*
Security to me - - - -	70	0	0				

Fourth Account. Francis Blake D^r.	*l.*	*s.*	*d.*	Fourth Account. Per Contra C^r.	*l.*	*s.*	*d.*
Security to me - - - -	90	0	0				

Fifth Account. Aaron Goddard D^r.	*l.*	*s.*	*d.*	Fifth Account. Per Contra C^r.	*l.*	*s.*	*d.*
Security to me - - - -	50	0	0				

Now suppose the three First of these Securities [51] to become dubious, *viz. John Jones, Jacob Tonson,* and *Isaac Newton,* either from the Persons themselves absconding, or otherways being incapacitated for paying their respective Debts. Hence then it's plain, that in regard to the Manner of my Estates consisting, it differs from what it was before; that is, in plain Terms, the Sums there charged, as they are doubtful whether they may be ever received, are not so absolutely to be depended on as the Rest of which I have no Manner of Reason to doubt; but it is most evident if these Accounts were to be let alone, in the Manner they now stand stated the whole Set in general would appear alike substantial Securities, because as yet no Distinction has been made to render them obvious to the contrary. Now the Error of letting them stand being thus manifest is therefore avoided, by entering as much on the Creditor

[51] " Securities " is Stephens' term for " assets "; see extract 109, below.

of each of these Accounts as they appear to be Debtors for; and from thence carrying their Sums and placing them to the Debtor Sides of others capable of demonstrating the true Nature and Quality of the Debts. *Example*; Such Accounts being ballanced, or equalled, in their Debtor and Creditor Sides, are render'd as followeth, according to their present Stating.

First Account. *John Jones* desperate D^r. Security to me - - - -	*l.*	*s.*	*d.*	First Account. *Per Contra* C^r.	*l.*	*s.*	*d.*
	100	0	0				

Second Account. *Jacob Tonson* desperate D^r. Security to me - - - -	*l.*	*s.*	*d.*	Second Account. *Per Contra* C^r.	*l.*	*s.*	*d.*
	63	0	0				

Third Account. *Isaac Newton* desperate D^r. Security to me - - - -	*l.*	*s.*	*d.*	Third Account. *Per Contra* C^r.	*l.*	*s.*	*d.*
	70	0	0				

Thus I am informed of the true Nature and Quality of the Debts, and consequently, as they are Part of the computed Value, whether the Extent in general be not liable to be diminished from such Securities; but admit these Accounts were all reduc'd into one only, as thus:

Desperate Debts D^r.	*l.*	*s.*	*d.*	*Per Contra* C^r.	*l.*	*s.*	*d.*
John Jones owes me - - -	100	0	0				
Jacob Tonson - - - - -	63	0	0				
Isaac Newton - - - - -	70	0	0				

Here the Securities appear equally evident to what they did from the last Stating, notwithstanding they were allowed each a particular Account to itself; and the same Method may be used with the Rest happening of this Nature. For whatsoever Number they may happen to increase to, will not in the least obscure them, seeing when any of them are discharged I have no more to do than place such Discharge on the Creditor Side of the Account, right just opposite to the Security on whose Part it was made, and that will clearly relate at all Times who remains indebted to me and who not. . . .

83

(Peele, *Pathewaye to Perfectnes*, 1569.)

In folio 9 in thaccompt of fine clothes,[52] ther is founde at takinge of the ballaunce,[53] to remayne vii. clothes, which being valewed as the cost, be set on ye creditour syde, havinge the letter. R. to make the clothes of that accompt even, & be removed to thaccompt of goodes remayninge, then is subtrayed the totall somme of all the clothes bought standinge on the debitour side, from the totall somme of the sale & remayne on the creditour side, and the difference is gayned by the sales made which is set on the debitour side with the letter. R. to make even that accompte of fine clothes & is borne to accompt of proffitt and losse to the creditour syde.[54]   And in suche like sorte are thaccomptes of all goodes to be cleared and shut up at taking of the ballaunce and closing up of the bookes.

84

(Mair, *Book-keeping Methodiz'd*, 1741, pp. 76–7.)

An accompt of goods.

Contains, upon the Dr. Side, the prime Cost and Charges; and, upon the Cr. Side, the Sale or Disposal of them.   So that there are here three Varieties: 1. When the Goods are all disposed of, the Difference of its Sides is, the Gain or Loss made upon the Sale; and so is balanced, by charging it Dr. to *Profit and Loss*, for the Gain, if the Cr. Side be heaviest; or giving it Credit by *Profit and Loss*, for the Loss, if the Dr. Side be heaviest. . . . 2. When none of the Goods are disposed of, then it is closed by *Balance*,[55] for the whole Sum on the Dr. Side. . . . 3. When only part of the Goods are disposed of, which will appear by the Inequality of the Quantity-columns; this Case requires a double Balance, *viz*. First, the Accompt must be credited by *Balance*, for the Goods remaining,

---

[52] Plates IV and V reproduce the '' Fine Clothes '' account on folio 9 of Peele's illustrative ledger.   The opening balance is introduced via the inventory.   The columns for quantities are on the extreme left of each side of the account.

[53] This refers to the drawing up of the balance account on the closing of the ledger.

[54] It will be seen that in the illustration in Plates IV and V there is no profit or loss, since all the credits are at cost.   The other goods account on the same folio (not reproduced) for '' Sortinge Clothes '' does show a profit entry.   The closing stock of 43 cloths is entered at cost: '' which cost all after v £ per clothe ''.

[55] Balance account.

valued at the prime Cost; which equals the inner Columns [56]: After this, it must be made Dr. to, or Cr. by *Profit and Loss*, for the Gain or Loss made upon what are sold; which evens the outer Columns,[57] and closes the Accompt. . . .

Note 1. If the Goods are of different kinds or Prices, as they should be distinguished, when posted to the *Ledger*, by different Numbers, or separate inner Columns; so care must be taken, in balancing the Accompt, to mention the kind of Goods remaining unsold, and to value them at their own Price.

Note 2. A Merchant may, at any time, know what Goods he has on hand, by comparing the inner Columns of the *Accompts of Goods*, without being put to the Trouble of inspecting his Warehouse, and weighing or measuring the Goods themselves.

Note 3. If there be Inlack or Outcome of Goods, that is, Defect or Excess in Weight or Measure, it will happen, when the Goods are all disposed of, that the inner Columns will not be equal. In this Case, the *Balance* or *Equality* must be restored, by inserting as much in the deficient Column as will make it equal to the other, writing the Word *Inlack* or *Outcome* before it, as the Reason why it is added; but nothing goes to the Money-columns.

85

(Dowling, *Complete System*, 1770, p. 33.)

Wares.

The Debit shews the Cost and Charges, the Credit shews the Produce.

1st, If none be sold, credit the Account by Balance for the Amount of the Debit.

2d, If all be sold, debit the Account to Profit and Loss for the Gain, or credit it by Profit and Loss for the Loss.

3d, If Part be sold and Part unsold, 1st, credit the Account by Balance for what remains unsold, valuing it at the Rate it stands you in, and 2d, close it afterwards with Profit and Loss for the Gain, &c.

4th, If in the last Case, you cannot without Trouble calculate to the Value of what remains unsold, or if you desire to have the

---

[56] The quantity columns.
[57] The money columns.

Account appear in the next *Ledger*, in the same State it is in here, then you may close the Account with a double Balance, that is, debit the Account to Balance for the Total of the Credit Side, and credit the Account by Balance for the Total of the *Dr.* Side.

86

(Malcolm, *Treatise of Book-keeping*, 1731, p. 90.)

For *Accounts of Houses* and *Ships*: You may value them at the first Cost; and when that is stated on the Creditor-side, the Difference of the Debt and Credit is Gain or Loss, arising from the Difference of the Reparations, &c. and the Rents or Freights. Or you may take the Difference of the two Sides, and state as the Balance due to you; by which means the Value of the Thing will appear less and less at every balancing, till it's nothing.[58] And then in a new Inventory you enter it again, at what Value you think proper; and sometimes also you may appear to be a Loser, which must go to *Profit* and *Loss*; but the first Method I think the best: And though these Subjects do not really keep up their Value, yet I would continue them at the first Value till they were disposed of, or lost; or you may chuse to state them at another Value from Time to Time, as you think they are then really worth.[59]

---

[58] That is, the net income on the use of the asset is not carried to the profit-and-loss account, but simply reduces the value of the asset as recorded in the account.

[59] In this passage Malcolm refers to three different methods. Their different effects can be shown by means of a simple example, as follows (where the three sets of columns distinguish the three methods):

Asset Account

	1	2	3		1	2	3
To Cost of Asset	£100	100	100	By Gross Revenues during year	£25	25	25
,, Repairs during year	10	10	10	,, Closing Balance (per Balance Account)	100	85	105*
,, Profit for year (to Profit - and - Loss Account)	15		20				
	125	110	130		125	110	130
,, Balance	100	85	105				

* New valuation.

For further discussion and exemplification of the three methods, see pp. 197–9, below.

87

(Mair, *Book-keeping Methodiz'd*, 1741, p. 79.)

Wagers Accompt.

Contains, upon the Dr. Side, the Consignments made when the Wagers were entered into. The Cr. Side contains the Decisions of the Wagers. So that here occur two Varieties, *viz.* 1*st*, If all the Wagers are determined, the Difference of the Sides will be the Gain made upon these decided in favours of the Merchant; and the Accompt is closed, by being charged Dr. to *Profit and Loss*, for the said Difference. 2*dly*, If any of the Wagers are yet undecided, the Accompt must first be credited by *Balance* [60] for them: After which, if the Sides are still unequal, it must be charged Dr. to *Profit and Loss*, for the Difference.

Accompts of Ships, Houses, or other Possessions.

Contain, upon the Dr. Side, what they cost at first, or are valued at, with all Charges, such as Repairs, or other Expences laid out upon them. The Cr. Side contains, (if any thing be writ upon it) either what they are sold or exchanged for, or the Profits arising from them, such as, Freight, Rent, &c. Here there are three Cases: 1*st*, If nothing be written upon the Cr. Side, it is closed, by being credited by *Balance*. 2*dly*, If the Cr. Side be filled up, with the Price of the Ship, House, &c. sold, or otherwise disposed of, then the Difference of the Sides is the Gain or Loss made upon the Sale; and the Accompt is closed, by being debited or credited to or by *Profit and Loss*. 3*dly*, If the Cr. Side contain only the Freight or Rent; in this Case, first charge the Ship, House, &c. Dr. to *Profit and Loss*, for the Freight or Rent; and then, close the Accompt with *Balance*. . . .

88

(Gordon, *Universal Accountant*, 1787, vol. 2, p. 56.)

Ships, Houses, &c. contain, upon the Dr. side, the original value, and charges of repairs, &c. and, upon the Cr. side, if any thing at all, the disposal of them, or profits arising from them, such as rents,

---

[60] Balance account.

freight, &c. Hence arise three varieties. 1. If the Cr. side is empty, fill it up with *Balance*. 2. If it contains the disposal, the sides are evened with *Profit and Loss*, for the gain or loss. 3. If it contains only the freight or rent, &c. credit the account by *Balance*, for the cost, and debit it to *Profit and Loss*, for the difference of its sides thereafter; unless the charges at the debit exceed the profits at the credit, in which case, close it by *Profit and Loss* for the excess.

89

(Dowling, *Complete System*, 1770, p. 36.)

Ship.

The Debit shews the Cost and Charges you have been at on this Account, the Credit shews the Produce by Freight or Sale. 1st, Credit the Account by Balance for the Value of the Ship or your Part thereof. 2d, Close the Account by Profit and Loss for the remaining Difference.

Houses, Lands, &c.

These Accounts are not unlike the last, and are closed the same Way.

Moveables.

The Debit shews the Cost, the Credit shews the Produce, if by Chance you have sold any. This Account is closed by Balance.

90

(Hamilton, *Introduction to Merchandise*, 1788, pp. 490–91.)

If a sum of money, suppose L.500, be expended to improve the farm, which the proprietor does not expect to draw back in less than 10 years, the whole sum, at the end of the first year, is considered as part of the stock on the farm; but, at the end of the second, when one-tenth part, or L.50, was expected to be drawn back, the remainder only, or L.450, should be considered as part of the stock; and this allowance is gradually diminished L.50 each year, till it be exhausted. If no returns be expected for several years, the allowance is not diminished till the time when benefit was expected. This, however, should be regulated by the hopes entertained when the money was expended, and not by the success of the improvements; and then the balance of the farm-accompt, in the successive years, will show how far the improvements have exceeded or fallen short of expectation.

The Balancing and Closing of the Ledger

91

(Weddington, *Breffe Instruction*, 1567.)

> The manner for to cleare olde great boks, that are full writton, and how to transsport the net restis of all the accomptis standinge in them into other new bokes.

When your principall great Boke or lidger, shalbe full writton, then you most ballance up all the accomptis not clearid, and carri the net restis therof into another new great Boke, in this manner, to saie all the accomptis that restethe Debitor on the Debitor side, the same rest you most make Creditor in the same accompt, and from thens carri the same in debito, unto the ballance of the same olde boke, made at thende of the same, and all that you shall finde to rest in the Creditor side, make the same Debitor in the saide accompt, and Creditor, in the saide ballans, and in this manner you most go throughe all your saide olde great Boke, and bringe all the net restis of the same into one ballance, at thende of your saide olde great Boke, as well the Debitors as the Creditors. And that beinge don, Some up the saide ballans, and you shall finde it to agre in Some, bothe in the Debitor, and in the Creditor side, yf your boke, be trewly kept, and the net restis well taken out. And this beinge all don as a fore saide, then you most have a like new Boke, as your olde boke was, and then enter or write into the same the saide ballance of your olde great Boke,[61] In this manner, fyrst make the Debitor perte of the ballans Creditor at the beginninge of your newe great Boke, to saie apon the seconde leaff in all thingis, like as it standethe in your olde great Boke, and the Creditor perte of the same ballance apon the Debitor side or fyrst leaff of your saide newe Boke,[62] and by this manner you shall in Debitor and Creditor lincke, the one great Boke, withe the other, And all this beinge don, make

---

[61] Plates II and III reproduce the opening balance account in the new ledger of Weddington's set of illustrative accounts.

[62] From the reproduction (Plates II and III) it will be seen that the entries on the debit side of the balance account are headed " Creditors " and that the phrase " owithe to have " (ordinarily used for credit entries) is used; conversely, the credit side is headed " Debitors " and the debit-entry phrase " owithe to give " is used.

other newe, accomptis in your new great Boke, for the same restis, to saie for the Creditor side of the ballans make Debitors alonge in your newe great Boke, and for the Debitor side of the ballans, make Creditors alonge in your saide newe great Boke, and so you shall finde all the net restis of the saide accomptis to stande in like order, as in your olde great Boke, wherin you maie write all your businis untill it be full also, and then do withe that as you have don withe your other olde Boke, unto the wiche this maye suffice——as more plainly aperethe at thende of this Boke in fo. 43.——

92

(Hayes, *Gentleman's . . . Book-keeper*, 1741, ch. 8.)

The way to balance your accounts, without shutting up your leger.

When you would balance your Books without shutting up your Leger, you must furnish yourself with a suitable Quantity of clean Paper, ruled in the same Manner that your Leger is.

Then open an Account for Profit and Loss upon the said Paper; and having done this,

Cast up the Dt. Side of Profit and Loss in your Leger, and place the total Sum upon the Dt. Side of the Account of Profit and Loss on your Paper.

Then cast up the Ct. Side of Profit and Loss on your Leger, and place the total on the Ct. Side of the Account of Profit and Loss on your Paper.

Having thus prepared an Account for Profit and Loss upon your Paper, the next Thing you are to do, is to open another Account upon your Paper for Balance, calling it Balance Dt. and Ct.

And having opened this Account of Balance, and ruled it in the Manner of the Leger, according to the Directions beforegoing,

Begin with the Account of Cash in your Leger, and having cast up the Dt. and Ct. Sides, the one being the total of what you have received, and the other being the same of what you have paid away, substract what you have paid away from what you have received, and for the Difference, being the Cash remaining,

Dt. Balance Account for what Cash remains by you.

And in the like Manner you are to proceed from one Account

to another, in successive Order as they stand in your Leger, only reserving the Account of Stock, and Profit and Loss, to the last.

Now you are to consider, that your Leger contains various Sorts of Accounts, and those being of different Kinds, different Methods must be pursued in balancing the same.

And, *First*, If it be an Account of Goods, if the whole Quantity of those Goods do remain unsold,

Dt. Balance on your Paper for the whole Quantity remaining unsold, valuing the same at the present Market Price, or at the Price they cost you.

Secondly, If only Part of the Goods be sold,

Dt. Balance Account on your Paper for the Value of those Goods that remain by you unsold, either at the Price they cost you, or at the Market Price.

N. B. It is usual with Merchants, when they make a general Balance of their Books, to value the Goods that they have by them at the Market Price they then go at, at the Time of their balancing; but some do not so.

Thirdly, If all the Goods are sold relating to the Account that you are now balancing;

If you have lost by them,

Dt. the Account of Profit and Loss upon your Paper.

But if you have gained by them,

Ct. the Account of Profit and Loss upon your Paper.

Now there are several Things to be considered in relation to balancing an Account with a Chapman, as well as in other Accounts.

As, *First*, In relation to Chapmen, if the Dt. Side of their Accounts amounts to more than the Ct. Side, it is plain they are indebted to you for the Difference; therefore,

Dt. Balance Account (upon your Paper) for what is due to you.

Secondly, If the Ct. Side of their Accounts amounts to more than the Dt. Side of the same, shews that you are indebted to your Chapman, and therefore you must (upon your Paper)

Ct. the Account of Balance for what is due to him.

Thirdly, When the Dt. and Ct. Sides of such Chapman's Account do both agree, it shews, that such Chapman's Account is finished; because there is nothing due on either Side.

Fourthly, and *lastly*, If there should any Difference arise in your Chapman's Account in relation to Abatements that have been made on either Side, between your Chapman and yourself; if the Difference does arise from Abatements that have been made by yourself,

Ct. the Account of Profit and Loss on your Paper for the said Abatement.

But if the Abatement has been made to your Chapman,

Dt. the Account of Profit and Loss (on your Paper) for the Sum that you abated to him.

And for all such Accounts as are of the same Nature with Stock, being such as you can make no Demand upon, nor them upon you; such as House Expences, Pocket Expences, Charges of Merchandise, &c. to make even such Accounts, you must

Dt. the Account of Profit and Loss upon your Paper.

And having thus run through all other Accounts in your Leger, but the Account of Stock, Profit and Loss, and Balance; the next Thing you are to do, is to open an Account for Stock upon your Paper; but first turn to the Account of Stock in your Leger, and cast both Sides up, and put the total of the Dt. Side upon the Dt. Side of Stock on your Paper, and the total Amount of the Ct. Side upon the Ct. Side of Stock on your Paper.

Then, to make even those three Accounts, *viz.* the Account of Stock, Profit and Loss, and Balance,

First, Begin with the Account of Profit and Loss upon your Paper, and cast it up in the same Manner as you did your other Accounts in your Leger, and if the Ct. Side (which is your Gains) amounts to more than the Dt. (or losing) Side of the Account, you will be a Gainer, and for whatever Sum your Gains does amount to,

Dt. the said Account of Profit and Loss on your Paper, and Ct. Stock on the Paper.

But if, upon casting up, you do find that the Dt. Side of Profit and Loss amounts to more than the Ct. Side, you will be a Loser by so much as the Difference does amount to; and for whatever the Sum does amount to,

Dt. the said Account of Stock, and Ct. Profit and Loss.

The next Thing you are to do, is to make even the Account of Stock on your Paper, by casting up the Dt. Side, being what you owe, and the Ct. Side, being what is due to you; and whatever Sum the Ct. Side does amount to more than the Dt. Side, so much will be the Value of your Estate at the Time of your balancing; for which you must

Dt. Account of Stock, and Ct. Account of Balance.

But if the Dt. Side of your Account of Stock amounts to more than the Ct. Side, by so much as that Difference does amount to at the Time of your balancing, so much you will be worse than nothing; for which Sum you are to

Dt. Account of Balance, and Ct. the Account of Stock.

Lastly, After you have made the foregoing Entries in the Account of Stock, then cast up the Dt. and Ct. Side of the Account of Balance, and if the Balance of this Account agrees with the Balance of Stock Account, it shews that your Books have been kept right, and your Work is done.[63]

This being the usual Method that the skilful Book-keeper takes to balance his Books, when he has so much spare Room in his Books, as not to want a new Pair; and these Balance Papers are to be carefully laid up in your Escruittore or Desk, to turn to at any Time hereafter, if you should want to know how much your Estate was worth, or in what Posture your Estate lay, in any particular Year.

93

(Mair, *Book-keeping Methodiz'd*, 1741, pp. 87–9.)

How the balances are collected, the ledger closed, and a new inventory formed.

When you design to balance your *Ledger*, in order to begin a new Set of Books, proceed in the manner following.

Take two Sheets or Folios of loose Paper, rule them like the *Ledger*, and write on the Heads or Tops of them, the Titles of the two following *Accompts, viz.* on the Head of the one, *Profit and Loss Dr.* and *Contra Cr.*; on the other, *Balance Dr.* and *Contra Cr.* Then, beginning with the *Accompt of Cash*, go over every Accompt in the *Ledger*, (omitting only the *Accompts of Profit and Loss* and *Stock*, which must be left open to the last) and, adding up their Dr. and Cr. Sides, carry the Articles of Gain or Loss found on any of them, to the *Profit and Loss* Sheet; and the Articles of

---

[63] The test of the books described in this paragraph should have been made *before* the balance of stock account was transferred to the balance account; for this transfer would —if the books were correct—close all the accounts. The appropriate procedure is described by Hayes in his chapter 11 " Shewing the Way to close a Leger, in order to open a new Pair of Books ".

Debt, or Goods remaining, to the *Balance* Sheet, without touching the Accompts themselves: *e.g.* After adding up the Dr. and Cr. Sides of the *Cash-accompt*, subtract the one Sum from the other, and, on the *Balance* Sheet, make *Balance* Dr. to *Cash*, for their Difference, being the ready Money in your Hands. Again, in an *Accompt of Goods* that are all sold, after adding up the Dr. and Cr. Sides, subtract the one from the other, and, on the other Sheet, make *Profit and Loss* Dr. or Cr. to or by the said *Accompt of Goods*, for the Difference of its Sides. And in this manner proceed with every other Accompt in the *Ledger*, according to their Nature, as explained in the last Section.

Having advanced thus far, your next Step is, to add up the Dr. Sides of the *Profit and Loss* Sheet, and the *Profit and Loss Accompt* in the *Ledger*, into one Sum, and their Cr. Sides into another; and, on the said Sheet, make *Profit and Loss* Dr. or Cr. to or by *Stock*, for their Difference: Which Difference being carried to the *Stock-accompt*, add up its Dr. and Cr. Sides, and carry their Difference to the *Balance* Sheet. Which being done, the total Sums of the Dr. and Cr. Sides of the *Balance* Sheet will be equal to a Farthing, if the Books be right, and the balancing Work truly performed: As may be thus demonstrated.

It is obvious, that the *Balance* Sheet, before the Balance of the *Stock-accompt* is brought to it, contains, upon the Dr. Side, the Money and Goods you have on hand, or at Sea, or in the Hands of Factors, with the Debts due to you; the Articles on the Cr. Side are the Debts due by you to others: So that the Difference of its Sides is your present Worth, or *neat Stock*. Now, if the Balance of the *Stock-accompt* be also equal to your present *neat Stock*, it is plain, that it will even the Sides of the *Balance-accompt*: But that it is so, appears thus.

Your present neat Stock is equal to your neat Stock when the Books were begun, with the Addition of the Gain, or Diminution of the Loss made since that Time: But the Difference of the Sides of *Stock-accompt*, before the Balance of *Profit and Loss Accompt* be brought to it, is your neat Stock when the Books were begun; and the Balance of *Profit and Loss Accompt*, is the Gain or Loss made since that Time; which, consequently, being brought to *Stock-accompt*, makes the Balance of *Stock-accompt* equal to your present neat Stock: And therefore the Balance of *Stock-accompt* evens the Sides of *Balance-accompt*. Q.E.D.

If, after the Balance of *Stock-accompt* is brought to *Balance-accompt*, the Sides happen to be still unequal, there has unquestionably some Error been committed; which you must find out by a careful Review of the balancing Work: For here the Error must ly, since the Books are supposed to have been examined, and found right, or made so, before the balancing was begun. On the other hand, if the Sides of *Balance-accompt* be equal, all may be presumed right. There is not indeed an absolute Certainty in the Case; for if you imagine two Mistakes committed, either both in the Articles of *Profit and Loss*, or both in the Articles of *Balance*, or one in the former and the other in the latter, both Excesses, or both Defects, equal, and on opposite Sides, it is plain this would not impede the Equality of the Dr. and Cr. Sides of the *Balance-accompt*. But then, this is so great a Chance, that it is more than probable such a thing can never happen, and pass too, without being discovered.

Having brought the two Sides of the *Balance-accompt* to an Equality, which is the Test of every thing being right, proceed to close the *Ledger-accompts*, thus: First, to the *Profit and Loss Accompt*, transfer the Articles on the *Profit and Loss* Sheet. Next, at the End of the *Ledger*, erect an *Accompt of Balance*, into which transcribe the *Balance* Sheet. After which, return to the Beginning of the *Ledger*, and, giving the *Cash-accompt* Credit by *Balance*, for your ready Money, draw a Line cross the Money-columns on each Side, at the Foot of the Accompt; below which set down the total Sums, which will be now equal. Proceed in like manner with all the following Accompts, transferring to each the respective Articles that belong to them, from the two Sheets of loose Paper, inserting the referring Figures in the *Folio-column*, and writing the total Sums on the Foot of the *Accompt*; by which means all the Accompts in the *Ledger* will come to be balanced and closed; that is, evened and finished.

The *Ledger* being now closed, the next thing to be done, is, to begin a new Set of Books; in order to which, a new *Inventory* must be fetch'd from your old Books, as the Foundation of your future Trade in the new. Now it is plain at first View, that the several Articles on the Dr. Side of the *Balance-accompt*, being the particular *Items* of your Effects and Debts due to you, make up the first part of the *Inventory*; and the several Articles on the Cr. Side, except the last, being the Debts due by you to others, make up the second part of it: And accordingly, in your new Books, the several

Particulars on the Dr. Side must all of them be made Drs. to *Stock*, and *Stock* Dr. to the several Particulars on the Cr. Side, thus:

Stock Dr.	*Contra* Cr.
To *Jacob Russel*,	By *Cash*,
To *H. V. Beek*,	By *Indian Chints*,
&c.	&c.

I shall now conclude with one general Reflection upon the Stock or Inventory placed in the Front of a Merchant's Books. It is the Fund for Traffick; and it is worth while to observe how it spreads, and diffuses itself in a Course of Trade, branching out into a Multitude of various Accompts, which all depend and hang on it, as the Branches on the Root. It is to a Merchant some way like Seed to the Husbandman, which is sown in the Spring, adorns and beautifies the Fields in Summer, and appears with quite another Face than what it had before; is cut down in Harvest, and gathered into the Barn; where, being separated from Chaff and Straw, it again resumes its former Shape, with Increase or Diminution, according to the Nature of the Soil and Season, and becomes Seed for the ensuing Year. Thus, when a Merchant begins to trade, his Stock dissipates and scatters, spreads, sprouts, and shoots out into a Variety of Accompts, and these again into others, proceeding in a constant Succession, and continual Flux, till by this Propagation a whole *Ledger*, consisting perhaps of 200 or 300 Folios, be replete, and ripened as it were into a Harvest. Upon this the Books are shut up, and the Articles of Stock that lay lately diffused through the whole *Ledger*, and seemed to possess so large a Field, being now separated from Refuse and Dregs, shrink again within the narrow Limits of the *Balance-accompt*, being enlarged or lessen'd, or only varied, according to Success and the Chance of Trade. From this it passes into the *Inventory* of the new Books; where it takes the same Turn as before, and again is brought to the *Balance-accompt*, and from it to the next *Inventory*; and thus goes on in a circulatory manner, while the Merchant continues to trade. In one Word, it gives Birth to, is the Burden, and proves the Burial of Accompts.

94

(Dafforne, *Merchants Mirrour*, 1660, p. 46.)

Leagers-Conclusion, or ballancing of the leager.

Phil.[64] What Causes may move a man to a Generall Ballance?

Sch. The same may be either of these three:

1. When the Journall, and Leager are full written; so that there must be New-Books: —————————
2. When a Merchant ceaseth from Trading: —————————
3. When the book-Owner departeth this world: —————————

} Then is a Ballance requisite.

Phil. What understand you by the word *Ballance*?

Sch. By *Ballance* I understand, *An Equall-making in Equivalent manner all the Open-standing Leager-accounts*; transporting all those Open-standing Leager differences under One last framed accounts Title, whose name Generally we call *Ballance*: for being that that account *includeth* all the Leagers remaining differences; so it *concludeth* with *one* solely itself. *Nota*, the word *Ballance* seemeth to be borrowed from a pair of Scales: for as true Scales ought neither to be heavier then other; so a true taked Generall Ballance ought not to differ the least naming value: for the Generall Debitor and Creditor must justly counter-poize each other in even-monies nomination; *else*, the Book is out of square, the summes ill taken, or amisse added. In place of the word *Ballance*, I should rather enter *Estate-reckoning*: for by drawing the whole Book to a head, I draw with *one* an account of my *Estate*. . . .

95

(Hamilton, *Introduction to Merchandise*, 1788, pp. 284-5.)

Merchants generally balance their books once a-year. The design of this operation is, to collect the various branches of their business diffused through the books, into a concise abstract; to ascertain their gain or loss since the last balance; and exhibit the present state of

---

[64] Dialogue between Philo-Mathy and School-Partner.

their funds. If the business be of such a kind, that most of the branches naturally come to an issue at a certain time of year, that time is the proper one for making the balance. Otherwise the end of the year, or the least busy time, may be chosen.

It is proper, before balancing, to settle as many personal accompts as possible; to clear all arrears and small charges; to take an exact inventory of the goods on hand, as far as can be done; and affix a moderate value to each article, according to the current prices at the time; such a value as the owner would be willing at present to buy for. It is much more proper to value the goods on hand in conformity to the current prices, than at prime cost: For the design of affixing any value is to point out the gain or loss; and the gain is in reality obtained so soon as the prices rise, or the loss suffered so soon as they fall.

Errors and their Correction

96

(Jones, *English System*, 1796, p. 19.)

. . . When they have gone through the process for making the trial-balance, and unexpectedly find that the Debits and Credits are not equal in amount, how great is the disappointment they feel, and how painful the sensations they undergo on account thereof! They examine the balances; but to no purpose:——A fancied confusion appears on every leaf, and their minds are racked, because they cannot discover where the error lies. Some particular accounts, then, attract their attention: they investigate them; and after some hours spent painfully in the fruitless search, they are obliged to sit down in the same state of uncertainty that they were in when they began.——To examine all that they have been doing during the last twelve months wears a formidable appearance:——Yet, nothing short of this, perhaps, will have effect; and, unfortunately, this may be *done in vain*: In the mean time, they read nothing but dissatisfaction in the countenances of their employers; nor can they expect it should be otherwise, while their employers cannot get an accurate statement of their affairs. . . .

97

(North, *Gentleman Accomptant*, 1715, pp. 38–40.)

One Thing more is most needful to be animadverted upon, and that is the Matter of Errors in Accompts, and the best Means of setting them right. All Practice in the World is obnoxious to Error, and none more than the keeping and stating Accompts; as every Body, even the most dextrous and skilful, as well as young Beginners, must be sensible; and if Provision were not made for finding them out, and then to rectify them fairly, and not slovenly, this Art of regular Book-keeping would be much undervalued. I mentioned the surest Test of true stating in the Books, by a Balance of the *Drs.* and *Crs.* If that Proof fails, the Error is Ensconc'd, and will never, or rarely be discover'd, without Comparison with some other Check-Accompt, if any be kept against you. If by the Balance failing it appears there is Error, it must of Necessity, by some Means or other, be found out, *Costa che Costa*; for if the Variance be but 2d. the Error may be 10*l*. For Errors may be many; and perhaps one countering the other may reduce the Effect into a small Sum, whilst the Falsity may be in many and great Instances.

Therefore as the surest Expedient to find this Failing out, the Merchants use to prick over their Books, as they call it; that is, go from the Journal Entry to the Ledger, and see every Sum is posted true and properly *Dr.* and *Cr.* and when a Parcel is entred, they put a Point in the Margin of the Ledger, to shew that is examined; for they will not endure cancelling, tho' with only Crayon. Thus going on Parcel after Parcel, till every Line is pointed, if the Work be deliberately or carefully done, what Errors are therein will be found out. For then, after Adjustment made on a By-Paper, and the Balance found to fall right, so far is fixed; and the Points stand for a Remembrance, that is not needful to prick those pointed Parcels over again, but hereafter only to go on with what come in after.

Before I come to shew how Errors are to be adjusted to Truth in the Books, I must repeat the Advice before given for preventing Errors, which is, to enter in the Journal, and post into the Ledger, with the greatest Care and Deliberation possible. When an Accomptant hath been once or twice punish'd with the Drudgery of hunting for Errors, and pricking (which Work of it self is subject to Error) fails the Accomptant, and he must do it over and over again, he will bethink himself in Time, and be very solicitous to save that Trouble by early Care; this being liable to Errors; and drudging to find them out, makes a regular Accompt very fastidious to a Person of Estate, who deals only for himself; for he will not think the Time and Pains, subducted from his more favourite Pastime, compensated by the Fruits of Care to prevent, and Industry to find out Errors in his Accompts: Let them (says he to himself) go, his Loss and Gain will be the same. Therefore it must be one that hath a Zeal or Warmth towards Exactness and Justice in Accompts, that will bear the Fatigue of keeping Books regularly, which not done with Pleasure, will never be done tolerably well. The careless, lazy, and voluptuous must find somewhat else to do, and not sit to Accompts, which require Mercury in the Head, and Lead in the Tail.

98

(Ympyn, *Notable . . . Woorke*, 1547, ch. 13.)

How to remedy and amend parcelles evill written in the boke by negligence.

It is to be considered that there is no persone so perfight but that he shall sometyme misse, and entre some thyng wrong, howbeit yet maie not that faute be taken for deceipt and fraude, so that it be doen by ignoraunce. And if it fortune that any parcell be evill entred by negligence, yet maie you not therfore blot it out, for in the boke shuld be no blottyng: but there are other remedies and ordres for it, by the whiche there shalbee no cause to blame or suspecte the boke. And firste ye shall understande that this boke muste be kept as men use a paire of balaunce, that the one side bee never hevier or more of some then the other, that is to saie that ye make nothyng a debte, but ye make a credite to it as is said sufficiently before. Wherefore if it fortune that a parcell be evill entered, like as in the exemplary ye shall finde in the parcell of Jhon Leis accompte, whiche ought to have been set upon the accompte of Gyles Houte, ye muste correcte it in suche sorte as ye shall fynde it there doen, shewyng the cause of the faute, and so in all other like, for as the olde saiyng is, he never lerned that never erred. And thus with addyng these fewe wordes folowyng upon the side of the creditor ye maie amend all fautes: The wordes are these, to make a like some unto the parcell written on the other side marked with + betokenyng that it was entred by negligence, have I written this. And this so corrected, ye maie then entre the parcell in his right place where he should have been entred. But if it fortune you to entre any parcell wrong into your Jornall or Memorial, and perceive the same before ye entre it into the greate boke, then maie ye strike it out in suche wise as ye shall se doen in the Jornal the xxvij. daie of June whiche is striken out, and the cause therof shewed under the parcell.

99

(Ympyn, *Notable . . . Woorke*, 1547, ch. 25.)

How to make the ballaunce of this boke and all other, and how to searche the fautes, if the ballaunce agree not.

When your boke shalbee so full that ye can write no more therin : before that ye entre into your other boke, it shalbe necessary that ye first make up the ballaunce of your old boke, the whiche must be doen with greate diligence, for it must come out so justly that the one side surmount not one mite more then the other, for if it doo, the keper of the boke hath committed some faute as it is aforsaied in the xi. Chapiter. And this ballaunce shall ye make in suche maner as the exemplary shall shewe you, where ye shall finde all parcelles brought together as it wer on an heape in one shete of paper, that is to saie, al that is owyng on the one side, and al that is to discharge it withal on the other side. When ye have doen this, then shall ye note in a paper the somes on bothe sides, and if the somes come bothe a like, then is there none error or faute committed in your boke, whiche seldome happeneth, (for the waies to faile & make fautes are many, and men have not Angelles memory.) Then is there no more to do but begin your other boke as is aforsaid. But if it fortune any faute to be made, then first searche it in the somes least thei in removyng from boke to boke hath been written amisse, and if it be not founde there, then must you take more labor and call one to helpe you for ye cannot do it well alone, and take first the Jornall boke and peruse it parcell by parcell with your greate boke, and ever as ye finde the parcelles entred justly out of your Jornall into your greate boke, so let hym that kepeth the Jornall make a pricke or poinct with a penne heard before the nombre of the leaves that stande in the margent of the Jornall [65] as ye se dooen in the exemplary : and let hym that kepeth the greate boke make likewise a pricke or poyncte before the poundes of the greate boke [66] as ye se also dooen in the exemplare of the greate boke. And this shall ye examamyne all your parcelles aswell in debte as in credite till the faute be founde, and this is called poyntyng of the boke. And if it shall fortune any parcelles to be found in the Jornal that are not written on both sides, but was forgotten

[65] That is, in front of the posting reference, showing the numbers of the ledger accounts debited and credited.
[66] That is, in the column immediately preceding the money column.

to be doen, then must you correct and amend theim, as the matter shall require: Or if it shall fortune the somes to be made greater on the one side then on the other, it must also bee corrected that every reconnyng maie apere perfight of it self. And likewise if any accomptes wer closed up ignorantly, thei must be brought and set upon their accompt of profite and losse or gaynes and losse. And therefore it is necessary that ye write the somes in a pece of paper and peruse the accompt, and se that it come just out before ye close up the accompt of profite and losse: And thus dooyng shall the balaunce of your boke be juste. When you have thus poyncted and marked all the parcelles of your Jornall boke, yet shall there remain some whiche paradventure are not poyncted as the somes of those parcelles that be brought forward from one accompt to another, and parcelles that are growen by error of misentraunce,[67] whereof is spoken in the xiij. Chapiter, these muste also bee examined and poyncted like the other. And likewise if any parcell be founde in the Jornall the whiche is not entered into the greate boke, ye muste streight waie entre thesame in his right place, and thus shall ye make the balaunce of your boke to come just.

100

(Hayes, *Gentleman's* . . . *Book-keeper*, 1741, pp. 84-6.)

Of mistakes in posting, shewing how to rectify the same in the leger.

When you find out a Mistake in your Leger by false posting, &c. you ought not to erase, nor scratch the same out, that is to say, if you should write an Article on the Dt. Side of an Account, which should have been wrote on the Ct. Side, or write an Article on the Ct. Side of an Account, that should have been wrote on the Dt. Side, or should post an Article to the wrong Account, and, upon examining your Books, you should afterwards find such a Mistake out, none of these Mistakes should be erased, nor scraped out, but must be rectified in the following Manner.

If you have wrote an Article on the Dt. Side, which should have been wrote on the Ct. Side, you must rectify it, by writing upon the Ct. Side of the Account,

---

[67] This refers to entries in ledger accounts which do not originate in journal entries.

By itself for an Error, as *per contra*, setting down the Sum.

Having made this Entry, enter the Article underneath the above-said Entry, as it should be.

And if you have put an Article on the Ct. Side of the Account, which should have been placed on the Dt. Side, write on the Dt. Side of the said Account,

To itself for an Error, as *per contra*.

And underneath the said Entry post the Article, as it should be.

Or, if you have posted an Article to one Account, which should have been posted to another; in this Case, turn to the Account wherein the Entry is false made, and if it be made on the Dt. Side, write on the Ct. Side,

By itself for an Error, as *per contra*.

But if it be made on the Ct. Side, then you must write on the Dt. Side,

To itself for an Error, as *per contra*.

And having wrote the Errors off in this Manner, turn to the Account that the Article most justly belongs to, and there make your entry in its proper Manner. . . .

101

(Gordon, *Universal Accountant*, 1787, vol. 2, p. 54.)

Errors in the *Leger* are of four kinds.

1. If a *Dr.* or *Cr.* is omitted, supply that defect, by entering it in its proper account.

2. If the *Dr.* or *Cr.* is charged too much, make the opposite side Dr. to, or Cr. by *error*, for the excess.

3. If a *Dr.* or *Cr.* is charged with too little, charge it again Dr. to, or Cr. by its correspondent account, for the deficiency.

4. If the *Dr.* and *Cr.* are both entered on the same side, adjust it, by making the opposite side Dr. to, or Cr. by *error*, for the sum of the article misplaced; and then enter the article in its proper place; by which means the mistake will be balanced, and the account properly stated.

OBSERVATION

Were merchants to admit of erasings or total cancellings in their books, it would be impossible to trace fraud with any degree of certainty; but when every thing stands fair and naked as it happened, it would be impossible, without a long premeditation, to contrive or carry on a designed fraud: and it would be difficult, even in that case, to give a false account, in all its circumstances, the colour of a true one, even if it could be supposed, that a man would voluntarily form a design of throwing up his credit by becoming bankrupt, and imposing on his creditors by an account of losses which he never sustained. It is therefore to avoid inconveniencies which might arise from erasing or cancelling totally any thing in the books, that practices of that kind are prohibited by law, and discountenanced by merchants.

102

(Hamilton, *Introduction to Merchandise*, 1788, pp. 282–3.)

Some accomptants correct all errors in the ledger, without erasing any thing, by the following methods: 1st, If the sum be entered too small, they make a second entry for the deficiency. 2d, If it be entered too large, they make an entry on the opposite side for the excess. 3d, If it be entered on the wrong side of the accompt, they enter it twice on the other; once to counterbalance the error, and a second time for the true entry. 4th, If it be entered on a wrong accompt, they charge the wrong account Dr. to, or Cr. by, the right one.

We do not much approve of these methods, as they give the books a confused appearance; and would rather recommend the following rules.

1st, If an article be omitted, do not attempt to interline it at the place where it should have been; but insert it under the last article when you discover the omission, and mark a cross × against it on the margin, and another at the place where it should have been.

2d, If you discover a mistake immediately when committed, correct it without cancelling any thing, as in this example. *To Cash, say, To James Spiers received to account.*

3d, If you have written a line entirely wrong, or in a wrong place, write the word *Error* at the end, prefix a cross, and omit or cancel the sum.

4th, Cancel errors, by drawing a line lightly through them, so that the old writing may still be legible; by which it will be evident, that the book has not been vitiated for a fraudulent purpose. The same method should be followed in correcting errors in the journal.

103

(North, *Gentleman Accomptant*, 1715, pp. 42–3.)

These are Errors, which pricking the Books will find out; but there are others that happen in making States, collecting Sums, and the like, which stand in the Waste or Journal Entry, and not in the Ledger, and are often found by Accident, as when Men are diligent in perusing their Books; but else there is no Rule, but a Check Accompt to find them out. When such are found, the best way to adjust them, is the framing an Accompt of Errors. For it is likely, that the Accompts have been rendered, or are closed, and the Error past retrieving in real Dealing. And then consider, if the Error is Profit to you, or Loss: If the former, then write, Profit and Loss is Dr. to Accompt of Errors, &c. If Loss, then Accompt of Errors is *Dr.* to Profit and Loss: And so after many Lines wrote in the Accompt of Errors, perhaps the Loss or Gain shall not be a Shilling; but if Accompts are open and currant, they may be rectified by a Line in a proper *Dr.* and *Cr.* for then Right may be done when it fails. The other way is more for the sake of Exactness and Truth, than Justice to the concerned.

But after all, it is not necessary a Gentleman should be so nice, but in Case of small Errors of Figures or Words, he may be allowed to use his Pen-knife and Pounce: For perhaps his Books will go no farther than his Cabinet, and the Use of them terminates only in himself and Family. But Merchants are so nice, that if a Word, nay, a Sentence be wrote amiss, they will not raze or cancel, but set down the right with a *Dico*, or, I *say*, before it, as thus: Paid, *Dico*, Received, &c. which I mention only to shew their extreme Affectation of pure and fair Writing.

104

(Jones, *English System*, 1796, p. 13.)

It frequently occurs, that Books kept by Double Entry do not balance, and several months in each year are spent in some compting-houses to discover the cause: Some I have known to undergo seven or eight examinations before they were found to balance; and others I have seen in use *fifteen* or *twenty* years, which were *never balanced*; although great pains had been taken to make them correct.

105

(Hamilton, *Introduction to Merchandise*, 1788, pp. 286–7.)

Though the books must balance, if free from error, yet it is sometimes difficult to adjust them exactly, especially when the business is extensive, and the error trifling.   If there be still a difference, which we do not think it worth while to make further search for, we may close the books, by making Profit and Loss Dr. or Cr. for the same.   This introduces an article on one side of the ledger, which has none corresponding to it on the other, but is balanced by some undiscovered error.

The Structure of the Double Entry System

106

(Hatton, *Merchant's Magazine*, 1712, p. 196.)

. . . Your present Stock and what you owed when you began the Account now ballanc'd, will be always equal to your Stock when you began your Accounts, and what you have gained since, to the Day the general Ballance is made. And the Reason of this is plain: For my former Stock and what I have gained since must be my present Stock; as in the Example foregoing of Stock, my former Nett Stock (Debts deducted) is 2649 l. 10s. 00d. and I have gained since, as appears by the Account of Profit and Loss 896 l. 10s. 01d. the Sum of which is 3546 l. 00s. 01d. = my present Stock. But if (because the Method of the Account of Stock requires it) I add my Gross Stock when I began Trade to what I have since gained, the Sum will consequently be just so much more than my present Nett Stock as was the Sum I owed when I began Trade; which if I therefore add to my present Stock, the Sum must be equal to my former Gross Stock and the Sum gained, as 'tis plain in the Example;

For if 3159 l. 10s.[68] − 510 l. + 896 : 10 : 01 be = 3546 : 00 : 01;

Then it follows,

That 3159 l. 10s. + 896 : 10 : 01, is = 3546 : 00 : 01 + 510 l.

(*Note*, That (−) is less, (+) more, and (=) equal to.)

107

(Hamilton, *Introduction to Merchandise*, 1788, p. 286.)

We shall prove that this equality [69] must always hold, from the nature of the articles collected. The Dr. of the balance-sheet contains every kind of property belonging to you, and every debt owing to you; and the Cr. contains every debt owing by you: Therefore

[68] In the original this sum appears as £2649. 10. 0—an obvious slip.
[69] The equality referred to is that between net assets (on the balance account before the capital account balance is entered) and the balance of the capital account after the profit has been entered.

the difference of the sides exhibits your nett estate. The profit and loss sheet, when the articles from the ledger are included, contains every thing you have gained on the Cr. and every thing you have lost on the Dr.; and the difference of the sides is your nett gain or loss. The stock accompt contained your effects and debts at the time the books were opened; and, therefore, when the gain or loss is added to the proper side, it must show the extent of your nett estate at present. Thus the stock accompt and the balance-sheet both point out how much you are worth at present; the one from your former stock, allowance being made for your gains or losses; the other from a view of your present effects and debts; and they will correspond, because both must be agreeable to the truth, if the books be correct.

108

(Thompson, *Accomptant's Oracle*, 1777, vol. 2, pp. 68–9.)

   . . . Your Profit and Loss accompt contains on the credit side your particular profits on the several articles sold, legacies left you, wagers won, interest on money lent, &c. The debt side is, in like manner, a particular account of your several losses.

The difference therefore between those two sides is your neat gain or loss, which sum must be exactly equal to the difference between the neat of your stock accompt, when subtracted from the neat of your ballance accompt.

The neat therefore of your gain or loss being carried to your stock accompt, viz. to the credit side, if gain, or to the debt side, if loss, the difference then between these two sides being carried to the deficient side of your ballance accompt, the debt and credit sides of the latter must of course come even: For it is self-evident, that the neat of what you was worth when you begun trade, (which was the difference of your stock accompt) increased by adding the neat of your gain to it, or diminished by subtracting the neat of your loss from it, will then be equal to your present neat worth, which is the difference between the debt and credit side of your ballance accompt; consequently then, such sum or difference being carried to the deficient side of your ballance accompt, the two sides of the said accompt will then be equal, and finally close the whole.

Or, in brief, thus: The whole of your stock (which is the credit side of the said accompt) when you begun trade, your neat gain, (which is the difference of your profit and loss accompt) and the debts you now owe, (which is the credit side of your ballance accompt) being all added together, the sum will be equal to the sum of the debt you owed when you begun trade, (which is the debt side of your stock accompt) and your present stock, (which is the debt side of your ballance accompt) and on the contrary when you lose by trade. Then the debts you owed when you begun trade, your neat loss, together with your present stock, will be equal to your stock when you began trade, and the debts you now owe.

109

(Stephens, *Italian Book-keeping*, 1735, pp. 6–9, 13–14, 16–17, 18.)

Of Italian book-keeping in general; and the certain principles on which the whole is founded.[70]

Italian Book-keeping is an Art by which the present Condition and Extent of a Man's Estate are discover'd, as they are the certain Consequences arising from the first Condition and Extent, with the Alterations that have happen'd to them, recorded.

This Art is comprehended under these two Heads:

First, The rightly applying the Alterations as they happen to the first Condition and Extent, that the present at all Times may appear as conspicuous as the first did.

Secondly, In the exact and regularly recording the Matter of Fact, as a standing Proof of these Alterations.

Now to begin with the former, before we can apply the Alterations, the first Condition and Extent must be disposed in a proper Order to receive them; nor can that be done, unless we know what Alterations may, and after what Manner they do happen. But it is evident, all the Alterations that can happen, are such as either happen to the Condition alone, the Extent alone, or the Condition and Extent together.

When by any Transactions our Securities become different from what they were, but yet are charged with the same sum that is call'd an Alteration in the Condition only, thus our Securities being divided, according to the different Natures of them, we discern

---

[70] The discussion in Stephens' book is long and somewhat tedious. For this reason four parts of the discussion have been selected here instead of reproducing the whole. The selections are sufficient to show the nature of the argument and its development, and also the flavour of the exposition. Stephens devised his own terminology; the meaning of his terms becomes clear as the discussion proceeds.

what they are, and the Charges and Values depending on each. *Example*; I have 10,000 *lb*. Weight of Tobacco for 300 *l*. as also *A. B.* owes me 100 *l*. Now I bargain with another, and give him 5000 *lb*. Weight of my Tobacco, worth 150 *l*. for five Pieces of Cloth of the same Value; by this Transaction the Sum of the Extent is not alter'd in the least, notwithstanding my Condition is, by reason whereas before I had 10,000 *lb*. Weight of Tobacco for 300 *l*. now I have only 5000 *lb*. Weight for 150 *l*. and whereas before I had no Cloth, now I have five Pieces of Cloth remaining in my Hands, worth 150 *l*. and so the Condition may be alter'd in respect to the personal Security; as suppose I agree with *A. B.* to give me a Note upon *C. D.* for 100 *l*. whereby *C. D.* becomes indebted to me such Sum in Place of *A. B.* who is discharged; it is plain, I say, that nothing here but the Condition of my Estate is alter'd, and that the Extent remains as it was before.

As the Condition is divided according to the various Natures of Securities, so must the Extent be divided according to the Variety of Properties. And when one Proprietor comes in Place of another, that is call'd an Alteration in the Extent only. As for *Example*; my Extent we'll suppose to be in all 540 *l*. whereof due to *A. B.* 150 *l*. to *C. D.* 100 *l*. the remaining 290 *l*. clearly my own, then *A. B.* assigns 50 *l*. of what I owe him to *G. H.* whereby *G. H.* becomes Proprietor for 50 *l*. in Place of the said *A. B.* so that the Securities continue the same, tho' the Extent be divided after a different Manner from what it was before.

An Alteration is said to happen to the Condition and Extent together, when by any Transaction we either receive new Securities, or add to the former, and at the same time get one or more new Proprietors, or add to the Sum of the former, or otherways give out some of our Securities, and diminish the Proprietors in Number, or lessen their Sums. As for *Example*; If I buy Goods from *B. D.* to wit, 2000 *lb*. Weight of Tobacco, and owe him the Sum of 50 *l*. for it, then I have more Goods than I had, and *B. D.* is a Proprietor more than he was before: so if I had bought the Tobacco from any one who was a Proprietor before, he would have increased his Property, as also should I my Security Tobacco, provided I had any such Goods to have added to; on the other hand, if I pay *A. B.* 60 *l*. of what I owed him, I shall have less Money than I had before, and *A. B.*'s Property will be lessen'd by 60 *l*. and so if I pay him all that I owed him, the Number of Proprietors is diminished by one.

Whatever Alterations can happen possibly to the Estate, being reducible under these three Heads, we come next to the Consideration of the first Condition and Extent, how to dispose of them, so that these Alterations as they happen, may be properly applied to them. To begin then with the Condition:

I say, the various Securities must be so divided, that when by any Transaction it becomes necessary to add to, or take from them respectively any Quantity, Number, or Sum, we may do it so, that the remaining Quantity, Number, or Sum, with the Alterations that produced them, may appear: for which Reason there must be a competent Space allow'd each Division (wherein the first Quantities, Numbers, or Sums are noted) for the Recital of the Alterations of adding to, or taking from, as Occasions offer. *Example*; I have in Money 200 *l.* 1000 *lb.* Weight of Sugar worth 100 *l.* and *A. B.* is indebted to me 100 *l.* the Money must be allow'd a Space by itself, the Sugar a Space by itself, and *A. B.* a Space by himself, on the Top of each of which Spaces must be prefix'd a Title, shewing wherein it bears Part of, whether the Condition or Extent, and the State of the Matter would stand as followeth:

First Account.

	l.	*s.*	*d.*
A. B. bears Part of the Condition of my Estate.			
He owes me - - - - - - -	100	0	0

Second Account.

Sugar bears Part of the Condition of my Estate.			
I have 1000 *lb.* Weight for - - - - -	100	0	0

Third Account.

Money bears Part of the Condition of my Estate.			
I have - - - - - - - - -	200	0	0

Note, the Lines drawn above, are for separating one Account from another.

By the abovesaid Accounts of *A. B.* Sugar and Money, I know, first, the Estate or Portion of Things, secondly, the particular

Securities of which such Estate consists, with their respective Values depending on them; and lastly, I can, by adding all these Values up together, understand the computed Value or Extent in general. Next I must consider the Extent as it is divided into its respective Properties or Parts; which will shew how much of it is alienated from me, and what belongs to me as my own clear Share. *Example*; Admit I was indebted to *C. D.* 40 *l.* and *E. F.* 30 *l.* for the same Reasons then as before, each Proprietor must be allow'd a competent Space, &c. and the State of the two Articles would stand as followeth:

Fourth Account.

	l.	*s.*	*d.*
C. D. bears Part of the Extent.			
I owe him - - - - - - - -	40	0	0

Fifth Account.

E. F. bears Part of the Extent.			
I owe him - - - - - - - -	30	0	0

These being all the Proprietors the Extent hath, excepting myself, it follows, if we deduct the Sum of the two Articles from the general Extent, that from thence will come out what my own clear Share is; after which the whole Condition and Extent, according to their respective Divisions of Securities and Properties, will stand as followeth:

First Account.

	l.	*s.*	*d.*
A. B. bears Part of the Condition of my Estate.			
He owes me - - - - - - -	100	0	0

Second Account.

Sugar bears Part of the Condition of my Estate.			
I have - - - - - - 1000 *lb.* for	100	0	0

Third Account.

Money bears Part of the Condition of my Estate.			
I have - - - - - - - -	200	0	0

Fourth Account.

C. D. bears Part of the Extent.

I owe him -   -   -   -   -   -   - | 40 0 0

Fifth Account.

E. F. bears Part of the Extent.

I owe him -   -   -   -   -   -   - | 30 0 0

Sixth Account.

My own clear Share of the Extent.

I have clearly my own -   -   -   -   -   - | 330 0 0

Thus I have the first Condition and Extent discover'd to all Intents and Purposes, and dispos'd in such a proper Order as to be capable of receiving any Alterations as can possibly happen to them.

. . . . . .

'Tis to be observ'd, that one who is a Proprietor to Day, may to Morrow make a Part of the Condition of my Estate; and one who makes Part of the Condition of my Estate now, may to Morrow become a Proprietor for Part of the Extent; for as nothing can be charged with any Part of the Condition, but when by some Transaction it becomes Security for more than depended on it before, nor the Sum charg'd on any Thing suffer the least Abatement unless by some Transaction it ceases to be Security for a certain Part of the computed Value; and so on the other Hand, there is not any Thing can have Share of the Extent given it, but when by some Transaction it becomes Proprietor for more than it was: Nor can the Property of any Thing be lessen'd, but when by some Transaction it ceases to have such Share in the Extent as it had before that happen'd. So if I pay a Man what I owed him, he ceases to have any Share of the Extent of my Estate; and if I advance him more, then he becomes Security for that Sum, which did not depend upon him before; and so on the other Hand, if a Man not only pays me, but advances, &c. For *Example*, in the Case of *C. D.* above, he appears to remain Proprietor for 60 *l.* but if I pay him (whether by several Parcels or at once) the Sum of 100 *l.* then it is plain, he not only ceases to have 60 *l.* Share in the Extent, but he becomes Security for 40 *l.* of the Condition of it: Again, if he pays me 60 *l.* then is it as plain, that he not only ceases to be Security for 40 *l.* but becomes Proprietor for 20 *l.* and so has Share of the Extent; which Revolution obliges us to shift the Spaces, in the former Method, at least as often as these Changes occur; therefore I say, to prevent this, we apply the Alterations to the respective Places, of the Condition and Extent, without any Regard to what the Result of them may be in several, for that will appear at all Times, when we proceed to a Comparison of the Condition and Extent together: *Example*; these Alterations apply'd to the foregoing Account of *C. D.* would render it in its Appearance as thus:

Fourth Account.

		l.	*s.*	*d.*
	C. D. bears Part of the Extent.			
	I owe him - - - - - - -	40	0	0
Alter. 2.	Receiv'd from him - - - - -	100	0	0
Alter. 5.	Receiv'd from him - - - - -	60	0	0
	Total -	200	0	0
	C. D. bears Part of the Condition of my Estate.			
Alter. 1.	Paid him - - - - - - -	30	0	0
Alter. 3.	Paid him - - - - - - -	50	0	0
Alter. 4.	Paid him - - - - - - -	100	0	0
	Total -	180	0	0

And thus I add to the Sum of the Extent, whether I intend to make it more, or lessen that of the Condition; and I add to the Sum of the Condition, when I would lessen the Extent Sum, or augment the Charge of the Condition.

For where there are two opposite Sums to add to the one, makes it the Difference or Agreement the same between them as if the like Sum had been substracted from the other: For *Example*, suppose *A.* 50 *l.* one, and *B.* 100 *l.* the other; if I add 25 *l.* to the 50 *l.* then it will make 75 *l.* and the Difference between 75 *l.* and 100 *l.* is 25 *l.* which the latter exceeds the former by; or if instead of adding 25 *l.* to the 50 *l.* I had substracted the like Sum of 25 *l.* from the 100 *l.* then would there have remained 75 *l.* which is likewise just 25 *l.* more than the 50 *l.* and so the Difference is the same.

. . . . . .

Now the Uncertainty of the Prices of Things renders my Share of the Extent liable to increase or decrease with them: as for *Example*;

When any Thing stands charg'd with Part of the computed Value in the general Calculation or Division of the Securities and Properties already made, and afterwards purchases more, or appears to be of more Value than what depended thus on it, the Sum of the computed Value of my Estate is greater, and consequently the Extent is increased; but all the Extent consists of other Men's Properties or my own, and none can claim any Title to this, by Reason it is purchased with my own Securities, which no Person has any thing at all to do with. *Example*;

Suppose I have 2000 *lb.* Weight of Tobacco, which I value at first at 50 *l.* I sell this Tobacco some Time afterwards for perhaps 60 *l.* I say by this Transaction I have made myself richer than I was before; or suppose when I come to calculate anew, I find the Tobacco, at the present Rate, able to purchase more than 50 *l.* which it was reckon'd worth at first, then I am so much richer; as set the Case, it were able to purchase 56 *l.* it is plain I am 6 *l.* richer than I was.

So when any Proprietor having Share of the computed Value, has such Value settled at the first general Calculation; if some Time afterwards he should be discharged the Thing upon which such Value was settled, with less, his Share of the Extent is consequently lessen'd by so much as remains after his being discharg'd; for the Thing I am owing is properly the Proprietor's Share of the Extent, only we are oblig'd to value it in order to bring it into the general Calculation or Estimate of the Extent, that we may know the Proportion or Share he bears in it: Therefore, I say, if he be discharg'd with less, the Surplus is still a Part of the Extent in general, which not being claim'd by any other, must be my own; so that it is indeed barely removing of what was said to be his Share of the Extent to mine, as if his was over valued.

. . . . . .

Again, when the Property of any one who has Share in the Extent, takes more of the computed Value, to discharge it, or appears to be of a greater Value than it was reckon'd to be of at first, then is my clear Share of the Extent decreas'd by so much as the Sum of the common Measure which discharg'd the Property exceeds that of the common Measure allow'd it formerly; for the Extent is in general lessen'd by just the Sum that I give him, because I have so much the less in Possession; but seeing what I give him entirely discharges his Property, the Sum of the Extent is lessen'd in the Particular of his Share only as to the Difference from what it was, and therefore the Remainder of the Value of what I have given out, in the Discharge of his Property, must come of my own clear Share, I having receiv'd nothing at all as my Security for it. . . .

110

(Fulton, *British-Indian Book-keeping*, 1800, pp. 5–9.)

. . . To push our enquiries, however, a little further here on the subject of double entry, let us advert to the familiar form of an Account Current. In this, the several debits being collected on one side and the credits on the other, their difference exhibits the balance due to or from the proprietor; and this balance, being stated on the deficient side, makes the amount of the debits and credits even; for it is evident *that the furnisher or proprietor of an Account Current is Dr. for the deficient amount of debits, or Cr. for the excess thereof*, as the case may be. A set of books, kept according to the principles of double entry, is but a larger account current, exhibiting the state of the proprietor's accounts, not individually only, but also generally : the net amount of the stock current, which is the balance either for or against him on the whole, by being added to the deficient debits or credits, makes both even; for here again it is evident, that the proprietor of a concern is generally a Dr. where the amount due by him to his Crs. exceeds that due to or possessed by him, for which various accounts are his Drs.—and the contrary. So that the position in book-keeping, of there existing *a debit for every credit*, and *a credit for every debit*, should not be considered, which it too generally is, as a precept of deliberate art, invented for the elucidation of a particular process, but rather as a maxim, containing the controvertible principles of a simple truth on which the process in question has been founded; and under this consideration of the subject, it will be easy to conceive why the followers of the imperfect plan of single entry, by neglecting or despising the maxim in question in the progress of their work, have only the greater difficulty and uncertainty to encounter, in finally adjusting the general balance of their accounts; or, in other words, arriving at a precise knowledge of the state of their affairs whenever the same may be necessary.

In further elucidation of the principles of double entry, let us suppose two lines (*A B* and *C D*) to represent the Drs. and Crs. respectively of any regular set of accounts, and consequently that these lines are equal to each other:

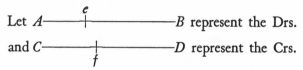

Let *A*————————*B* represent the Drs.

and *C*————————*D* represent the Crs.

and let the Drs. be divided at *e*, or any other part at pleasure, and the Crs. at *f*, or any other part likewise; and *A e* and *C f* represent respectively (the sums carried to) the Dr. and Cr. sides of the stock account, whilst *e B* and *f D* in like manner represent the collective Drs. and Crs. of all the other accounts on the books. It must be very evident then, that the difference between, or say the balance of, *A e* and *C f* is equal to the difference between *f D* and *e B*, and must be equal to it, let the marks of division be placed at what part of the lines they may; or if we suppose that one of those marks be taken away entirely (say *f*) it must still be evident that *A e* is equal to the difference between *C D* and *e B*. Hence it follows, that the balance of the stock account is equal to the net balance of all the other accounts.

But this comparative equality is not restricted to the stock account only; for if we assume the cash account or any other, or even any number of the accounts on the books, the same reasoning will still hold good. For instance, let us suppose the lines *A e* and *C f* to represent, as before, the cash instead of the stock account; or let us suppose them to represent any proportion or number of the accounts on the books, and it will follow, that the balance of the cash account is equal to the net balance of all the other accounts; and that the net balance of any proportion of the accounts on the books is equal to the net balance of the remaining proportion, with this obvious distinction, however, in each case,—if the net balance of the account or accounts assumed is Cr. the net balance of the remaining account or accounts must be Dr.—and *vice versa*.

Thus much being established, let us turn our attention to such distinction as is necessary to be made in the several accounts on a set of books. This, as far as the rudiments of book-keeping are concerned, is very simple and easily remembered; *viz.* on the *one* hand the stock account, and on the *other* all the rest of the accounts on the books. The distinction in these last between *real* (for goods, commodities, &c.) and *personal*, is by no means invariably obvious, when, for instance, bills receivable, sometimes classed with other commodities, as well as bank-notes, are merely the representatives, each for its amount, of those persons bound to discharge them. Nor is the purpose to be answered by such distinction less immaterial in regard to the purposes of book-keeping than the distinction itself is equivocal; but that between the stock account and all others is equally obvious and necessary: the stock account is that of the principal (or partnership account of the principals) of a concern: it is not composed of a particular independent property, like each of the other accounts, but arises from the state of all these collectively taken, which thus form merely the particulars of it: and the grand aim of double entry is, to ascertain the true state of the stock account (taken abstractedly in as far as regards the several entries made to its immediate debit and credit) and to check the balance thereof, by the net balance collectively of all the other accounts.

The learner adverting to the equal lines $A B$ and $C D$ as representing the Drs. and Crs. of a set of accounts, may perhaps conceive that, notwithstanding these are at the outset allowed to be equal, yet, as transactions must occur to alter their extent, it is possible also for such an alteration to occur as shall operate to the unequal extension or diminution of the one or the other; and of course to the subversion of the whole reasoning here founded on their equality. But such a circumstance can never happen; for in every species of pecuniary or accountable transaction whatever, it will be found that an equal amount of Drs. and Crs. must be affected. If a *gain* be made, the Cr. side of the stock account is thereby increased, and of course the whole Cr. line; but at the same time the Dr. side of cash or some other, one or more, accounts must be *equally* increased. A *loss* will increase the Dr. side of stock, and increase in an *equal* degree the Cr. side of some other account or accounts. In *buying* and *selling, receiving* and *paying, drawing* and *remitting, bartering,* &c. this *equality,* in the amount of the respective Drs. and Crs. affected by each of these various transactions, will still be found to hold good; so that the extension or diminution of the two lines in question must ever be equal in regard to each other. . . .

111

(Cronhelm, *Double Entry by Single,*[71] 1818, ch. 3.)

Principle of equilibrium.

It is a primary axiom of the exact sciences, that the whole is equal to the sum of its parts; and on this foundation rests the whole superstructure of Book-keeping. It considers property as a whole composed of various parts: the Stock Account records the whole capital; the Money, Merchandise, and Personal Accounts record the component parts. Hence, in complete Books, there must necessarily and inevitably be a constant equality between the Stock Account on the one hand, and all the remaining Accounts on the other.

The introduction of Credit and Bills into commerce, produced two kinds of property directly contrary in their natures:

1st, Positive Property, consisting of Goods, Cash, Bills Receivable, and Debts Receivable.

2d, Negative Property, consisting of Bills Payable, and Debts Payable.

And as these two kinds of property mutually destroy each other, it is evident that the Stock, or entire capital, must always be equal to the difference between them, and be of the same nature as that which preponderates.

Hence arise three varieties of Stock or Property; the Positive, the Neutral, and the Negative; in the first two of which the proprietor is solvent, in the latter, insolvent. An example of each case is here adduced.

---

[71] The full title of this book, which is not included in our bibliography because it falls outside the period covered, is: *Double Entry by Single, A New Method of Book-keeping, Applicable to All Kinds of Business; and Exemplified in Five Sets of Books.* By F. W. Cronhelm. London. Longman, Hurst, Rees, Orme, and Brown, Paternoster-Row.

CASE I. POSITIVE PROPERTY.

Positive Parts: Goods £2000
                Cash 1000
                Bills Receivable 500
                Debts Receivable 1500
                                    ——— £5000

Negative Parts: Bills Payable 800
                Debts Payable 1200
                                    ——— 2000

                Stock, Positive £3000

The Proprietor is here solvent, with a surplus of £3000, his net capital.

CASE II. NEUTRAL PROPERTY.

Positive Parts: Goods £2000
                Cash 1000
                Bills Receivable 500
                Debts Receivable 1500
                                    ——— £5000

Negative Parts: Bills Payable 1800
                Debts Payable 3200
                                    ——— 5000

                Stock, Neutral .... £   0

The Proprietor is here solvent, but worth nothing.

CASE III. NEGATIVE PROPERTY.

Negative Parts: Bills Payable £2000

Debts Payable 4000

—— £6000

Positive Parts: Goods £2000

Cash 1000

Bills Receivable 500

Debts Receivable 1500

—— 5000

Stock, Negative £1000

The Proprietor is here insolvent for One Thousand Pounds, the amount of his deficiency.

From the view of property as a whole composed of positive and negative parts, constantly equal to the collective result of those parts, we must now ascend to a higher and more general consideration of it, as a mass of relations between Debtors and Creditors. The application of these terms is originally personal; but it is extended by analogy to every part of property, and to the whole capital itself.

A man's positive property consists of Debts Receivable, Bills Receivable, Cash and Goods: and all these parts are consequently in the same relation to him as proprietor. But the first, or Personal Accounts, bear the relation of Debtors: therefore the others equally bear this relation; and Bills Receivable, Cash, and Goods are Debtors to him for their respective amounts. So also with the negative parts: persons to whom he owes money being his Creditors, Bills Payable are also Creditors for their amount.

Thus all the component parts of property are distributed into Debtors and Creditors; the positive parts constituting the former, and the negative parts the latter. The Stock, or whole capital, must also come under one of these classes; for the proprietor, being Creditor for all the positive parts of his property, and Debtor for all the negative parts, must, upon the whole result, be either Creditor for the excess of positive parts, or Debtor for the excess of negative parts; in other words, Creditor for the excess of Debtors, or Debtor for the excess of Creditors; the direct Inference from which is the Equilibrium of Debtors and Creditors throughout the Books.

But without thus deducing it from the connexion of the Accounts, this correspondence is immediately evident from the very signification of Debtor and Creditor, which being relative terms, the one always implies the other, and cannot exist without it. If, therefore, for every Debtor there must be an equal Creditor, and for every Creditor an equal Debtor, the respective sums of these equalities must also be equal.

To illustrate this principle, let us repeat the examples of the three cases of property, under a different arrangement.

CASE I. POSITIVE PROPERTY.

POSITIVE PARTS, OR DEBTORS.		NEGATIVE PARTS, OR CREDITORS.	
Goods	£2000	Bills Payable	£ 800
Cash	1000	Debts Payable	1200
Bills Receivable	500	Stock (Proprietor's Capi-	
Debts Receivable	1500	tal)	3000
	£5000	——Equilibrium——	£5000

CASE II. NEUTRAL PROPERTY.

POSITIVE PARTS, OR DEBTORS.		NEGATIVE PARTS, OR CREDITORS.	
Goods	£2000	Bills Payable	£1800
Cash	1000	Debts Payable	3200
Bills Receivable	500	Stock (Proprietor's Capi-	
Debts Receivable	1500	tal)	0
	£5000	——Equilibrium——	£5000

CASE III. NEGATIVE PROPERTY.

POSITIVE PARTS, OR DEBTORS.		NEGATIVE PARTS, OR CREDITORS.	
Goods	£2000	Bills Payable	£2000
Cash	1000	Debts Payable	4000
Bills Receivable	500		
Debts Receivable	1500		
Stock (Proprietor's Deficiency)	1000		
	£6000	Equilibrium	£6000

Should it be inquired why the Stock appears to be negative when the property is positive, and positive when the property is negative; this seeming contradiction will be removed by the following consideration. In these general relations of Debtors and Creditors, the estate or concern itself is abstracted from its proprietor, and becomes a whole, of which the Stock or proprietor's Account is now also one of the component parts. If, therefore, his property be positive, the Concern is Debtor to him for that property, the same as to any other person; and he classes among its other Creditors. If, on the other hand, his property be negative, or himself insolvent, the Concern is Creditor, and he classes among the other Debtors.

We are now arrived at the most comprehensive view of the subject, having generalized the three specific cases of property into one. For, when we thus abstract a Concern from its Proprietor, and place the account of Stock or entire capital among the component parts, the Concern itself is constantly neutral, consisting of a mass of relations between Debtors and Creditors, in perpetual and necessary equilibrium. The Concern thus abstracted, is always a cypher; and all its component parts are equally and mutually dependent upon each other, and upon the whole. It is no longer merely the Stock which is the result of all the other Accounts collected together: every Account has the same property, and may be found or proved in the same manner. For example, if in Case 1. the Account of Goods be required, it is ascertained by collecting all the other Accounts into one result; thus,

Creditors: Bills Payable .... £ 800
Debts Payable 1200
Stock 3000

_____

£5000

Debtors: Cash £1000
Bills Receivable 500
Debts Receivable 1500   3000

_____

Result: Goods £2000

By a similar process any other Account may be obtained; and hence it is evident that each of the Accounts is equal to the aggregate of the remainder, and that all are in mutual dependence and harmony.

The same reasoning may be more concisely expressed in an algebraic form. Let a, b, c, &c. represent the positive parts, or Debtors; l, m, n, &c. the negative parts, or Creditors; and s the Stock, or proprietor's real worth. Then, as the whole is equal to the sum of its parts,

$$a + b + c, \&c. - l - m - n, \&c. = \pm s.$$

By transposition, we obtain

$$a + b + c, \&c. - l - m - n, \&c. \mp s = o,$$

or that general equation, in which the whole Estate is neutral or a cypher, and includes the Stock as one of its component parts. Here too, it may be observed that the transposition of s changing its sign, explains the reason why the Stock, when positive in itself, becomes negative or creditor as a component part of the estate, and positive or debtor when negative.

Again, by transposing any one of the terms in the general equation, it may be proved to be equal to all the rest. Thus,

$$b + c, \&c. - l - m - n, \&c. \mp s = -a;$$
$$a + b + c, \&c. - m - n, \&c. \mp s = l;$$
$$a + b + c, \&c. - l - m - n, \&c. = \pm s.$$

Hence the truth of that general proposition already laid down, that any debtor or creditor in the books is equal to the collective result of the other debtors and creditors, an affection which has been commonly supposed peculiar to the stock account.

In tracing the principle of equality, we have hitherto considered property in a state of rest; but we shall find it equally essential to property in motion. This is evident from two considerations:

Firstly, At any two periods of time, as the beginning and the end of a year, the equilibrium of debtors and creditors exists in the concern considered in a state of rest. From the axioms, that if equals be added to equals the sums will be equal, or if equals be taken from equals the remainders will be equal; it is evident that the same equilibrium must exist in all the intermediate occurrences.

Secondly, The same thing is apparent in the very nature of all transactions relating to property. The component parts of property in trade are in a state of continual fluctuation and change. In purchases, cash is converted into goods; and in sales, goods are re-converted into cash. Or, if credit is allowed, the changes are still more numerous. Purchases create personal creditors and goods; sales convert goods into personal debtors; receipts convert personal debtors into cash; whilst payments destroy cash and personal creditors. The introduction of bills would multiply the changes by an intermediate stage between personal debts and cash. But all these creations, metamorphoses, and destructions of the parts, resolve themselves into the single case, that in every transaction two accounts are affected, the one receiving what the other communicates. The imparting account is always creditor, and the recipient always debtor; so that in each occurrence debtor and creditor must perfectly equilibrate.

We must proceed to shew that the harmony of debtors and creditors is not disturbed by profits and losses, or, in other words, by the augmentations and diminutions of the capital. Each alteration in the whole mass can be produced only by a correspondent alteration in one of the parts; and hence two accounts are always affected by the change, namely, the stock account and the account of the part, between which the equality of debtors and creditors is maintained. Thus, when a legacy is received in money, Cash is debtor, and Stock creditor; when the sale of goods exceeds the cost, Merchandise is debtor for the surplus or profit, and Stock is creditor; when the sale falls short of the cost, Merchandise is creditor for the deficiency or loss, and Stock is debtor. In all these cases, there is a transfer between the whole and the part, the one receiving what the other transmits; but, as it would be inconvenient to record in the stock account every individual alteration of capital, the transfer is made periodically; and, when the profits and losses proceed from various sources, accounts are opened to collect the particulars, and transmit the general result in one entry to the stock. Till the time of this transfer, the profits and losses remain latent in the particular accounts, without at all disturbing the equality of debtors and creditors, which exists in all the transactions that have produced the profits and losses. Thus, goods bought of A. for £900, and sold to B. for £1000, leave a profit of £100, which remains latent in the merchandise account till the periodical transfer. Debtors and creditors are in the mean time perfectly equilibrated; for in the purchase, Merchandise is debtor £900, and A. is creditor £900; whilst in the sale, Merchandise is creditor £1000, and B. is debtor £1000.

The Equilibrium of debtors and creditors having been demonstrated, as well from the nature of these relations, as from the axiom that the whole is equal to the sum of its parts; and having been shewn to exist essentially in property, in every state, whether of motion or of rest; we may justly lay it down as the fundamental principle of Book-keeping—a principle not of art or invention, but of science and discovery; not of mere expediency, but of absolute necessity, and inseparable from the nature of accounts. . . .

Part Two

A SURVEY OF BOOKS ON
ACCOUNTING IN ENGLISH, 1543–1800

Oldcastle and Mellis

DOUBLE entry bookkeeping had been practised in Italy for more than two centuries by the time the first printed exposition of the system was published. It forms part of Luca Pacioli's great compendium of mathematical knowledge, the *Summa de Arithmetica Geometria Proportioni et Proportionalita*, written in Italian, and published in 1494 in Venice. The section on accounting is the eleventh "tractatus" of the ninth "distinctio", and is entitled *Particularis de Computis et Scripturis*. Almost exactly fifty years later the first book in the English language on accounting was published, the *Profitable Treatyce*[1] of 1543, of which Hugh Oldcastle is commonly given as the author. By this time further works on accounting had already appeared in Italian and also in German; and the first books in Dutch and French were published in the same year as Oldcastle's.

No copy of the *Profitable Treatyce* is known to have survived to the present day. The last recorded sale (at eight shillings) of a copy took place in 1779, by which time the book was already a rarity: it is not listed in the first edition (1749) of Ames's *Typographical Antiquities*, but was included in the second edition (1785) on the basis of an entry in the sale catalogue issued in 1779. Neither of these sources gives the name of the author of the book; its omission from the sale catalogue suggests that it was not readily apparent on the title page (perhaps this was missing) or similar obvious place. The attribution of the authorship to Oldcastle is in fact traceable to the sixth book in English on accounting—the *Briefe Instruction* of John Mellis, published in 1588. In his preface to the reader Mellis explains: "And knowe ye for certaine, that I presume ne usurpe not to set forth this worke of mine owne labour and industrie, for truely, I am but the renuer and reviver of an auncient old copie printed here in London the 14. of August, 1543. Then collected, published, made and set forth by one Hugh Oldcastle Scholemaster, who, as appeareth by his treatise then taught Arithmetike, and this booke in Saint Ollaves parish in Marke-lane." Mellis does not mention the title of this book by Oldcastle; but as no other book on accounting is known to have been published in 1543, the inference is that Oldcastle's book,

---

[1] Fuller titles of English books on accounting before 1800 are to be found in the Bibliography, pp. 202 to 224, below. Abridged titles are used for convenience here.

which Mellis was "renewing and reviving", was none other than the
Profitable Treatyce [2]—an inference which is supported by the appearance
in Mellis's exposition of phrases which form part of the full title of the
Profitable Treatyce, the only part of that work which has reached our
times without Mellis's intermediation.[3]

It is, of course, not possible to determine how closely Mellis adhered
to the contents of Oldcastle's book. It certainly is not a straight copy.
Thus in a reference to the "canons and rules" in Oldcastle's book, Mellis
says that "in divers places I have bewtified and enlarged [them]
according to my simple knowledge". Occasionally he has examples in
the exposition which could not have been the same in the original; and
he added a full set of illustrative accounts at the end of the exposition:
"Here endeth my Authour, and for the better and plainer understanding
and practise of these rules, I have hereunto added a little Inventorie,
Journal, and Leager, as followeth: . . ." Thus, like Pacioli, Oldcastle
had not illustrated his exposition with a set of specimen account-books
and accounts, and Mellis, who by this time had access to the treatises (in
English) of Ympyn, Peele and Weddington, each with its set of worked
examples, repaired the omission. Mellis also added a brief discussion of
arithmetic, "for suche as lacke the knowledge of Arithmetike by the
penne . . .".

It is therefore not possible to ascribe to Oldcastle all of what Mellis
wrote in his book, especially as it is obvious from Mellis's illustrative set
of accounts that he took more or less directly from Peele and, to a lesser
extent, from Weddington, and also that the exposition itself contains
borrowings from predecessors other than Oldcastle.[4] Thus ascribing to
Oldcastle what is in Mellis may be misleading in detail; yet it seems most
reasonable to assume that the texts of Oldcastle and of Mellis coincide
in the main.

The great similarity in content, chapter headings, treatment and
numerous details between Pacioli's "tractatus" and the Oldcastle-Mellis
book is so striking that Oldcastle has been said by some to have
translated Pacioli.[5] Others, however, have emphasised the differences

---

[2] B. F. Foster (in his *The Origin and Progress of Book-Keeping*, 1852) is said to have
been the first to have linked the name of Oldcastle with the authorship of the
Profitable Treatyce.

[3] In the title of the *Profitable Treatyce*: ". . . the famouse reconynge called in latyn,
Dare and Habere, and in Englyshe, Debitor and Creditor . . ."; in Mellis's foreword
"To the Reader": ". . . with these three bookes is this famous reckoning ordered
and guyded, which reckoning in the parts of *Itailie* is named, Dare & Habere. Which
in our language of English is called Debitor and Creditor".

[4] Specific borrowings from Peele are noted in P. Kats, "Hugh Oldcastle and John
Mellis", *The Accountant*, vol. LXXIV (1926), *passim*.

[5] R. Brown, *A History of Accounting and Accountants*, Edinburgh, 1905, p. 126 (the
relevant chapters of this book are by J. Row Fogo); A. H. Woolf, *A Short History of
Accountants and Accountancy*, 1912, p. 132; D. Murray, *Chapters in the History of
Bookkeeping, Accountancy and Commercial Arithmetic*, Glasgow, 1930, p. 219.
The 25 chapters in Mellis are on the following subjects: (1) Of good order in

between Pacioli and Oldcastle-Mellis. From these differences it has been inferred that Oldcastle had based his treatise on some pre-Paciolian unpublished exposition of double entry,[6] and that Pacioli, also, had availed himself, without acknowledgment, of the same production. The Italian scholar, Besta, went so far as to suggest the identity of the author of this document: one Troylo de Cancellariis, of whom there is documentary evidence for the period 1421–54, and who, being expert in accounts, may well have compiled a manuscript manual on double entry for use in mercantile academies in Venice.[7] On this view, Pacioli is not the key figure in, or the *fons et origo* of, the literature of accounting; and, moreover, his reputation for plagiarisation is enhanced.[8]

We need not consider these questions in detail, except to explain why the Oldcastle-Mellis treatise itself does not provide strong support for the view that Pacioli had used an earlier model for his own "tractatus".[9] Besta referred to three main points of difference between the Pacioli and the Mellis texts. First, the Mellis text omits several chapters which are in Pacioli, dealing with matters such as the procedure for the authentication of account-books in Perugia, and accounting for transactions with banks. Besta suggests that these chapters were also absent in the original document allegedly used by Pacioli and Oldcastle, were added by Pacioli and

keeping accounts, and things necessary for the merchant, after the form of Venice. (2) Of the inventory. (3) Example of inventory. (4) "Holsome exhortation" to every merchant. (5) The three principal account-books. (6) The memorial. (7) How to make entries in the memorial. (8) On buying and selling. (9) The journal. (10) How to make entries in the journal. (11) The ledger. (12) Posting from the journal to the ledger. (13) Entries for cash and stock in the ledger. (14) Entries for merchandise in the ledger. (15) Entries for voyages, including factorage. (16) Company (partnership) accounts. (17) Ordinary expenses. (18) The profit-and-loss account. (19) Carry-forward of balances of filled-up accounts. (20) Correction of errors in ledger. (21) How to make a balance of the ledger. (22) How to record transactions while books are being balanced. (23) Accounts for a retail shop. (24) The care of letters and advices (25) Summary of the work.

Broadly, the chapters in Mellis and Pacioli correspond as follows:

Mellis:	1	2	3	4	5	6	7	8	9	10	11	12	13	14	15	16	17	18	19
Pacioli:	1	2	3	4	5	6	8	9	10, 11	12	13	14	15, 28	16	26	21	22	27	28

Mellis:	20	21	22	23	24	25
Pacioli:	31	30, 32	33	23	35	36

It will be noted that several chapters in Pacioli (*e.g.* 7 and 20) are not represented in Mellis.

[6] *Cf.* P. Kats, *ibid.*, p. 484: "It is therefore the writer's belief that the *Profitable Treatyce* was originally based on a tract of other than Paciolian authorship, or a compendium possibly written in Latin. . . ."

[7] F. Besta, *La Ragioneria*, vol. III, Milan, 1932 (2nd edition), pp. 369–78.

[8] Luca Pacioli has frequently been accused of publishing as his own the mathematical writings of his friend, the famous painter Piero della Francesca, in *De Divina Proportione*, of 1509 (with illustrations by Leonardo da Vinci). "It is now proved beyond question that a great part of the *Divina Proportione* is an unacknowledged, but practically direct, translation into Italian of Piero's Latin MS. *De Quinque Corporibus Regolaribus.*" (Sir Kenneth Clark, *Piero della Francesca*, 1951, p. 51 n.) Pacioli did, however, pay "an enthusiastic tribute to Piero, both as an artist and as a master of perspective, in the dedication of his *Summa de Arithmetica*" (*ibid.*).

[9] See F. Melis, *Storia della Ragioneria*, Bologna, 1950, pp. 623–5, for a critical examination of Besta's position.

therefore do not appear in Oldcastle-Mellis. But it is more reasonable to suppose that Oldcastle omitted these chapters in Pacioli simply because they were of no interest to merchants in England, for whom his book was intended.[10] The second point is that the Mellis text does not include the material in the concluding part of Pacioli—some examples of entries according to Tuscan usage, the rest of the exposition conforming to Venetian usage. Here, again, the " omission " could be explained on the grounds of the lack of relevance of the material for the new, intended readers. Finally, several sentences or expressions appearing in Latin in Mellis are in Italian, or partly in Latin but completed in Italian, in Pacioli.[11] This is supposed to show that both Oldcastle and Pacioli worked from an earlier document, written in Latin, and had diverged from each other in the extent of their translations. But it is likely that Oldcastle or Mellis, recognising the Latin equivalent of the Italian used in Pacioli, preferred the Latin version to a literal English rendering of the Italian.[12] It is reasonable to conclude—though with some hesitation —that Oldcastle worked from Pacioli rather than from some problematical fifteenth-century manuscript. Pacioli was a celebrated mathematician and his work was in print; the rival claimant, if he existed, may have been well known in his time in his native Venice, but he was unknown elsewhere and his work was not published. It is most unlikely that Oldcastle used the latter and not the former model.

To conclude our brief discussion of this issue, it is worthwhile looking more closely at two specific instances of correspondence between Pacioli and Oldcastle-Mellis. These show the difficulties in the way of reaching finality, but also some of the grounds for believing that Oldcastle-Mellis derives from Pacioli rather than that both works come from a common source.

Pacioli's chapter 28 instructs how, when a ledger account is full, its balance should be carried forward. The example taken is of the account of " Martino " on folio 30, the balance of which is carried to folio 60 of the ledger. Mellis's chapter 19 concerns the same topic. The example used is that of the account of " Marten ", and again folios 30 and 60

---

[10] The only "omission" which is puzzling is that of Pacioli's chapter 20 which concerns barter transactions. Barter was an important form of trading, and its accounting treatment figures prominently in contemporary treatises; but it is not discussed in Mellis (Kats, *ibid.*, p. 486). Does this suggest that Pacioli's chapter 20 is an addition by Pacioli to an earlier exposition used also by Oldcastle? The omission is the more curious because, in Mellis's edition of Recorde's book on arithmetic (*The Grounde of Artes . . . Made by M. Robert Recorde . . . diligently corrected & beautified with some newe Rules . . . by John Mellis*, 1582) the subject, Barter, is treated.

[11] For example, the Latin sentence towards the end of Mellis's chapter 23 (see extract 64) is in Italian in Pacioli. (Extract numbers refer to the selection of extracts forming Part One of this book.)

[12] This supposes that Oldcastle or Mellis knew Italian or had access to someone who knew both English and Italian.

are involved. This correspondence may, of course, be due either to a common source or to a copying of Pacioli by Oldcastle. But other considerations militate against the former interpretation. Pacioli advises that the carry-forward of the balance should not be passed through the journal, and refers to similar omissions of entries from the journal noted in his chapter 27 on the " famosa " account of profit and loss. Mellis, likewise, informs the reader that the carry-forward transfer should not go through the journal, " like as is touched in the canon of *Lucrum* and *Damnum* " (see extract 40). But in his chapter 18 on the " famous " account of profit and loss (see extract 56) there is no mention of the by-passing of the journal. The most likely explanation is either that Old-castle, in reworking Pacioli's text, accidentally omitted something from one chapter, or that he deliberately omitted it without making the consequential change. But, of course, it cannot be ruled out that Oldcastle had repeated an error which was in the postulated earlier document. Nor can we be sure that the specimen entries in Mellis's chapter 18 (see extract 56), which refer to discounts instead of gains and losses on merchandise as the text requires, are an example of Oldcastle's inexpert " improvement " of Pacioli (in whose chapter there are no specimen entries) or evidence of his slavish copying of an error, avoided by Pacioli, in the postulated pre-Paciolian original.

The second instance is in Mellis's chapter 14, where there is a reference to an *earlier* chapter stated, however, as being chapter 15. Now Mellis's chapter 14 corresponds to Pacioli's chapter 16; and in Pacioli's chapter there is a reference back to (his) chapter 15, which corresponds to Mellis's chapter 13.[13] The most likely explanation is that Oldcastle, when working from Pacioli, failed on this occasion to adjust for the fact that the chapter numbers were not the same. Besta's explanation [14] that it was a printing error is not convincing.

Ympyn

The next book in English on accounting also presents problems as to its origins. In 1547 an English translation appeared of a book which had already appeared in two versions, French and Dutch, in 1543—Ympyn's *Notable and Excellente Woorke*. The only known surviving copy of this book was discovered in a library in Reval (Estonia) in 1893. From a reproduction of parts of the text in a German journal, the Bohemian scholar, C. P. Kheil (whose remarkable collection of early books on accounting was acquired after his death by the Institute of Chartered Accountants) was able to show that it was a translation of Ympyn's

---

[13] Brown, *op. cit.*, p. 127, n. 1.
[14] Besta, *op. cit.*, p. 372, n. 2.

books of 1543. [The English version does not mention the name of the Dutch author or of the English translator, but states that the book is a translation of a French work: " And now (for the love I bere unto Merchantes of Englande) translated out of Frenche into Englishe "]. After some vicissitudes, the Reval copy of the book has come to rest in the Lenin Library in Moscow. The copy is incomplete, as the set of illustrative accounts was missing when the book was found in 1893.[15]

Again we have to do with a book of which the contents, general treatment and many particular passages and sentences give it a very strong family resemblance to Pacioli's.[16] But the precise connection between Pacioli and Ympyn is extremely difficult to determine. Ympyn acknowledged the pioneer writings of Luca Pacioli and Tagliente (whose first book in Italian was published in 1525), but recognised as his main and, indeed, direct influence, one Juan Paolo di Bianchi, an Italian whom he met in Italy. Nothing else is known about Bianchi. From the Prologue in the French version, the first of the three versions of Ympyn's book, we learn: " Further, I made the acquaintance of a man of good reputation, of Jehan Paulo de Biancy, who worked more in this matter [the science of bookkeeping] than all the others. Through his work one can grasp, understand and learn the said science, if one only studies the treatise [*i.e.*, Ympyn's treatise] that follows and devotes to it one's intelligence and diligence. This treatise I have got from the said Jehan Paulo de Biancy, and translated from his language into French for the profit and advantage of all who are concerned with it, particularly because the French language is closer to the Italian than the German or the Flemish or many other languages ".

Because Ympyn's book is so similar to Pacioli's, it has been generally assumed either that Bianchi's " work " (presumably in manuscript) was a reworking of Pacioli, or—perhaps more plausibly—that Ympyn was making use of Bianchi's own work only to the extent of specimen accounts compiled by Bianchi, there being none in the original (Pacioli). On these interpretations—and some statements in the French prologue complicate any reasonable interpretation—Pacioli is the source of Ympyn's books, and Bianchi at best an intermediary. But Besta, and also Kats whose studies of the earliest English books and of the Dutch

---

[15] A transcript of the surviving text was made for a Latvian scholar in 1910. This formed the basis for its reproduction in modern spelling by Kats in 1927: " The ' Nouvelle Instruction ' of Jehan Ympyn Christophle ", *The Accountant*, vol. LXXVII (1927), pp. 261-9, 287-96. Again using the 1910 transcript, Dr. de Waal published the text in its original spelling in 1934: P. G. A. de Waal, " De Engelsche Vertaling van Jan Impyn's Nieuwe Instructie ", *Economisch-Historisch Jaarboek*, vol. XVIII (1934), pp. 1-58. The extracts published in Part One, above, have been checked against a photocopy of the original book in the possession of the Library of the Institute of Chartered Accountants. De Waal's reproduction shows remarkably few deviations from the original.

[16] See C. P. Kheil, *Uber einige Bearbeitungen des Buchhaltungs Tractates von Luca Pacioli*, Prague, 1896, *passim*; and Besta, *op. cit.*, p. 385.

influences on early English accounting writings are invaluable, dissented from such interpretations.[17] For them, Ympyn's references to the work of Bianchi supply further evidence of the existence of some influential manuscript written before Pacioli's treatise, a manuscript which was worked on by Pacioli in the preparation of his "tractatus", and which was also translated by Ympyn. Moreover, Professor de Roover, who supports the view of Besta and Kats, has argued convincingly that Ympyn, a mercer in Antwerp, used his own account-books to supply material for the specimen set of accounts in his treatise.[18]

Again, it is not possible to prove or disprove the existence of a pre-Paciolian manuscript, or to establish its authorship. It is surprising, however, that Ympyn, the friend of Bianchi, would not have put the record straight if, indeed, Bianchi's work, or the manuscript on which it is supposed to be based, had preceded Pacioli's *Summa*, and had been used without acknowledgment by Pacioli. (Ympyn presumably met Bianchi after 1494.) Perhaps it is wisest to take the chronology as it stands,[19] to relegate Bianchi to obscurity until more is discovered about him, and to remember Ympyn not only as the author of an excellent book written in the Paciolian tradition, and in fact an improvement on the "original", but also for having complemented the Paciolian exposition with a fine set of specimen account-books.

It remains to note that Ympyn introduced some practices not found in Pacioli or his immediate Italian successors. Two examples may be given. First, in the opening inventory of assets and liabilities Pacioli merely lists the items, without stating their values. In Ympyn, on the other hand, there are both valuation and orderly extension; but no grand total of assets, or balance of net assets, is ascertained in the inventory itself. Second, Ympyn, on the closing of the ledger, transfers the unsold balances of goods to a separate collective account, and from there to the balance account. This feature is not found in the early Italian treatises, but was followed by Peele.

---

[17] See Kheil, *ibid.*, p. 8; de Waal, *ibid.*, p. 7, and his *De Leer van het Boekhouden in de Nederlanden tijdens de zestiende eeuw*, Roermond, 1927, pp. 93, 94–5; and compare Besta, *ibid.*, p. 385; Kats, " The ' Nouvelle Instruction ' . . .", *op. cit.*, p. 262.

[18] Raymond de Roover, " Something New about Jan Ympyn Christoffels ", *The Accountant*, vol. XCVII (1937), p. 658.

[19] Two particular matters in Ympyn's book suggest strongly its derivation from Pacioli, rather than from any other source. The twentieth chapter in Ympyn is a long chapter on bills of exchange, with very little on their bookkeeping aspects. Pacioli writes very briefly on bills of exchange in chapter 24 of his accounting " tractatus ", because this subject is dealt with fully in another part of the *Summa*, i.e., in the fourth " tractatus " of the ninth " distinctio ". According to Kheil (*ibid.*, p. 18), Ympyn's discussion is vividly reminiscent of the discussion in Pacioli.

Ympyn, unlike Oldcastle, included a chapter on the authentication of books, with special mention of the practice in Perugia (as in Pacioli). It is not a straight translation of Pacioli, but is sufficiently reminiscent of the earlier work to suggest its origin. Besta adduced the fact that Oldcastle's book does not contain some of the chapters in Pacioli's as pointing to the use of an earlier model. Ympyn's inclusion of the chapter on authentication on this basis works against Besta's conclusion that Ympyn used the same pre-Paciolian source (via Bianchi) as Oldcastle. (Besta, *ibid.*, p. 385.)

Peele and Weddington

James Peele, citizen and salter of London, and clerk of Christ's Hospital, wrote two books on bookkeeping by double entry. The first, his *Maner and Fourme*, appeared in 1553. It is well within the Paciolian tradition, though departures from the traditional pattern and some innovations suggest that Peele was both independent in his approach and knowledgeable about contemporary practices.

Kats has shown that some of the features of Peele's first book are best explained as the result of acquaintance with the work of the Italian, Domenico Manzoni,[20] whose book on double entry (the *Quaderno Doppio*) was very popular and, in terms of exposition and its illustrative material, an improvement on Pacioli's "tractatus" from which it derives. Thus, for example, Peele numbered his journal entries consecutively, as Manzoni had done. This, presumably, was done to help the reader or user of the book.[21] Again, both Manzoni and Peele speak of the memorial (waste book), but neither gives an example of one. Further, Peele's set of accounts runs for a period of one year, while all earlier examples, other than Manzoni's, cover shorter periods. Finally, both Manzoni and Peele introduced more system in the exposition of the journal and its entries. Manzoni's specimen journal is preceded by a " table " in which 300 entries are grouped in convenient sections. Peele did not do this; instead, the journal entries themselves are grouped by type of transaction, and in each entry there is an indication in a special column of the nature of the transaction. For example, journal " parcels " (entries) numbers 70 to 73 are stated as:

" 70. Wares bought for moneie
71. Wares bought for time
72. Wares bought for part mony and the Reste for tyme
73. The moneye payde."

Peele also borrowed from Ympyn. Thus the opening inventory includes valuations and extensions into a money column, as in Ympyn (see above). But, unlike Ympyn's, Peele's inventory goes further, includes a summation of the debits and the credits, and concludes with the net balance, " the substaunce of the owner " (see extract 13).[22]

---

[20] P. Kats, "James Peele's 'Maner and Fourme'", *The Accountant*, vol. LXXXII, (1930), pp. 41–2.

[21] It is interesting that the entries in Sir Thomas Gresham's surviving journal (1546–51) are numbered consecutively. See Peter Ramsey, "Some Tudor Merchants' Accounts", in A. C. Littleton and B. S. Yamey (eds.), *Studies in the History of Accounting*, 1956, p. 190, and Plate VII.

[22] In the second book by Peele, the *Pathewaye to Perfectnes* of 1569, this "neat substaunce" is referred to as the owner's "proper stocke or capitall". (See extract 14.) This seems to be the earliest recorded use of the term "capital" for a man's (net) wealth; see E. Cannan, "Early History of the Term Capital", *Quarterly Journal of Economics*, vol. 35 (1921), p. 471.

Peele also referred to the "goods remaining" account (see p. 161), but did not use it in his worked example.[23]

In some respects Peele's *Maner and Fourme* represented quite new departures. One innovation (at least as far as the literature of accounting is concerned) was his method for keeping secret some of the details of the business man's assets and liabilities (see extract 26). Another was his prescription that the underwriters be debited with the insured value of the goods at the time the premium was paid to them.

In 1569 Peele published his second book, the *Pathewaye to Perfectnes*; it was a great advance on his earlier work, as indeed on all earlier expositions of double entry,[24] though some readers no doubt found the device of a dialogue between teacher and student both contrived and tedious. (Nevertheless, the method was used after Peele by writers in several languages.) Between the two books of Peele, however, another book in English had been published; and as it seems clear that Peele was influenced by that book, we first turn to it.

John Weddington, an Englishman who spent many years in Antwerp and was active as factor (and probably merchant) and bookkeeper,[25] published his *Breffe Instruction* in Antwerp in 1567. Though the fact of its publication has been well known, no copy of the book was known to have come down to the present day, until a few years ago a copy was located in the Library of Blairs College, Aberdeen. Examination of this book shows that, apart from some unavoidable echoes of earlier English works, it is in many ways original, and in some respects right outside the Paciolian tradition.[26] Indeed, Weddington's book and Peele's second book broke the strong links which had previously bound the English literature of bookkeeping to the pioneer works of Pacioli and his followers.

The chief originality of Weddington's book lies in the organisation of the account-books, which represents a considerable departure from what may be called the classical system of Italian double entry. In that system there are three account-books: the waste-book or memorial, the journal and the ledger. Each transaction was first entered in the waste-book, from where the entries were taken in proper form to the journal,

---

23 He used the "goods remayning" account in his second book (1569); see extract 83, and Plates IV and V.

24 This assessment was made by Kats in "De Invloed der Nederlanders de 16e en 17e eeuw op de Engelsche literatuur van het Boekhouden", *Maandblad voor het Boekhouden*, vol. 32 (1925), p. 170, and "James Peele's . . .", *op. cit.*, p. 41.

25 On Weddington, see O. de Smedt, *De Engelse Natie te Antwerpen in de 16e Eeuw*, Antwerp, 1954, vol. 2, pp. 487–9.

26 Murray (*op. cit.*, p. 228), who had not seen the work, expressed the view that it "appears to have been a reissue of an already published book, and to be either a reissue of the book of 1547 [the English version of Ympyn], or a new translation of Ympyn or of Mennher de Kempten". It is certainly not a re-issue or a translation of any known earlier book, though, as we suggest, it probably was influenced by Mennher's works.

which was the medium for posting to the accounts in the ledger. Weddington's plan—presumably he had seen it in practice or had practised it himself—was to have separate books of original entry, one for each distinct type of transaction, instead of a single all-inclusive book (or pair of books). Each of the "parts" of the waste-book was the source from which entries were made in the ledger; and the journal was dispensed with. The plan has a modern flavour about it. It is not followed by any of the authors after him, until it re-appears, in altered form, in 1789, in Booth's *Complete System* (below, p. 174). Of course, some authors before (and also after) Weddington had described the use of subsidiary account-books, the entries from which might not be passed through either the waste-book or the journal; and Manzoni had carried the process quite far, though retaining the journal. But Weddington went the whole hog; and he did this to make possible the division of labour in keeping the accounts in large businesses, and also partly (with other changes) to relieve the ledger of some detail.

While Weddington's main innovation attracted no followers, other changes were taken over. His influence on Mellis is clear. (It may be noted, incidentally, that the title of Mellis's book is almost identical with the first 25 words of Weddington's title. And Mellis took other things as well. His inventory entry for "lands and rents" is almost the same as Weddington's, with only superficial differences.) Peele also seems to have borrowed from Weddington; his borrowings are more substantial and more interesting. Four of these may be noted.

First, Weddington is the first English book in which the goods accounts have separate columns for entering the quantities received or sent away. They appear on the left-hand margin of each side of the account, where they can also be found in Peele (see Plates IV and V) and in Mellis. In the earlier Peele (1553) these columns are absent. Weddington may have acquired his columns from the books written by the German Valentin Mennher from 1550 onwards in both German and French. But, as Mennher placed his quantity columns next to the money columns, Weddington may have been following what he saw in practice rather than what he saw in books. However, Weddington must have known some of Mennher's books, for several were published in Antwerp during his sojourn in that city. Second, Weddington introduced multiple or compound "journal" entries: that is, in some parts of his waste-book there are examples of entries which involve more than two accounts in the ledger. This device was taken up by Peele in 1569, though it is not to be found in his earlier book: it is referred to by him as "reperticion". Again, Mennher was the first writer to refer to multiple entries. Third, in his examples of personal accounts, Weddington distinguished between "current accounts" and "accounts of time". Though this distinction—relating to the difference between

transactions giving rise to amounts currently due or payable and transactions giving rise to deferred receipts or payments—is found in the early
practice of double entry, it is not described or illustrated in the Italian
writings of Pacioli and his more immediate successors.[27] Weddington
seems to have been the first author to illustrate the two classes of personal account, and Peele, in 1569, both described and illustrated their
use. Fourth, Weddington explained how a merchant could use a
" secreat greate Boke " to conceal parts of his estate from his counting-
house staff (see extract 27). His short discussion of the secret ledger is
unambiguously the first in the literature of accounting, though secret
ledgers had, of course, already been used in practice. Peele's book of
1569 also discusses secret ledgers (see extract 28), and does not refer to
the quite different method of concealment which he had described in
his earlier *Maner and Fourme*. Moreover, while Weddington "for
breviation " did not illustrate his suggested division of the ledger into
the secret ledger and the trade ledger, Peele's exemplary set of account-
books demonstrates most successfully the procedure first referred to by
Weddington.

It seems beyond doubt that Weddington's book, itself in some respects
influenced by Mennher's writings and probably more pervasively by
accounting practice in the Low Countries, was an important influence on
Peele's *Pathewaye to Perfectnes*.[28] Nevertheless, Peele not only effec-
tively absorbed Weddington's "innovations", but more generally
improved on his own earlier publication of 1553. In particular, the
didactic part of his second book marks a step forward in exposition. It
includes a convenient, detailed guide to the entries in the illustrative set
of accounts, and breaks new ground by giving the reader systematic
instructions as to how to close the accounts when balancing and
closing the whole ledger. Later writers of accounting manuals were to
develop further the exposition of instructions for finding the debitor
and creditor in each of a wide range of types of transaction, and for

[27] Kats, " De Invloed . . .", *op. cit.*, p. 175.
[28] Peele did not follow Weddington's major innovation—the new arrangement of the books
of original entry—presumably because it did not accord with typical practice. He also
did not follow another interesting " innovation ". Weddington describes the use of a
balance account to open a new ledger, and illustrates it in his specimen set of accounts
(see extract 91, and Plates II and III). In the opening balance account, the entries in
the closing balance account at the end of the preceding ledger are reversed, so that it
resembles the form of a modern English balance sheet. The use of this reversed opening
balance account is first described in Alvise Casanova's *Specchio Lucidissimo . . .* of
1558. Weddington's discussion of the opening balance account is the first recorded out
of Italy. It is unlikely that Weddington got the idea from Casanova's book; practice
was the more likely source. The narration of the opening entries in each side of the
account is quite different in the two books: Weddington heads his credit entries with
the word "Debitors ", while Casanova does not; and on the same (credit) side of the
account Weddington uses the form of words for a *debit* entry (" owithe to gyve ")—
because the items are asset balances—while Casanova uses the credit form of words.
Later writers in English who used the opening balance account did not use Weddington's
headings or form of words.

preparing the various types of ledger account for the closing of the ledger. Peele may fairly be regarded as the first systematiser of this practically important branch of the subject.

Carpenter, Handson and Dafforne

Apart from the re-issue in 1588 by John Mellis of Hugh Oldcastle's *Profitable Treatyce*, little happened in the publication of English books on accounting between Peele's *Pathewaye to Perfectnes* of 1569 and the early 1630s. In 1589 appeared the *Merchants Avizo* by John Brown, merchant and mayor of Bristol, written for the guidance of the sons and servants of merchants when first sent " beyond the seas, as to Spaine and Portingale or other countreyes ". This book, which went into six editions, contains some instruction on the keeping of accounts by a factor for his master. The system illustrated ("the forme of a Spanish accompt") is not in double entry, and the specimen accounts have more interest for their information on various costs associated with trading ventures than for the technique of accounting they reveal.

In 1596 the *Pathewaye to Knowledge* was published "written in Dutch, and translated into English". The translator was "W.P." probably one William Phillips, an Englishman who at the time was making translations of several books from the Dutch. The English book was re-published in 1613, as the *Path-way to Knowledge*, by John Tap, "which in its turn was re-edited by Peter Ray, gentleman, in 1658".[29] There is no reference in either book to the source of the translation, but Kats[30] established that each is a translation of Nicolaus Petri's (Claesz Pietersz) *Practique om te Leeren Rekenen Cypheren ende Boeckhouwen*, first published in 1583, and revised and enlarged in 1591.[31] Pietersz' book includes expositions of arithmetic and algebra, and the accounting part consists of a rather condensed worked example, without preliminary explanation or discussion. The English translation of this part is somewhat abridged, but largely faithful to the original.[32] It would have been better if another book of Pietersz, the *Boeckhouwen op die Italiaensche Maniere* (first edition, 1576), devoted exclusively to accounting, had been translated; for in this, the exposition is more comprehensive and helpful. One imagines that the three *Pathways* were found to be of use mainly for their sections on arithmetic and algebra.

---

[29] Murray, *op. cit.*, pp. 236–7.   [30] Kats, " De Invloed . . . ," *op. cit.*, p. 172.

[31] On the strength of misreading " N.P." for " W.P." on the title-page of the 1596 *Pathway*, Murray stated that " the translator was Nicholaus Peters of Deventer ". (*Ibid.*, pp. 233–4.)

[32] One interesting difference is noted by Kats, *ibid.*, p. 173. In the Dutch original, on the receipt of goods by a factor from his principal, no entry is made for the value of the goods. Tap, on the other hand, credits the principal for the amount and debits an account of goods opened in the name of the principal.

Gerard Malynes' *Consuetudo vel Lex Mercatoria* was first published in 1622, and further editions appeared in the course of the century. This compendium of the "law merchant" included a chapter on "merchants accounts kept by Debitor and Creditor", which shows traces of the influence of Ympyn as well as of acquaintance with Spanish practice.[33]

In the 1630s there was a spurt in the publication of works on accounting: Carpenter's *Excellent Instruction* came out in 1632; in the next year the third (and earliest known) edition of Ralph Handson's broadside, *Analysis of Merchants Accompts*, was issued; and in 1635 came the first edition of Richard Dafforne's *Merchants Mirrour*, the first book in English on the double entry system to go into several (at least four) editions. These publications were all curiously linked together. Moreover, together they mark the high point of Dutch influence on English writing in our field; after this group of publications, direct Dutch influence becomes progressively attenuated.

In his prefatory remarks Carpenter stated that his book was in part the work "of some well-experienced practitioners in the Art of Keeping Merchants bookes of Accounts", and in part the result of his "owne paines". "I send it out not as absolutely mine owne worke, nor doe I goe about hereby to detract from the due merit of him, whoseover he be that hath so well deserved in framing the chiefe groundworke thereof." Carpenter professed to be ignorant of the identity of his indicated source, and gave the impression that his own contribution was substantial: "some slight directions to this purpose have been heretofore published, but never any so compendious, perfect and absolute a forme as this". In fact, almost the whole of his book is taken, mostly without real alteration, from earlier books; and it is difficult to believe that he himself had not handled at least some of these books. The principal work plagiarised, though indirectly, was a French text, itself a translation by the author of his own Dutch original text. This particular borrowing was angrily unmasked by Handson in the preface he wrote for Dafforne's book. He explains that a large part of Carpenter's book was taken from notes which he (Handson) had at one time collected "out of Henry Wanninghen in French",[34] which notes "were surreptitiously gotten from me, and with them, and other examples, a Book of Accompts is patch't up, and printed for an Exact one, without my privity". Dafforne confirmed that Waninghen was Carpenter's main source.

The bulk of the didactic part of Waninghen's *Le Thresor de tenir Livre de Comptes a l'Italienne*, 1615,[35] consists of a large number of

---

[33] Kats, *ibid.*, p. 173.

[34] Carpenter seems to have adhered so closely to Handson's "notes" that he retained the initials "R.H." in some illustrative formulations of the titles of some accounts.

[35] This is a translation of his *Tresoor van't Italiaens Boeckhouden*, the first edition of which may have appeared as early as 1607.

questions-and-answers which explain the required debits and credits for different types of transaction. These questions-and-answers are grouped conveniently into a smaller number of sections (for example, the seventeenth section consists of ten questions-and-answers relating to the entries for the assuring of goods). These sections appear almost unchanged in Carpenter: the order is changed, and each pair of question and answer is replaced by a single proposition.[36] There can be little doubt that Handson's " notes " were a version of Waninghen's sections.

Not content with taking over Waninghen's instructions via Handson's notes, Carpenter also presented two further sets of instructions for the guidance of practitioners. One set is a straightforward copy of a portion of Peele's *Maner and Fourme* of 1553 (and Carpenter's specimen set of accounts is also essentially the same as Peele's). The third set, called " The Contents " (a small part of which is reproduced as extract 51) and appearing at the end of the book, shows close similarities with Handson's broadside; and in view of his proclivities as copier, we may assume that Carpenter followed Handson (the first edition of whose broadside probably was published before 1632). Before turning to Handson, a further example of Carpenter's eclectic copying may be noted: his section on accounting for a retail shop is a direct derivation from the corresponding chapter in Mellis's *Briefe Instruction*, 1588 (compare extracts 64 and 65). Thus there is very little that is original in Carpenter[37]; it is almost entirely patchwork.[38]

Handson's broadside consists entirely of a tightly compressed presentation of an analytical classification of types of transaction, indicating for each type the accounts to be debited and credited (see extracts 49 and 50).

---

[36] The fidelity of the translation, and the slight difference in treatment, can be shown in the following random example:

Waninghen
" De ce qu'on recoit a mariage, ou qu'on donne comme aussi de recevoir & desbourser des biens hereditaires.
Pour la somme qu'on recoit on fait Cassa, ou tels biens Debet, & Capital Credit. Au contraire pour autant qu'on donne on fait Debet son Capital, & Cassa ou tels biens Credit.
1. *Demande.* Quand vous recevez & argent & biens en votre mariage?
    Response. Cassa & tels biens Debet a mon Capital, ou a mon nom, y adjoutant par qui on l'a receu. . . ."

Carpenter
" On that which you receive upon Mariage, or that which you pay; as also receiving and disbursing hereditary goods.
For the summe that you receive, you make Cash, or such goods, Debtor; and Capitall Creditor,
And on the contrary, for as much as you pay, he makes your Capitall, Debtor; and Cash, or such goods, Creditor. *As*
1. First, if you receive both monie and goods in Mariage; Cash, and such goods owe to your Capitall, or to your name; adding therewithall by whom you have received them. . . ."

[37] He even followed Waninghen's proposterous prescription for secrecy in the books of account, and was duly chided for it by Dafforne (see extract 29).

[38] Brown (*op. cit.*, p. 150) was wrong, however, in suggesting that Carpenter derived from Manzoni's *Quaderno Doppio* and Ympyn.

With this guide in the counting-house, a clerk could without undue trouble discover how to deal with a particular transaction. Being all on one sheet, it was a particularly handy form of guide. And where Handson pioneered, others followed. Thomas Browne seems to have published a similar broadside in 1666 [39]; and his book, *The Accurate-Accomptant* (1668, and subsequently), begins with a Handson-like "Analysis of Accompts" spread over an opening. In 1711 (and again in 1733) John Alleine prepared a broadside sub-titled *Rules to Find Debtors and Creditors in the most Usual Transaction of Trade*; its content and construction are similar to Handson's. But the culmination of the development of Handson's method of serving up instructions in potted and classified form, with a minimum of words and in a small space, is to be seen in Malachy Postlethwayt's *Universal Dictionary of Trade and Commerce* (2nd edition, 1757), in the entry "Mercantile Accountantship or Merchants Accounts". Part of this entry consists of several pages of summarised and classified instructions for debits and credits; and in one or two of the details one may perhaps glimpse the original Handson, though the whole is far more comprehensive.[40]

Dafforne's *Merchants Mirrour* is lavish in its acknowledgments to those from whom its author learnt or borrowed; in this respect it is a refreshing change from Carpenter. Dafforne had lived and worked in Holland, before returning to the land of his "breaths first drawing"; his "Great Waste-Book" was printed in Amsterdam in 1621 in English and Dutch. On returning to England, he discovered—he says—that the stationers' shops in London had no books on accounting, unlike the state of affairs he had known in Holland. He concluded that while merchants in the Lòw Countries "are generally enamoured of this Art" of bookkeeping, in England, "alas, the small love that a great part of our merchants bear to this science, daunteth the Pen of Industry in our Teachers". But the pen of Dafforne was not daunted, and he wrote his lengthy *Merchants Mirrour*, and subsequently, the *Apprentices Time-Entertainer Accomptantly*.

In spite of his "egregious style",[41] the *Merchants Mirrour* is a

[39] *Cf.* Murray, *op. cit.*, p. 251, n. 4.

[40] Thus, for example, the item for money received as interest on a continuing loan:
Handson: "For Interest of Money (formerly lent, the Principal being continued) Dr. Mony: Cr. the Accompt of Interest, or Profit and Loss".
Postlethwayt: "For interest of money formerly lent, and principal continued: Dr. cash to account of interest, or profit and loss, (which you please)".
The similarity between Carpenter's "Contents" (see text, above) and Handson is far closer:
Carpenter: "For Interest of monies formerly lent (the principal being contained [error for "continued"]. . . .".
To take another example, Handson comments that the sale of wares for cash on delivery is rare. His words are: "which is seldom in use". With Carpenter it is: "which is *raro aut nunquam*, little in use".

[41] Brown, *op. cit.*, p. 154.

competent exposition, though it is rendered unnecessarily laborious by the use of the device of a dialogue between Philo-Mathy, the teacher, and his scholar, School-Partner. It owes, as its author acknowledged, a good deal to the books, in Dutch, of Waninghen and his pupil, Buingha; he also mentions other Dutch authors in acknowledgment, including the celebrated mathematician and man of affairs, Simon Stevin (whom he refers to as a friend), Coutereels, Claesz Pietersz and Jan Willemsz of Leuven.[42] Moreover, he refers the reader from time to time to contemporary bookkeeping practice in Holland. But Dafforne was not a passive assembler and copier. He expresses dissent from some of the observations and prescriptions of his teachers, including even Stevin; and praises the Englishman, Peele, to the discredit of Waninghen, Buingha and Carpenter, for their respective treatments of how to achieve secrecy in the account-books (see extract 29).[43]

We have already remarked that the *Merchants Mirrour* went into several editions, which testifies to its success. After Dafforne, books on accounting appeared in increasing numbers. He seems to have shown the way; or, perhaps, the demand for manuals of instruction was increasing. Between 1543 and 1640 eleven productions in English had appeared (excluding Browne's *Avizo* but including Malynes' and Handson's publications); between 1641 and 1740, over 30 new authors contributed books on accounting (some more than one book), and several of these books went into a number of editions.

Scottish Ascendancy

It is difficult to trace foreign influence on the books in English published after Dafforne and his immediate successors. The principal treatises of the last quarter of the seventeenth and the whole of the eighteenth century were essentially home-grown, with a preponderance of the best works being published in Scotland, or in England by Scottish authors. And though there was naturally a substantial variation in style, competence, lucidity, length and appearance, a fairly standard pattern of content and treatment did in fact begin to emerge. The main accent in the better treatises is on the treatment of the different types of ledger account and different types of transaction, and on the closing of individual accounts and of the ledger as a whole on the formal closing of the books from time to time. Subjects which preoccupy accountants today, notably the valuation of assets and the calculation of profit, take

---

[42] He also mentions Passchier Goessens, a merchant who fled from Brabant, settled in Germany, and wrote a serviceable German treatise on bookkeeping.
[43] See Kats, "De Invloed . . . ," *op. cit.*, pp. 174–5.

up very little space, and are generally touched upon *en passant* in connection with the closing of the accounts. Even where, exceptionally, methods of stating asset " values " are referred to in more than a few words, the effect of the methods on the calculation of profit is not discussed (see extract 90 as an exception). Modern preoccupations enter the literature of accounting only in the latter half of the nineteenth century, with the rise of the joint stock company form of business organisation, when the very term " company accounts " ceased to have its earlier connotation of partnership accounts and acquired its present meaning. Again, in the manuals of the eighteenth century and earlier it is rare to find discussion of the application of the double entry system to the problems of recording and measuring activities in manufacturing (as distinct from trading) enterprises. There are some exceptions [44]; but the specific subject of cost accounting received little attention before the second half of the nineteenth century, whenceforth the subject is more frequently discussed in general books on accounting and, increasingly, in specialised books.

Robert Colinson's *Idea Rationaria*, 1683, was the first book on accounting to be published in Scotland. We may agree with Brown that " there was no particular merit at this period in producing a good work on book-keeping, so that it would be out of place to bestow special praise on Colinson." [45] His book is sensible and reasonably straightforward and without frills (though he has some). One of its attractions today is the two pieces of verse, by other hands, praising Colinson, his book or the double entry system, it not being clear always who or what is being praised. [46]

---

[44] In the period up to 1800 some discussion of accounting for manufacturing enterprises can be found in books by John Collins, James Dodson, Wardhaugh Thompson and Robert Hamilton. We do not reproduce extracts from these portions of their books, because detailed extracts are presented, with an instructive commentary, by Ronald S. Edwards in " Some Notes on the Early Literature and Development of Cost Accounting in Great Britain ", *The Accountant*, vol. XLVII (1937).

[45] Brown, *op. cit.*, p. 155.

[46] The following are extracts from the laudatory verse by Ninian Paterson:

" Thy *Idea* hath brought home a more complete,
And richer *Cargo* than the *Indian* fleet
By which the Stuards of the Kingdoms Stock,
Our Merchands now shall never more be broke. . . .

This the kind *Ariadne's* Silken thread
Conducts them through the Labyrinths of trade:
While *Colinson* like *Theseus* doth devour
CONFUSION that monstrous Minotaure. . . .

This was the fam'd and quick invention, which
Made *Venice*, *Genoa*, and *Florence* rich:
The Th[en?] Low Countries, (in all senses such)
By this Art now *speaks high and mighty Dutch*. . . .

The want of which (till now) did still abate
The Kingdoms stock, and private mens estate.

The principal Scottish authors in our period were Alexander Macghie, Alexander Malcolm and John Mair, and somewhat later, William Gordon and Robert Hamilton. All five were teachers, Macghie and Malcolm in Edinburgh, Mair in Ayr and Perth, Gordon in Glasgow where he was co-founder of a Mercantile Academy, and Hamilton in Perth.[47] Hamilton was the most distinguished person in this group. After being a master of the Academy at Perth, he became professor first of natural philosophy and then of mathematics at Aberdeen; and, as an economist, he is famed for having exposed the economic fallacies of Pitt's policy of the sinking fund.[48]

The treatises of these authors are all good in relation to their objective of giving instruction and advice methodically and clearly. Mair was the most successful. His first book, *Book-keeping Methodiz'd*, of 1736 reached its eighth edition by 1765. In 1768, " as forms and fashions in accountantship, as well as in other things, are in a perpetual flux and continuously changing ",[49] he revised his book and presented his *Book-keeping Moderniz'd*, which reached its ninth edition in 1807, and later formed the basis of Langford's *Merchants' Accounts*, published in several editions between 1822 and 1853. Mair's book was not only popular with the public, but also with his fellow-authors. An anonymous author, a " Teacher of Book-keeping ", who had a book published in Glasgow in 1758, wrote: " It must be confessed, that Mr. Mair's treatise on Book-keeping is the most perfect of the kind, it particularly merits the attention of every man of business ". (He added, however: " but without derogating from his merit, it must be owned that the subject is still capable of further improvement ".[50]) Writing in 1818, Cronhelm, himself a writer on accounting, could say: " In 1736, Scotland had the honour of producing, in the Book-Keeping Methodiz'd of John Mair, the most complete and elaborate exposition of the old Italian Method, ever published." [51]

While the merits of Mair's works are undeniable, in some ways Malcolm's books are more satisfactory, at least for those now enquiring into the nature of the practice of accounting in the eighteenth century. Thus, for example, Malcolm is apt to give more information than Mair

> Which Noble Art (when it augments our store)
> This shall admire, and the next age adore."

And a couplet from the verse by J. Kniblo:

> " By this Ingenious Pilot safely may
> We trade at home, to Indies find a way. . . ."

[47] Murray, *op. cit., passim.*
[48] See H. R. Hatfield, " An Historical Defense of Bookkeeping ", reprinted in W. T. Baxter and Sidney Davidson, eds., *Studies in Accounting Theory*, 1962.
[49] Quoted from Murray, *ibid.*, p. 325.
[50] Quoted from Murray, *ibid.*, p. 337.
[51] F. W. Cronhelm, *Double Entry by Single*, 1818, Introduction, p. xiii. The " old " contrasts with the " modern " Italian Method; see p. 174, below.

on variants in the treatment of particular matters. Hamilton's *Intro-duction to Merchandise* has yet other virtues. His approach was more enquiring than that of Mair or Malcolm. On occasions he considers the rationale of particular practices, or discusses the relevance of particular procedures for the business man who might look to his ledger account for guidance in decision-making.[52] In many ways it has the most modern appearance of all the early books.

Before returning to England, we should take a quick look at publications in Ireland. The first recorded publication on bookkeeping is that by S. A.[mmonet] entitled *The Key of Knowledge*, of 1696. Murray reports a suggestion that it might be compiled from the earlier *Pathway to Knowledge*[53] (see p. 166, above). Daniel Dowling's *Complete System* (second edition, 1770) was the first considerable Irish work on the subject.

Booth's Modern Italian Method

Writers on accounting in England had not, of course, been idle. Stephen Monteage wrote his *Debtor and Creditor made easie* in 1675, which appeared in at least four editions. It is an interesting work, though not out of the ordinary. Its importance lies in the fact that, according to the *Dictionary of National Biography*, Monteage, a " mer-chant and accountant ", " did much towards bringing into general use the method of keeping accounts by double entry ". Hatton and Webster's books went into many more editions, but are undistinguished. Edward Hatton's *Merchant's Magazine* of 1695 reached its eighth edition by 1726; and William Webster's *Essay on Book-Keeping* of 1719 notched up its fifteenth edition by 1772.

Quite different, and far more interesting and entertaining, is the book by " A Person of Honour ", entitled *The Gentleman Accomptant*,

---

[52] *Cf.* also the following extract from his discussion of accounting for manufacturers (quoted from Edwards, *ibid.*, p. 253):

" When a person is engaged in several branches of manufacture, whether on different materials, or on the same materials through several successive stages, he should keep his books in such a manner as to exhibit the gain or loss on each.

Take the example of a linen manufacturer who purchases or imports rough flax, dresses it by his own servants, and sells such kinds as do not suit his purpose; delivers the rest to be spun, and receives the yarn from the spinners; weaves part in his own workhouse by journeymen and delivers the rest to other weavers; gives out the linen to be bleached, and receives and sells it when white.

If all these branches of business were necessarily connected and the manufacturer had no other choice than to purchase the rough flax, and carry on the successive operations, it would be sufficient to keep his books in a form that should exhibit the gain or loss on the whole; but if he has an opportunity of beginning or desisting at any stage of the manufacture, his books should exhibit the gain or loss on each operation seaparately ".

[53] Murray, *ibid.*, p. 360.

1714. The author has been identified as Roger North (1653–1734), the sixth and youngest son of Dudley, fourth Lord North, and author of the well-known *Lives of the Norths*. As Murray has put it, "the style and matter of the book [on accounting] are quite consistent with this [identification] ".[54] Another interesting short book is that by Richard Hayes, *The Gentleman's Complete Book-keeper*, 1741.

The English writers come fully into their own again towards the end of the century. Benjamin Booth, a merchant "late of New York and now of London", expounded the "modern Italian Method" in 1789; and Edward Jones invented and published his *English System* in 1796.

In Booth's *Complete System* he "gave to the world . . . the first English work illustrative of the modern Italian Method. The latter system differs from the former [the old], in dividing the Waste Book into various subsidiary Books, and in journalizing each of them separately once a month. This Method was rendered elementary, and adapted to schools, in 1801, by the popular treatise of Dr. Kelly ".[55] Booth himself claimed that "the system here laid down, which is the result of thirty years experience, is calculated to obviate every objection that can be made to double-entry, even among Tradesmen and Manufacturers; since it possesses both the facility and expedition of the *single-entry*, with all the advantages of the *double*. All extraneous matter being lopped off from the Journal, every article is brought to its respective account in the Ledger, by the shortest and most expeditious means ".[56] Booth, in effect, repeated (no doubt independently)[57] what Weddington had done: the dismemberment of the books of original entry. But he went much further than Weddington in prescribing the summarisation of entries preparatory to the writing up of the ledger accounts. Of course, some other writers before Booth had also recommended that certain types of transaction should be entered separately in particular subsidiary books, with periodic total entries to the relevant accounts in the ledger. But Booth's is the first exposition in English of the completed process; and this part of his system was presumably directed primarily at larger business firms.[58] His book was greatly

[54] Murray, *ibid.*, pp. 261–2.

[55] Cronhelm, *ibid.*, Introduction, pp. xiii–xiv. The reference to Kelly is to P. Kelly, *The Elements of Book-Keeping*, 1801 (twelfth edition in 1847).

[56] Booth, *Complete System*, p. 6. The reference to "Tradesmen" is probably to small-scale craftsmen and retailers.

[57] De la Porte, in his *La Science des Negocians* (first edition, 1703) had also described the dismembered memorial.

[58] *Cf.* Booth, *ibid.*, p. 6: "Upon the failure of one of the most capital houses in London, I remember it was remarked, that the insolvency was more owing to the want of a proper Book-Keeper, than to any other cause; or rather, that the Book-Keeper wanted a proper method. The business of the house was become so extensive, that without a summary mode of bringing those immense sums which were daily circulating, to the debtor and creditor of their respective accounts, it was impossible to know how any one

praised in McCulloch's *Dictionary of Commerce* (new edition, 1859):
" The reader of his work finds a great deal of information in short
compass, without being perplexed either by superfluous detail or by
fanciful theory ".

The 'English System' and After

Booth had claimed rashly that his improvements to the Italian system
of double entry would " obviate every objection that can be made to
double-entry ". He did not reckon with Edward Thomas Jones, an
accountant in Bristol, whose *English System of Book-keeping* was published in London in 1796. In 1795 he had issued *An Address to Bankers,
Merchants, Tradesmen &c.* as a form of prospectus to announce his new
system. This *Address* appears substantially unchanged as the " Intro-
ductory Address " to his book published in the following year. He
made extravagant claims for his invention, and coupled them with
searing criticisms of the Italian system of double entry; and his criticisms,
if just, would have applied equally to the traditional and to Booth's
" modernized " system of double entry. The prospectus was carefully
prepared, and was strengthened by a number of favourable testimonials.
One of these, signed, *inter alia*, by D. Giles, governor of the Bank of
England, and Robert Peel, M.P., reads: " The Simplicity on which
Jones's *New System of Book-Keeping* is founded—the Expedition with
which Books may be examined and balanced—the ingenious, certain,
and yet simple Method of discovering Errors, or false Statements, makes
it a valuable Acquisition to Persons in anywise concerned with Trade ".
On the strength of the respectable auspices under which his *System* was
appearing, Jones was able to forestall criticisms that he was indulging
in a " take-in ". He also explained that his miraculous system would
not cause redundancy in the ranks of bookkeepers. Their work would
be purged of its tedious and unpleasant parts, but otherwise " the office
of the Book-keeper is still the same ". Moreover, he did not claim
superiority over others. He explained that others had no doubt discerned
the inadequacies and dangers of the Italian system: " (for I do not
mean to arrogate to myself any exclusive or superior intelligence to other
men) but it is not every man who reflects upon an Evil, that chooses to
set about providing a remedy; and the labours of an Accomptant
occasion him, in general, gladly to devote his leisure moments to relaxa-
tion rather than study. What might have been produced by the efforts

account stood, without having recourse to vague and uncertain expedients, depending
chiefly on imagination and conjecture."
The main appeal of his system for very small firms probably was his use of a single
goods account in the ledger, instead of a series of particularised ones (see extract 59).

of others, I know not: but, certainly, no new method of Book-Keeping has been offered to the world since the Italian invention, except the English System ".

The prospectus, the testimonials, the nationalistic title, the general desire for simplicity and safety in accounts, and, no doubt, the fact that the " system " had been patented, all contributed to the success of the launching of Jones's book in 1796. Over 4,000 subscribers are listed in the first edition, and Jones is said to have profited to the extent of £25,000 from his " invention ".[59] Translations appeared in six European languages, and there were at least two American editions. It was the first book on accounting by an English author to have influenced, however fleetingly, developments in Europe. According to Brown (writing in 1905), Jones's book " is the most widely known book on the subject in the English language ".[60] Moreover, for the first time a book on accounting gave rise to acrimonious debates, both in England (where Jones seems to have stood alone) and on the Continent (where he had some supporters as well as critics). His critics gained a rapid victory. Jones's claims and criticisms were preposterously insupportable, and his critics, some of whom were sometimes as intemperate as Jones had been, were able to point this out.[61]

We need not elaborate here on Jones's system, on the debates and on his very limited influence.[62] Jones himself abandoned his own invention, though this abandonment was accompanied by further inventions, some of which may well be regarded as early moves in the direction of modern practice, *e.g.*, in the use of sectional balancing and control accounts.[63] We turn, instead, to one of the more direct consequences of

---

[59] E. Jäger, *Die Berechtigung der einfachen Buchhaltung*, 1868, p. 13.

[60] Brown, *op. cit.*, p. 159.

[61] Some of his critics claimed, not surprisingly, to be as much actuated by serving the public interest as was Jones. Thus Gosnell, *An Elucidation*, 1796: " . . . although many, and perhaps the greater part of the Readers of Mr. Jones's Book may be fully competent to judge of it, yet it is very probable that, among those who are about to commence business, and others who have not had sufficient experience to determine for themselves, some might be persuaded, by the confidence which pervades Mr. Jones's own account of his System, to give it a preference; and if at a future day they should find themselves in inextricable confusion, might very justly consider as criminal the silence of those who were competent to the task of exposing the deception, and of guarding them against the seducing danger which it is the duty of professional men to point out." Gosnell practised (in London) the " Examination and Settlement of every Species of Account ".

[62] For further details, see B. S. Yamey, " Edward Jones and the Reform of Book-keeping," in Littleton and Yamey (eds.), *op. cit.*, pp. 313–24.

I have not seen any surviving account-book, the form or content of which reflects the English system. Professor Osamu Kojima has kindly drawn my attention to the ledger of 1812–18 of Bryant and Sturgis (in the Baker Library, Harvard University) which seems to be modelled on Jones's patent ledger described in his book.

[63] McCulloch's *Dictionary of Commerce*, new edition 1859, singles out Booth's *Complete System* and Jones's *The Science of Book-keeping exemplified*, 1831, as the two most serviceable books on accounting. Jones's book of 1831 does not, however, expound the " English system " of 1796. The *Dictionary* makes an unfavourable reference to the high price (£4.4.0) of the book.

the publication of his system, though it is one which was not intended by Jones.

One direct result of Jones's publication was a crop of " new " systems of bookkeeping, all exploiting the usefulness (or alleged usefulness) of the addition of various classificatory columns to the journal and/or ledger.[64] Another was the more limited copying of Jones's peculiar method for the instant calculation of net profits in the journal or ledger. This innovation was the subject of strong criticism by supporters of the double entry system; and some of the published criticisms are interesting in that they improved on the prevailing methods of explaining the articulation of the various parts of a set of ledger-accounts kept on the double entry system.

Stated briefly, Jones omits all ledger-accounts other than those for persons, capital, cash and bills. It follows that, with a suitable adjustment for the closing stock of merchandise, in a simple case, *i.e.*, where there are no other assets, the excess of total debits over total credits in the journal is the net profit for the period. It measures the net balance of the entries to the omitted accounts which would have been included in the double entry system and which would in effect have constituted the profit-and-loss account. Jones did not explain for the benefit of his readers why his method got the right answer. It appears that some of

---

[64] See Yamey, *ibid.*, *passim*.

The main purpose of Jones's extra columns was to provide an independent check on the accuracy of posting to the ledger. Thus he provides columns in the ledger which enable one to ascertain readily the total of debits (or credits) entered in the ledger in any particular quarter, which total could then be checked against the total of the debits recorded in the journal.

In the same year as the publication of Jones's *English System*, a book was published in Philadelphia, William Mitchell's *A New and Complete System of Book-keeping*, which is one of the earliest American works on accounting. Some of the main features of the system expounded by Mitchell seem to come from Booth. A passage in the preface echoes one in Booth: " . . . combining, in a considerable degree, the simplicity of single, with all the advantages of Double Entry " (Mitchell); " it possesses both the facility and expedition of the *single-entry*, with all the advantages of the *double* " (Booth). But Mitchell, like Jones, introduced a balance check on the ledger, additional to the usual straightforward check, which seems to be new. His method, he says, is so complete " as scarcely to admit the possibility of the smallest error existing, without being detected " (*cf.* part of the title of Jones's book: " in which it is impossible for an error of the most trifling amount to be passed unnoticed.") The balance check is to compare the total of all debits (or credits) in the ledger with a total made up of a collection of amounts, which at first glance appears to be haphazard. In fact, however, the second total must be equal to the first if there are no errors. This collection consists of two parts: the totals of the debits to certain ledger-accounts (*e.g.*, the cash account) ascertained from these accounts directly; and the total of debit entries to all other accounts, obtained indirectly. Thus the collection includes, for example, the sum of the debits to the bills receivable account as well as the sum of the credits to the bills payable account (which measure, of course, the debits to the otherwise omitted personal accounts in connection with the issue of bills payable); and it includes both the sum of the debits and of the credits to the cash account, the debits for obvious reasons, and the credits because they measure the debits to other ledger accounts not otherwise included in the calculation.

It is not possible to ascertain whether the publication of Jones's book preceded that of Mitchell's book, or *vice versa*.

his critics, in probing into his somewhat mystifying procedures, were stimulated to examine the logic of the double entry system.

Broadly, in our period the treatises on accounting taught how to make entries in debit and in credit by one or more of several methods [65]: the formulation of rules (see, for example, extracts 46 and 47) to be learnt by rote and applied more or less unthinkingly [66]; the personification of non-personal accounts, so that, for example, one was to regard the cash account as an account in the name of the cashier; and the multiplication of cases with detailed instruction in distinguishing the debits and credits in each case (see, for example, extract 76). There was no attempt (with one exception to be noted immediately below) to explain the making of particular entries in terms of the grand structure of a system of accounts. Hustcraft Stephens in his *Italian Book-keeping*, 1735, was the first to break away from the traditional methods of approach. In a long discussion at the beginning of his book he sets out to explain how the disposition of assets, liabilities and proprietorship interests is recorded in the double entry system, and how changes in these components are incorporated in the system. A careful and persevering reader who followed the tortuous path of the exposition would have been able to deal appropriately with the recording of any particular type of transaction without having had to be drilled separately in the debits and credits of the case. It is apparent, however, that Stephens' pioneering effort had little influence on later treatises. His style and terminological innovations probably contributed to this neglect (see extract 109). Moreover, his more abstract approach was probably not to the taste of practitioners and schoolmasters who constituted the demand for manuals. The same fate of neglect in fact attended the later writings of Fulton and Cronhelm, who were his closest successors though they were not influenced by his book. Incidentally, these two " theorists " of accounting were practical men; and Stephens also was both practitioner and teacher.

Fulton's more satisfactory and more readable attempt to explain the internal equilibrium of the double entry system was undoubtedly inspired by Jones. James Williamson Fulton, a book-keeper with the Board of

---

[65] For a detailed discussion of this subject, copiously illustrated with quotations from early books, see J. G. C. Jackson, " The History of Methods of Exposition of Double-Entry Book-keeping in England ", in Littleton and Yamey (eds.), *op. cit.*, pp. 288–312.

[66] Thus the following verse precedes Dafforne's ledger in *Merchants Mirrour* (quoted from Jackson, *ibid.*, p. 291):

" In brief
The owner, or the owning thing,
Or what-so-ever comes to thee:
Upon the LEFT hand see thou bring
For there the same must placed be.
But
They unto whom thou dost owe,
Upon the RIGHT let them be set:
Or what-so-e'er doth from thee go
To place them there do not forget."

Revenue, Bengal, India, published his *British-Indian Book-keeping* in 1800. He criticised Jones for his " absurd attempt . . . to conform to single entry "; and he explained that to derive a figure of closing stock Jones must have records of purchases and sales " so that the principles of the Italian system are unavoidably adhered to " without its full advantages being enjoyed. Moreover, in following up his criticism of Jones, Fulton set out a crisp statement of the structure of accounts kept by double entry, though his objective was more limited than that of Stephens' exposition (extract 110). Eighteen years later Cronhelm returned to the subject, and presented an exposition of the algebra of double entry which can stand comparison with similar treatments in modern text-books (extract 111). It is reasonably clear from certain echoes that Cronhelm had read Fulton's book; and Cronhelm, like Fulton, seems to have been stimulated by Jones's wrong-headedness. Cronhelm sought to establish " the equilibrium of debtors and creditors " as the " fundamental principle of bookkeeping "—" a principle not of art or invention, but of science and discovery; not of mere expediency, but of absolute necessity, and inseparable from the nature of accounts ". He explained that Jones "has attempted to ridicule it as the ' common saying, that for every debtor there must be a creditor ' ", but that he (Jones) "was guided imperceptibly by the principle which he imagined to reject ".

With Cronhelm, the Italian system was triumphant, and the over-throw of the English system complete. With pride Jones had claimed his invention for England: " And surely it should be the boast of an Englishman, that he can change his system of bookkeeping [the Italian] for a better ". Cronhelm on the other hand, ended the Introduction to his book with a question: " Is it too much to hope, that England may yet enjoy the honour of perfecting the science of Accounts; and that, as she eclipses all that was wealth and glory in the commercial empires of the Mediterranean, so she may repay the debt of instruction and restore to Italy the Doppia Scrittura, purified from its repetitions, and guarded from its liabilities to abuse? "

It is not appropriate here to attempt to answer Cronhelm's question. It is, however, unlikely that any later English book had a greater impact on Continental accounting literature than Jones's nine days' wonder; for many decades it was apparently believed by some that the English kept their accounts on Jonesian lines, and that their counting-houses were enmeshed in the copious columns of the " English system ". But if the " debt of instruction " was not repaid via the literature of the subject, the world-wide influence of British professional practitioners and practice, especially in the later nineteenth century and the earlier decades of the twentieth, may be regarded as appropriate recompense for the earlier borrowings from Continental practice and printed expositions.

DOUBLE ENTRY IN PRACTICE IN THE SEVENTEENTH AND EIGHTEENTH CENTURIES[1]

In this essay some characteristics of early accounting by double entry are discussed in the context of an examination of some surviving business records. The account-books examined, ranging in time from 1655 to 1774, are not in any way a representative selection; they are records which have been brought to my notice and which have been readily accessible to me.[2] No attempt is made to describe or analyze the accounts comprehensively; the discussion is confined largely to their scope and to a group of related questions concerning balancing, profit calculation and the statement of asset values. These, perhaps, are the topics that will interest present-day practitioners of accounting most. They are also of concern to economic and business historians who may use old account-books as source material.

A considerable diversity of practice is revealed in the eight sets of records, though almost every one of the individual practices and procedures in these records is mentioned in one or other of the large number of contemporary treatises on accounting. In the course of the discussion some comparison with present-day procedures will be made; but there is no implication that present-day practice is the appropriate standard against which to test the adequacy and suitability of earlier practice. Indeed, insofar as one can put oneself in the position of the owners of the enterprises or properties dealt with in the books, it seems to me that the records and accounting procedures were well designed to meet their needs.

The Business Men and the Scope of their Accounts

The eight sets of account-books belonged to seven individual business men and one partnership:

William Hoskins, ledger A, 1655–1667
Sir John Banks, ledgers B, C & D, 1657–1699
Sir Robert Clayton and John Morris, ledgers 9–12, 1669–1680

[1] This essay consists largely of a combination of two articles by B. S. Yamey, " Some Seventeenth and Eighteenth Century Double-Entry Ledgers " in *The Accounting Review*, vol. XXXIV, No. 4, October 1959, pp. 534–546, and "" A Seventeenth Century Double-Entry Journal " in *Accountancy*, November 1960, pp. 639–641. Some additional material has been added.

We are grateful to the editors of the two journals for allowing the reproduction of the published material.

[2] The author is grateful to Dr. K. Burley, Dr. D. C. Coleman and Mr. R. Davis for having introduced him to the records in question.

Sir Dudley North, great ledger, 1680–1691
Sir Charles Peers, journal A, 1689–1695
Richard Du Cane, ledger D, 1736–1744
Peter Du Cane, ledgers C & D, 1754–1758
William Braund, ledgers F & G, 1758–1774.[3]

Before describing the selected aspects of these account-books, it is appropriate to introduce the business men for whom—and in some cases, by whom—they were kept. In the process it will be noted in each case whether the records discussed embraced the whole of the owner's assets and activities, or only a part of these.

Little is known of *William Hoskins*. From his ledger it appears that he lived in Cherbourg, and that until about 1661 he had close business relations with a John Haysome, also of Cherbourg until he returned to England in 1657. The ledger refers almost entirely to business transactions, in many of which Hoskins acted as agent for others, or in partnership, first with Haysome and later with Richard Berien. The scale of business done was small. It is clear from certain entries, however, that the ledger, "keept and written by mine owne hande", did not cover all his possessions or, presumably, activities. Several debit entries in the profit-and-loss account in the 1660s refer to the removal of assets from the scope of the ledger; for example, an amount owed by his brother was removed in this way from the ledger, presumably because it was to be paid (or had been paid) to Hoskins (or on his behalf) in England.

Sir John Banks (1627–99) was a wealthy merchant-cum-landowner. He was "born in middling circumstances in Maidstone, became a member and later Governor of the East India Company and acquired a very considerable fortune. He died with nearly £200,000, and left an income of almost £5,000 per annum to his daughter and co-heir who married Heneage Finch, subsequently Earl of Nottingham and Aylesford." [4] His ledgers embrace all his assets and financial activities, as is specifically stated in the inscription on the title-page of ledger C:

[3] The provenance and catalogue references of the account-books are:
    Hoskins: Goldsmiths' Library, University of London; MS. 265.
    Banks: ledgers B and D: Kent Archives Office, Maidstone; U 234 A 2,5.
        ledger C: Guildhall Library, Corporation of London; MS. 458.
    Clayton and Morris: Guildhall Library, Corporation of London; MS. 6428/1–4.
    North: Kent Archives Office, Maidstone; U 471 A 244.
    Peers: Guildhall Library, Corporation of London; MS. 10,187.
    R. du Cane: Essex Record Office, Chelmsford; D/Dc A 4.
    P. du Cane: Essex Record Office, Chelmsford; D/DDc A 13,14.
    Braund: Essex Record Office, Chelmsford; D/DRu B 3,4.
    The author is indebted to those in charge of these collections for having facilitated his examination of the records, and having attended so promptly to queries which have arisen in connection with the revision of this study for inclusion here.
[4] D. C. Coleman, "London Scriveners and the Estate Market in the Later Seventeenth Century", *Economic History Review*, 2nd ser., vol. IV (1952), p. 225. Dr. Coleman's book on Banks, *Sir John Banks, Baronet and Businessman*, has been published recently.

Leager No. C: or booke of accompts for all Marchandize, Land, Things and Persons, that concerne the reall or personall Estate of myne. or of whom ever I have to doe with: as well for what I doe owe to others, as what others doe owe to me—The Ballance of my last booke No. B being brought forward into this, wch God Prosper. And this booke begins to be written the 2^d Aprill 1672: the last booke No. B as aforsaid being fully written out:

John Banks.

The ledgers are concerned with land-owning and property transactions, financial dealings and some trading activities.

Clayton and Morris were in partnership as scriveners in the City of London.[5] Of the two partners, Robert Clayton, described by John Evelyn as "this prodigious rich scrivener", was by far the more important person. Both men were aldermen, but Clayton also served as sheriff and was Lord Mayor of London in 1679–80. He was active in Whig politics and sat in the House of Commons on several occasions. He was knighted in 1671, and "his riches provided delectable fare for satirists who noted his failure to secure a peerage." His rapid progress in civic affairs and status is well illustrated in the title, in the first of the surviving ledgers (1669–72), of the "general account" (which is best described as a combined profit-and-loss account and capital account in the name of the two partners). At first "Mr. Robert Clayton" came after the name of his partner. It then became "Robert Clayton, Esq.", and next, as "Alderman Robert Clayton", it preceded the name of his partner. It then appears on successive pages as "Sherife Clayton" and "Sr Robert Clayton".

The firm of Clayton and Morris was engaged in a variety of activities, including some which today are the concerns of financiers, bankers, solicitors, and estate agents. The surviving ledgers naturally deal with the affairs of the partnership, though the distinction between the individual partners on the one hand, and the partnership on the other, seems to have been somewhat blurred.[6] An interesting and odd feature of the ledgers is that they did not contain complete records of all partnership assets and liabilities. An example will make this clear. In 1669 the Earl of Manchester borrowed £9,500 from three lenders, the loan taking

---

[5] See Coleman, *op. cit.*, *passim*; also *D.N.B.*, XI (on Clayton).

[6] The two partners seem to have had a joint household, for the general account is debited with many entries for housekeeping expenses; for example, on 30 September 1670 it is debited with £863 "paid Mrs. Clayton at severall times to this day for housekeeping". Again, a large part of the expenditure (£3,785) in "The Accompt of Sr Robert Clayton's Mayoralty" was closed into the general account. On the other hand, the expenses of his sherifalty were transferred to Clayton's "proper" account. It is interesting that there was no division of partnership profits between the two partners during the eleven years of the ledgers. The fact that Morris left his estate to Clayton on his death in 1682 suggests the lasting intimacy between the two men, who had been fellow apprentices and then successful business partners.

the form initially of a credit on Clayton and Morris for the amount. The Earl's account was credited in full, and the accounts of two of the lenders were debited for their shares of the loan. But the £2,000 advanced by the third, Henry Avery, was not debited; instead, the amount was debited to the general account despite the fact that there was an account for Avery in the ledger. Thus a partnership asset disappeared from the books. Another example of analogous character may be noted. In the general account in ledger 11 an amount of £4,600 was credited for the sale of land to Sir William Langham. As no asset account was debited—there was in any case no account for land in the ledger—the entry almost certainly refers to the sale of land which had not been recorded in the ledger as an asset, for cash to Langham. (The cash accounts were not incorporated in the ledger and have not survived.) Here, then, a partnership asset was left outside the scope of the partnership ledger until it was transformed into cash. The credit to the capital account to record the sale of the previously unrecorded asset was the obvious double entry counter-weight to the debit entry for the receipt of the cash.

Thus the balance of the partnership capital account did not reflect the full extent of the partnership's assets and liabilities. But it is also apparent that some revenues from non-recorded assets were credited in the ledgers, presumably because the administration of these revenues was best dealt with in the organized accounting system, and the receipt of cash necessitated the usual accounting control. Thus the general account was credited with appreciable sums of rents received (£3,774 in 1674–5, £5,461 in 1679–80), though no commensurate investments in land and property appear in the ledgers. It is also probable that some of the revenues and expenditures on interest account pertained to principal sums not recorded as assets or liabilities in the ledgers. The ledgers are therefore imperfect documents for establishing the wealth of the partnership, the composition of its assets, and the rate of return on the capital employed in the business.

The exclusion of certain assets and liabilities may perhaps be explained on the grounds of the partners' desire to conceal some details of their wealth from their counting-house staff.[7] It is true that the entries for the first two transactions described above would have disclosed the

---

[7] One imagines that details of the excluded assets and liabilities were kept in other books or records, though the existence of such documents is not mentioned in the ledgers. However, in one case, at least, it is virtually certain that there were separate records. After the accounts had been closed on 30 September 1674, a large number of personal accounts of lenders and borrowers were introduced into the ledger, with corresponding entries in the general account. These clearly were for loans not previously recorded in the ledger, though, given their large number, some systematic records must have been kept. The effect of their introduction into the ledger was to convert a debit balance of £18,219 on capital (*i.e.*, the general) account into a credit balance of £1,921.

existence of the assets in question, so that the concealment would have been imperfect; but it would have involved a conscious and sustained effort on the part of any clerk to keep track of such entries over a period of years. If the maintenance of secrecy was the objective, the method used may be judged inferior to that proposed by two sixteenth-century writers on accounting, Weddington and Peele (see extracts 27 and 28). It is fair to add that by the end of the seventeenth century, secret ledgers had ceased to interest greatly the authors of accounting treatises.

Sir Dudley North (1641–91), the Turkey merchant, is well known as the author of *Discourses on Trade* (published in 1691) which has been praised as the first great exposition of free-trade doctrines.[8] At an early age he was apprenticed to a merchant in the Levant trade; later he spent many years in trade, mainly in Constantinople. He returned to England in 1680, a wealthy man, and engaged for a time in political activities. His surviving " great ledger " covers his years in London, and refers almost exclusively to his multifarious business and property-owning activities. His activities included trading with the Middle East, Lisbon, Antwerp and Hamburg, and also some insurance, money-lending and a silk-throwing venture. The ledger does not seem to include accounts for personal belongings. There is, however, an " acco. of my wifes fortune ", of which the credit balance of over £15,000 was eventually carried to the capital account.

Sir Charles Peers was knighted in 1707. He was a member of the Salters Company, and served as Lord Mayor of London in 1715–16. He was also a director of the Bank of England in 1705–07 and again in 1708–12. His surviving journal begins with his return to London from Malaga. His opening assets, set out in the first journal entry, consist largely (£2,136 out of £2,450) of his share as London partner in the Malaga partnership of William Morley and Company. Charles Peers had a one-third interest in the profits and capital, as is explained in the long narration of the opening entry. This narration contains the further information that certain of Peers's assets were not included in the ledger:

> Severalls [i.e., several different accounts] are D^{rs} to Stocke of me Charles Peers £2,450:18:02¼ for what Stockes I left behind me in Malaga as p^r our Bookes in Company wth Mr. William Morley & w^t my mother gave me since I came home; not making any acc^{tt} of my housses & lands in Brantery nor severall things of value that I have of my owne in Malaga & London; but for memorandums sake doe Booke heere how my partnershipp doth continue with Mr. Morley as p^r an article in our Journall att Malaga dated ye 30th October past from beginning of July

---

[8] For brief biographical details, see W. Letwin, "The Authorship of Sir Dudley North's 'Discourses on Trade'", *Economica*, new series, vol. XVIII (1951), p. 36.

next for two yeares more & I to have owne third part of yᵉ proffitts or losses & Mr. William Morley to have yᵉ other two third parts and soe to have our Stocks for sayd tyme in sayd housse at Malaga answerable to yᵉ shares; likewise yᵉ halfe of the furniture, horsses & cᵃ of our sayd housse in Malaga is myne for wᶜʰ Mr. Morley is to make it me good after the sayd two yeares of our Partnershipp is expired. . . .

Shortly after the opening of the journal, one of the excluded assets, " Estate in Brantery in Essex ", was introduced as an asset at £300, with a contra-credit to the capital account. Subsequently, further assets were introduced indirectly into the accounting. Thus from time to time small amounts (but occasionally a large one) were credited to profit-and-loss, representing the proceeds of sales of items not previously included as assets in the accounts. For example, £39. 16s. 0d. was received in cash for " 3 parsells for chayne ", £16 " for old plate sold ", £13 : 09 : 00 for " old quoynes my wiffe & I had by us ", and £6 : 09 : 00 " for a gold watch "; in each case the credit is to profit-and-loss account, not to capital account. Sometimes a previously excluded asset going back to Peers's sojourn in Malaga was brought into the ledger, with the balancing credit to profit-and-loss account. Thus in November, 1692, a debt of over £209 was entered to the debit of David Broad " owing to me & father Bands ". The credit to profit-and-loss is particularly striking in this case, for it is evident that the recovery of the debt was thought to be doubtful : the journal entry explains that the debt was really larger than the amount entered; but " I make no accᵗᵗ of same fearing will be all lost[,] if anything recovered whatever it is shall creditt the same to proffitt & Losse." A month later " Household Stuffe " to the sum of £600 was introduced, but with a credit to the capital account on this occasion :

> for so much I value my Jewells, plate pictures &cᵃ I have in my housse att the lowest rates are worth if was to be sold by an outcry as pʳ yᵉ particulars in a small booke intituled memorandum of C.P. in quarto.

Richard Du Cane (1681–1744) was member of parliament for Colchester in 1715–22, and a director of the Bank of England.[9] His son and heir, *Peter Du Cane* (1713–1803), was a director of the Bank of England and the East India Company. Richard's only surviving ledger covers his last years when he had withdrawn from trading. His ledger and those of his son largely concern their ownership of land and investments in joint stock companies, and their domestic expenditures. Not all the assets, however, were included in the ledgers. This is clear in repeated

---

⁹ He was a descendant of a family of Du Quesne who fled to England from Flanders during the rule of the Duke of Alva. His ledger and balance book are written in English with an admixture of French words.

entries in Richard Du Cane's "ballance book" (described below) to the following effect:

> N.B. I make no valuation of the Lease of my house in Pancrace Lane, house hold goods, Pictures, Plate Jewells &c. thô might be justly valued at £2,000.
>
> Coggeshall this 16 Jan. 1738.
>
> This day I ballanced my books and found all right.
>
> Richard Du Cane.

Moreover, an entry in a ledger account indicates that his house at Coggeshall was also not included in the accounting.[10] Peter Du Cane also excluded a similar collection of assets from his ledgers. Both capital accounts and balance accounts include such statements as:

> N.B. In the above Balance no valuation of Plate, Jewels, Household Furniture, Coaches or Horses are Included—nor Deer in ye Park.
> There are likewise standing in my Name the following Stocks—viz[t] . . . £3,800.

William Braund (1695–1774) is the subject of a monograph study by Dr. Lucy Sutherland.[11] He was "merchant, shipowner, and shipping insurer, Director of the East India Company and of the Sun Fire Office" and died "in prosperous commercial ease at the age of seventy-eight". His two surviving ledgers cover his last sixteen years, and the last asset accounts contain notes on the disposal of the assets signed by his three executors. The ledgers appear to cover all Braund's property, except household belongings.

The Balancing of the Books

This section describes the frequency of balancing the ledger, the accuracy of balancing, and the accounts specially involved in the balancing process (the profit-and-loss and balance accounts). The balancing procedures adopted throw light on the extent to which the owners of the ledgers needed brief, synoptic statements of the progress and position of their affairs and activities, as distinct from the type of information which they could obtain by paging through a ledger or by examining individual ledger accounts. My impression is that there was seldom a need for such summary statements, a conclusion which is not surprising in view of the apparently close connection between the owner and his enterprises. In several cases he was his own accountant. (Hoskins, Banks, Richard Du Cane and probably Peter Du Cane wrote

---

[10] The account entitled "Terres en Essex" included only £250 for the house and furniture at Coggeshall. This small amount was eventually written off in the ledger after the assets had passed to Peter Du Cane on the death of his father.

[11] L. S. Sutherland, *A London Merchant 1695–1774*, 1933.

up their own ledgers and Peers his journal; but Clayton and Morris certainly did not keep their books.) The balancing process, it seems, was mainly concerned with more narrowly-defined bookkeeping purposes, and the calculation of profits, for example, was probably an unimportant and incidental by-product. But such a conclusion is necessarily tentative, if only because one does not know whether other relevant accounting documents and records have disappeared.

Annual balancing was the rule in the Clayton, Peter Du Cane, and Braund ledgers. The ledger of Richard Du Cane was balanced irregularly, on six occasions in a span of nine years. The balance on the profit-and-loss account, called the "Esgalement", was usually carried to capital account (which until 1743 was not in the ledger), though on two occasions it was simply carried forward. Irregular balancing is also a feature of the Hoskins and Banks ledgers. The Hoskins ledger was balanced five times during ten years; the last balancing date is in 1665, after which the ledger entries continue in a rather ragged manner without subsequent balancing. The three successive Banks ledgers extend from 1657 to 1699, the year of Banks's death. The profit-and-loss account was balanced and closed into the stock account on 13 occasions in a period of 43 years, *viz.*, March 1658, December 1661, June 1663, May 1665, September 1666, December 1669, March 1672, June 1676, May 1679, June 1684, April 1686, October 1688 and January 1692.[12] (The irregular balancing is illustrated in the credit entries for profits in the capital account, Plate IX.) There is nothing in the Du Cane and Hoskins ledgers to indicate why the irregularly-spaced balancing dates were chosen. The same applies to the Banks ledgers, except that in one or two cases in ledger B the profit-and-loss account was balanced and closed into the capital account when the space allotted to the former had been filled with entries; and two of the balancings coincide with the opening of a new ledger.

The Peers journal, which runs to more than 390 pages and extends over more than five years, records only one complete balancing. This occurs at the termination of the journal and of the corresponding (but missing) ledger. However, on two earlier occasions some amounts of profit were transferred from the profit-and-loss account to the capital account. The first journal entry is as follows:

27 October 1690

Proffitt & Losse is D^r to stocke of me Charles Peers £649: 01: 09¾ for to make my sayd stock amount to £4000: starling judging I have att least sayd summe as appeares by sayd sume of profitt and losse not haveing att present tyme to make an entyre ballance as otherwise I would . . .

---

[12] In June 1696 several nominal account balances were closed into the profit-and-loss account, but its balance was not closed into the capital account.

In other words, there was no formal clearing of other nominal account balances into the profit-and-loss account; Peers, who was his own accountant, simply transferred an amount to raise his capital account balance to a round sum, not having the time to make a thorough balancing. At the second transfer of profits to capital, two days after Christmas 1694, he still could not find the time to balance his accounts properly:

27 December 1694

> Proffitt & Losse is D^r to Stock of me Ch: Peers . . . wch is ye least y^s day can carry from same to my Stock by ye nearest computation can make not having time to make a perfect ballance of these my bookes & begin new ones as intended but speedily hope to do it: in mean time leave in ye creditt syde of profitt & losse sufficient to countervaile household expences loss by Thompson ship D^n Carlos & Harts ship ye Larke & all other loosing acc^tts can think of at p^nt have or shall have of heithertos transactions to carry to s^d acc^tt . . .   £2400: 00: 00

(In fact, the loss on the ship *Lark* was written off to profit-and-loss less than two months later, the ship having been "taken by ye french privateers". A few months later the profit-and-loss account in the ledger was full, and both debit and credit totals were carried to a new ledger page—*i.e.*, without striking a balance. At this point debits fell short of credits by less than £1, which suggests that Peers had been none too cautious in estimating his profits.) The profit-and-loss account was finally closed to stock, to balance and close off the account as a preliminary to closing the entire ledger through the balance account. This was preparatory to the opening of a new ledger and journal. It was only when the old ledger was full that Peers could find time for a formal and comprehensive balancing.

The North ledger differs from the others in that there is no comprehensive closing of the accounts whatever. The profit-and-loss account was balanced whenever the ledger-page allotted to it was used up, but the balance was merely carried forward to the same account on the next page allotted to it. The timing of the balancing was therefore quite arbitrary. The profit-and-loss balances thrown up in the process were also arbitrary in the sense that they were not the outcome of a process of deliberate calculation; other nominal accounts were not balanced and closed into the profit-and-loss account when the latter was balanced [13]: they in turn were balanced only when their pages had been filled. Thus the balance of the "Acc^o of Rents in Bristoll", including both debits and credits and running over a period exceeding three years, was extinguished by transferring the net credit balance to profit-and-loss account as follows: "To Profitt & Loss carried to that acc^o to Ballance itt for want of room."

---

[13] The same is true of the profit-and-loss balances in the Banks ledgers whenever the filling up of the account-space did not coincide with general balancing.

The duality of entry in a system of double entry accounting provides, as is well known, a simple prima facie test of the arithmetical correctness of the ledger: at any time the sum of the debit balances in the ledger must be equal to the sum of the credit balances. Writers on accounting often praised this characteristic of the system, and instructed their readers to ferret out the source of discrepancy if the required equality was found to be lacking. It is difficult to know how often this advice was followed. In the account-books under discussion the accounts were found on at least four occasions to be out of balance, yet those concerned apparently did nothing to correct the books. The required equality was restored by cooking the books, in three cases openly, once covertly. In the Hoskins ledger there is a single entry of £53. 14. 6 (in debit) in the capital account: " Error on my books to ballance all acc°." In the profit-and-loss account in the Banks ledger C one finds a similar single entry, for £278. 3. 10: " By error wch I cannot yet finde." A sole single entry is also to be found in Peers journal: " Charges of Merchandize is D^r to no acc° . . . to ball^ce these bookes exactly to a farthing 15 : 08¾." [14]

These corrections are in line with the practice recommended by some writers (*cf.* extract 105). On the other hand, the concealed correction of error in Braund's ledger G would probably have found favour with few, if any, of them (though Roger North referred to the practice, *cf.* extract 103). The balance account of 1770, which is shown to balance, includes as a credit balance £675. 14. 6 for profit-and-loss account. (It was the practice in Braund's ledgers to carry forward some balance on this account after having transferred either a round sum of profit to capital account, or a sum sufficient to make the closing balance on capital account a round sum.) This entry raises suspicions, however, because a previously-entered amount has been erased, and this in a set of books which are generally impeccable in form and appearance. Reference to the profit-and-loss account shows that the corresponding balance is in fact £684. 6. 0; had the latter figure been inserted, the ledger's apparent equilibrium would have been upset.

It is not the point to criticise these failures to find errors and rectify the books. Not being responsible to anyone else, the owners were

[14] It would have been more appropriate to debit the profit-and-loss account. But this account had already been closed. So Peers did the next best thing, for the Charges of Merchandize account appears as a debit of over £1,000 in the balance account, *i.e.*, it had not been closed into profit-and-loss account. The explanation for this treatment of an expense account is that its balance represented outlays made by Peers which he hoped to recover by charging them against particular principals for whom he acted as agent, or against particular joint trading ventures, and so on. Indeed, earlier entries in the journal show that he had made a profit on this account by charging larger amounts than he had actually spent. On one occasion this profit had been carried to " Interest Money " account, and the narration suggests that he was, in effect, able to exact interest charges between the time of original disbursement and the time of subsequent recovery—" I here do carry it [the credit balance] to Interest mony, on acc^t pay allways ready cash in ye Custome house & in many of my sales charg'd Intrest on them . . .".

obviously at liberty to please themselves. There is evidence that in other respects, in matters touching the interests of others or in keeping check of particular assets, strict accounting was maintained, though errors of detail were made, then as now.[15] Hoskins had very detailed and careful accounts of his dealings as factor for others and in his partnership ventures. There are indications that Banks and Clayton brought " the bag and the book " together. (For example, there are occasional entries in the cash account in the Banks ledgers, " To Profitt and Loss misplaced.") And in the North ledger, where there is no sign that anyone bothered to try to balance the books as a whole, there are not only meticulous accounts for the various trading voyages, but there is also evidence of careful accounting in that the very active account with Sir Francis Child and partner, the bankers, agreed with the bankers' version, without any need for final adjustment except for an entry for twopence, " error in casting a bill of exchange."

The profit-and-loss accounts in the Peter Du Cane ledgers conform most closely with present-day practice in the sense that there is a good deal of grouping of individual incomes and expenditures into a few relevant headings. (See Plates XIV and XV.) The profit-and-loss account is preceded by an " Income " account, with debits (one for each) for " expences " and " charities " and credits for " produce of estates " and " dividends ". Each entry represents the balance of a more detailed account, which itself in some cases consists of balances of other more detailed accounts. Thus the " account of expences " brings together the balances of a number of different expense accounts (*e.g.*, " my expences ", " my childrens expences ", and " expences attending the sickness & Funeral of my most dear wife "). The profit-and-loss account takes up the balance of the income account, and also entries for losses or gains reflecting changes in the recorded value of investments in government and other securities, and building and repairs expenses. This grouping may be compared with the treatment in the Braund ledgers where the main entries in the annual profit-and-loss accounts are " sundries " entries,

---

[15] Lapses in the Clayton accounts were brought together in an " Accompt of Errors ", the balance of which was carried forward from year to year, an ever-suspended suspense account. (*Cf.* extract 103, where it is recommended that the suspense account be closed into profit-and-loss account.) The entries for errors record miscasts in the cash book (very small amounts), an instance where a debit entry in a personal account had to be reversed because " Mr. Colvil disownes ye receipt thereof ", and an opposite instance where a debit had to be made to a personal account for " a mistake of money he ownes to have been paid for him . . . not yet known whose money it is."

Similar errors in the Banks ledgers were simply corrected by adjustment entries to profit-and-loss account. The same ledgers also contain examples of two ways of correcting wrong entries as they arose. These are the neutralisation of the wrong entry by the passing of an off-setting entry, and the striking-out of the offending entry. (*Cf.* extracts 100, 101 and 102.) Errors in writing an entry are corrected as follows : " By Sund[ries] I say By Cash ", or " To new accompt in ballance : Error : O." (*Cf.* extracts 102 and 103.)

representing the totals of balances on other accounts transferred in omnibus entries to the profit-and-loss account via the journal. At the other extreme, in terms of detail, are the profit-and-loss accounts in, for example, the Banks and North ledgers. Here there is a jumble of entries with little grouping.

The Clayton ledgers are peculiar in that there is no separate profit-and-loss account. The " general " account, as has been explained, served both as a partnership capital account and as a profit-and-loss account. Thus, though there is an annual balancing, there is no single figure for the annual profit. Moreover, up to the year 1674-5 there was little grouping of similar profit-and-loss transactions in separate nominal accounts, with the exception of two accounts for petty expenses and rents, respectively; each of the numerous entries for interest was debited or credited separately to the general account. In that year, however, two new nominal accounts were opened, one for interest and the other entitled " contingent profits " (and apparently referring to incomes accruing to Clayton and Morris for acting as intermediaries in financial transactions and for " scrivening "). Subsequently the major items of income and expenditure were more conveniently grouped and annual totals presented in the " general account ", which still, of course, contained a large number of other (including capital) entries.

From contemporary treatises one learns that the profit-and-loss account was not reserved for items that would now be called of a " revenue " nature as distinct from those of a " capital " nature; and also that domestic or private expenditures were admitted to the account together with business incomes and expenditures. (*Cf.* extracts 66, 67, 68 and 69.) This is largely confirmed in the ledgers under discussion, particularly as concerns the mingling of business and private entries. Capital items (*e.g.*, the payment of marriage portions) were, however, relatively more often recorded directly in the capital account. (See Plate VIII for an example in one of the Banks ledgers.) The closest approximation to modern practice in the treatment of personal withdrawals of assets is found in the Braund ledgers. Braund's cash drawings were debited to capital account (" to cash paid Self "); this account was also debited for gifts of money to relatives and for the purchase of wine. Moreover, the capital account was on occasion credited for odd items, such as the proceeds of the sale of sheep, wool, and wheat; it is as if Braund was making a distinction between income from his main business activities and other incidental or extraneous incomes.

According to some of the treatises, a well-kept set of accounts would be completed, at balancing, with a balance account, which brought together all the account balances remaining after the closure of the profit-and-loss account into the capital account. (*Cf.* extract 91.) This balance account is the forerunner of the modern balance sheet; and like it, it was supposed to contain a listing of assets and liabilities and the equilibrating capital balance. In fact, in our group of ledgers, balance accounts appear infrequently. Only in the Peter Du Cane ledgers does the account appear regularly at each balancing, set out in the form of the modern English balance sheet, that is, with debit balances on the right-hand ("credit") side, and *vice versa*.[16] It is probable that Richard Du Cane also had a balance account at each balancing date; but in this case it did not as a rule appear in the ledger (a fact which points to the limitations of drawing conclusions from ledgers alone). A separate "ballance book" was employed, and one survives for the period 1706–1738. In it an account, roughly in the form of a balance account (again with debits and credits "reversed"), is drawn up for each of the first two balancing dates in the surviving ledger.[17] It may be assumed that the practice was continued in a lost successor to the surviving balance book.

There is only one balance account (a closing account in 1770) in the two Braund ledgers; and two closing balancing accounts in the three Banks ledgers; one at the end of each of the first two ledgers.[18] The Clayton ledgers have no balance accounts, and in this case it is unlikely that such accounts were compiled separately. (The closing entries for balances in individual accounts take the form: " By Ballance the 30th September 1672 posted to Liber 10 folio 2." Had there been a separate balance account, one would have expected the posting reference to have been to this.) There are also no balance accounts in the Hoskins ledger nor, of course, in the North ledger. From the Peers journal it appears that there was a closing balance account in the corresponding ledger, the only one in that book. This account almost certainly consisted solely of

---

[16] Some of the treatises recommend that the old set of accounts should be completed with a "closing" balance account, and that the next set of accounts should be inaugurated with an "opening" balance account, an account identical with the corresponding closing account, except for the reversal of sides. (*Cf.* extract 91.) (This practice is to be found in the ledgers of the Bank of England during the eighteenth century.) The Du Cane balances have the formal characteristic of an "opening" balance account. There is an opening balance account, appearing as the first account, in ledger C of Sir John Banks. (Plates VIII and IX.) It consists of only two entries, one omnibus entry in debit and the other in credit. The debit entry reads: "To Ballance my last Books No. B: as appears in fol 204 of sd Leager I say to Sundry Accots due to them on said Ballo as apps Jor fol. 2 . . . £100,212: 02: 11."
  Such uninformative balance accounts, both closing and opening, are to be found in some contemporary treatises.

[17] The Du Cane ledger did not have an ordinary capital account. Entries in the "Esgalement" account suggest that the periodic profit balances were transferred to a capital account in the "livre prive". A capital account was eventually introduced into the ordinary ledger in 1743.
  It seems likely in fact that the "ballance book" and the "livre prive" are the same book, in which case it is not of the type of secret ledger described by Weddington and Peele (see extracts 27 and 28).

[18] There is also one opening balance account in Banks ledger C, referred to in footnote 16. Unlike this account, the two closing balance accounts are set out in detail in the ledgers.

two equal but opposite omnibus entries, the journal entry for the debit being:

> Ballance is D^r to Sev^{lls} £18502: 16: 00¾ for ballance of these bookes N^o A wch y^s day do carry over to new bookes no B and are as p^r pticulars here underneath v^{zt} . . . [a long list of asset balances].

Pre-payments, Accruals and the Anticipation of Profits

In modern accounting the stress is on the calculation of periodic net income or profit. Much attention is paid to the correct assignment of items of revenue and outlay to particular accounting periods, and a number of rules and conventions have been established for dealing with the difficulties inherent in a situation in which the enterprise is continuing and the accounting periods are arbitrarily-determined short intervals. By contrast, in the group of account-books under discussion little attention seems to have been given to this aspect of the accounting problem; and it is rare to find deliberate procedures for the calculation, at general balancing dates, of periodic profits on continuing business activities.

The neglect of what today is called accrual accounting is evident in the treatment of interest on debts, a class of transaction prominent in several of the ledgers. There is no thorough-going attempt in any of the ledgers to make allowance for accrued interest at balancing dates, though sometimes, but not consistently, a number of entries for unpaid interest were put through at balancing dates in the Banks ledgers. The most common practice was to make the entry for interest when, or after, the interest payment became due, without adjustment at balancing dates. Thus in the Clayton ledger 9, for example, the personal account of Sir Robert Vyner, the noted banker, was debited on 4 January 1671 with an amount " Paid them [Clayton and Morris] more Intr of all moneys upon acc^t to this day " [19]; there were no adjusting entries on the preceding or succeeding balancing dates (on 30 September annually). Sometimes the entry was made when the interest was received or paid. A good example is in the Braund ledger F, where a personal account was debited " To Interest on £1017. 16. 8 for(?) 3 Febry 1757 to 3 Sep^t 1761 is 4 year 7 m at 5 per cent " on the day on which the debtor settled his account. There were no entries for accrued interest in the preceding four years. The same neglect of accruals is to be seen in the Clayton and Banks ledgers in the treatment of rents and, in the former, of " contingent profits ".[20]

---

[19] In the Clayton ledgers the terms " paid " and " received " are often used instead of " debit " and " credit ". The use of the terms does not necessarily indicate a cash payment or receipt.

[20] I have not found any example of the practice of entering interest as an addition to the face value of the debt, or of the rent for the whole period of tenancy, at the beginning

Braund, however, was careful to make year-end adjustments, with calculations of annual profits, in his Account of Assurances, which records his activity in marine insurance. At the end of each year a credit balance was carried down to the next year's account—this presumably was the estimate of probable claims against Braund on unexpired policies; and the credit balance on the old account, the profit, went to profit-and-loss account. In fact, these profit figures were calculated as round sums (*e.g.*, £500, £1,800).

This " modern " approach may be contrasted with that found in the Clayton ledgers. An important example is provided by the revenues and expenditures on postfines [21] recorded in the postfines accounts. These dealings were conducted in equal partnership with the banker, Vyner. In ledger 9, covering three years, a credit balance of over £7,000 was accumulated without any credit being taken to profit-and-loss. At the first balancing date in the next ledger a large sum was credited to the general account for profit (and, of course, an equal sum to Vyner's personal account), with a credit balance of over £1,600 remaining. No adjustment or division of profits was recorded at the next balancing date, but about nine months later the whole of the credit balance was divided equally between the general account and Vyner's account. At the end of the ledger (about three months later) the new credit balance of £1,300 was carried forward without adjustment. A similar erratic recording and division of profits is found in " An Accompt of the Coale Farme ", again a joint venture with other persons. In the first two ledgers (covering six years) profits were calculated and divided on seven occasions, but never on a general balancing date; and between November 1672 and July 1674 no profits were divided or entered. On each division of profit a credit balance remained undivided, and there were no adjustments on the general balancing dates. There are further examples of the same procedure—or lack of it as judged by the criteria of present-day practice. In two instances it would appear that no adjustment for profit or loss was made throughout the eleven years covered by the four ledgers. These are the " Accompt of Brownsea Island ", in which, among other entries, some sales of " coperas " are recorded, and the " Irish Adventure ", which seems to have been concerned, *inter alia*, with some iron workings in Ireland.

---

of the period of debt (or tenancy). Examples are present in Sir Thomas Gresham's accounts (see Peter Ramsey, " Some Tudor Merchants' Accounts ", A. C. Littleton and B. S. Yamey (eds.), *Studies in the History of Accounting*, 1956, pp. 197-8). The practice is also referred to in some later treatises. (*Cf.* extracts 70 and 71.)

[21] Postfines refer to the fees paid to some branch of the Exchequer on the writs which were taken out in connection with " final concords " (fictitious suits used to assure the title to land, *e.g.*, on conveyances or settlements). Rights to receive these fees constituted saleable assets, of which Clayton and Morris acquired a collection.

In the account-books there are several examples of the anticipation of profit, in the sense that the profit-and-loss account is credited for amounts which in modern practice would be regarded as belonging to the profits of later periods; though, as the Braund ledgers show in their treatment of the profit on assurance business, this was not universal. These anticipations are of two kinds. First, particular sums were credited to profit-and-loss account even though part of the sum related to payment for future services or obligations, and no adjustment for the unexpired obligation was made at the balancing of the accounts. Thus in both the Peers and Banks accounts, apprenticeship fees payable to them in lump sums were carried straight to profit-and-loss, although they entailed obligations for several years ahead. (See Plate XI.) It is apparent that the profit-and-loss account was credited as the obvious double entry counterweight to the payment by, or indebtedness of, the other party. Another example is in Banks ledger D, where Banks credited to profit-and-loss the whole of a single payment of £900 to him for a life annuity of £100. The narration in the journal entry (29 April 1686) is:

> For so much paid me upon condition that I do pay him £100 per ann. for his life half-yearly and after his life the £900 to me and the annuity to cease, for which sum he hath my receipt and he is paid in rent book in full to Lady Day 1686.

The accounting treatment is explicable in the same way as the treatment of apprenticeship fees, though the anticipation of profits was, in this instance, shown later to be especially "unrealistic", for the annuitant outlived Banks who died in 1699.

The second kind of anticipation of profits is also illustrated in the Banks ledgers. From time to time Banks bought for cash (or its equivalent) various types of promises to pay at some future date. He paid less than the face value of the instruments of debt; but in each case the face value was debited to the appropriate asset account, the balancing credit for the difference being to profit-and-loss account. Not only was this profit subject to hazard, but its very existence depended upon the expiry of time. It seems that for purposes of financial administration Banks was interested in the face value of the debts, and that he was not concerned with the careful statement of profits. (The same explanation probably holds for the anticipation of interest or rents inherent in the method of recording these items that is explained in footnote 20.) The discrepancy between the price paid and the face value was conveniently credited to the hold-all profit-and-loss account. Similar entries, but in reverse, with debits to profit-and-loss account, were made when Banks sold any of the debts in question (or parts of them) to others for cash.

195

Merchandise Accounts

Merchandise accounts are not common in our ledgers, and we do not know how Braund, Clayton, or Peter Du Cane—those whose books were balanced annually—would have dealt with them on balancing dates in order to reflect the profit or loss to date. The difficulty of accounting for unfinished merchandise trading ventures was avoided in the North ledger, for this was not balanced at all; for our purposes this is unfortunate, since there are many voyage and trading accounts in the North ledger. This leaves the Hoskins, Banks, Richard Du Cane and Peers account-books, all of which contain examples.

In the Hoskins ledger there is an important account for Cherbourg canvas. This account was carefully kept, with details of quantities bought and sold (in inner columns) in the ledger, amplified by more details in the entries in the journal which constitutes the first half of the volume. The detail may be explained in part by the fact that, except for a short time, Hoskins was in this branch of his activities in partnership with another person. The account runs from the beginning of the ledger in 1655 to 1665. It was balanced on eleven occasions; yet on only two (possibly three) occasions was it balanced on a general balancing date. There was clearly no attempt to assign profits on this account accurately to the (irregular) accounting periods marked off by the closing of the profit-and-loss accounts. Usually a balance of unsold stock was carried forward, but there is no indication of the basis of valuation. There is a similar lack of synchronisation between the general closing of the accounts and the particular closing of the " acc° of provisions " (*i.e.*, commissions received), another account the profits of which were shared with a partner.

In the Banks ledger C, an account for coffee, calicoes, and pepper, which includes both purchases and sales, was simply carried forward at the end of ledger C, without any calculation of profit or loss. An " Acc° Hopps ", with debits for receipts of hops in 1689, 1691 and 1693 and credits for disposals in 1689, 1690, 1694 and 1695, had no profit calculation at the balancing date in 1692, and was eventually closed in 1695. An account for horses, including quantity columns, showing both purchases and sales, was almost invariably closed simply by bringing down the difference between debits and credits. Only one entry for profit-and-loss has been found in the three ledgers. Generally, the Banks ledgers reveal no serious attempt to ensure that the profit-and-loss account for a given period included all gains and losses. A " brokeridge " account runs from 1660 to 1664 without any transfer to profit-and-loss account— there were general balancings in 1661 and 1663—until the account-space was filled.

There is only one merchandise trading account in the Richard Du Cane ledger, for " coccenille ". This account opens with a stock of six " sacs ". In two of the irregular accounting periods there were sales of one and two sacks, respectively. Yet there are no entries for profit or loss at general balancing dates; the simple balance, *i.e.*, debits less credits, was merely carried forward. It was not until after Du Cane's death that the account was closed, and the profit calculated, at the time when his son, Peter, took over the assets and closed his father's books.

In the Peers journal, the profit or loss on a completed goods account was taken to the profit-and-loss account; for example: " Profitt & Losse are D^{rs} to Hempe by Velez merch^t £15: 03: 06 to ballance sayd accompt lost by sayd Hempe . . .". But there are no entries for profit or loss to date on uncompleted accounts when the ledger was finally balanced and closed.

The Valuation of Fixed Assets

In seventeenth and eighteenth century accounting treatises it is common for a fixed asset account to record both the capital value involved in the ownership of the asset, and also the current payments and receipts arising from its ownership and operation. This method is found in our eight sets of account-books (for example, see Plates XII and XIII); though occasionally separate accounts were kept for an asset and for its attendant income and current expenditures.

In the accounting treatises, three alternative treatments of fixed assets and the income from them can be distinguished. First, the net income (receipts *less* payments other than the cost of the asset) is transferred to the profit-and-loss account, the asset being carried forward at cost. Second, the balance of the account is carried forward, that is, the original cost *plus* expenses *less* receipts is carried forward, with no entry to profit-and-loss account. Third, the asset is revalued and its new value is carried forward, the difference left on the account, whether gain or loss, being taken to profit-and-loss account. These three bases of " valuation " may conveniently be called the cost, arithmetical balance, and revaluation bases, respectively. The cost basis, or a variant of it, is of course the most usual in modern accounting.

All three valuation bases are to be found in the ledgers under discussion. There was no standard practice; and sometimes different bases were used for different assets in the same ledger, and even for the same asset at different balancing dates. As compared with modern practice, there was no aversion to the upward or downward revaluation of fixed assets (with the resulting difference taken to the profit-and-loss account); nor was there meticulous concern with the distinction between capital and revenue elements. In the valuation of fixed assets, as in the allocation of revenues to accounting periods, there was no consistent or rigorous application of any clear concept of periodic profit or income, or of any single set of accounting procedures.

The ledgers of the two Du Canes are perhaps the most consistent in their treatment of investments in that annual revaluation of securities is almost the rule, though simple arithmetical balancing occurs in the account for the investment in the Free British Fishery in the Peter Du Cane ledger C; and sometimes the previous year's valuation was repeated. On the accounts for land, etc., however, the cost or original valuation was simply carried forward without change; in this case the incomes were dealt with in separate nominal accounts.

Revaluation also occurs frequently in the Braund ledgers. The account for the investment in Sun Fire Shares opened at £3,000 in 1758. It was then raised to £4,000 and kept at this figure until 1764 when it was "valued at" £5,000. It was successively raised to £5,500 in 1769, £6,000 in 1771 and £6,250 in 1773. The accounts for 4% Consolidated Annuities, East India Stock, and East India Bonds include both revaluations and mere arithmetical balances. (The 4% Consols account for 1753–57 is shown in Plates XII and XIII.) Braund also revalued some of his landed property from time to time. For example, the estate at Hacton in Upminster was revalued downwards by almost £3,000 in 1766, and then upwards by about £160 in 1767 to produce a round asset "value" of £6,000. The balance in the account for Houses in Crane Court and Bucklers Bury in London was also raised, at intervals, from £1,500 to £2,600. The fairly numerous accounts for ships disclose examples of revaluations and also of arithmetical balances.

Banks had a substantial investment in the stock of the East India Company, and we may trace its inconsistent and apparently haphazard accounting treatment in ledgers C and D (1672–84, 1684–99). When the first account-space was filled, there was a revaluation: "now is worth 210 p.c.° God be praysed, to be sold and soe by me valued." There was another revaluation when the next space was filled, though no detail is given. About three years later there was a revaluation at 260, with a transfer to a new folio though the space was not filled. About a year later the procedure was repeated, at 270, and again, at the end of 1681, at 400, though this time the space was filled. In June 1682 there was a further closing: "the said Stock 2000 per contra [*i.e.*, £2,000 paid up] being doubled by a dividend so that it now is Stock 4,000 as appears by the Comp^a books—the wch 4000 stock is now worth 310[1] . . . and soe my 4,000 Stock worth this day God be praysed £12,400"—a capital gain of £4,400, carried with obvious pleasure to profit-and-loss account. A new account was opened on another page, though the old space was not filled. There were now several purchases at prices which ranged from 204 to 360, and one lot was sold "at cost". Nevertheless, at the closing of ledger C there was no revaluation, but the balance—in this case, however, after the dividends had been taken to profit-and-loss—was simply carried forward. It is interesting that in ledger C there were no revaluations on any general balancing date; the revaluations took place either when the account-space was filled or when Banks chose to make them. Hence, in effect, there were no more than simple arithmetical balances on the account at general balancing dates. The account in the new ledger D opens with a debit of £25,155. Nothing was done on the first balancing date. On the second date, in 1688, the £4,450 nominal—there had been a big sale in 1685—was carried forward at £15,531, " heer valued as was worth, & hoope may be." But this was an arithmetical balance (not a revaluation), after, however, dividends had been taken to profit-and-loss account; that is, no profit or loss on the disposal of part of the holding was computed or removed to profit-and-loss account. During the next thirty months the rest of the holding of stock was sold off, the last sale at 153½. A heavy book loss of £4,697 was incurred; this was taken to the account of " doubtfull debts ", a procedure which is quite inexplicable, except that it suggests that Banks was reluctant to admit his mistake. The same treatment was also followed for a loss on a small investment in " Ye Royall Fishery ".

Banks' account of " Fee Farme Rents Purchased from ye King "—rights to income acquired from the Crown—also has similar features, with the same tendency to disregard balancing dates and to record unrealised profits on revaluation. There was, however, no revaluation in ledger C: the costs of successive purchases were debited, the proceeds of sales credited, and the arithmetical balance carried forward, on one occasion misleadingly labelled " for the cost of my present fee farme rents." At the end of the ledger the account stood at £19,121 (in debit). On the first balancing date in ledger D, a profit of £8,052 was taken to profit-and-loss account. A detailed entry in the corresponding journal indicates that the new valuations were based on a capitalisation at 12 years' purchase for those rents held " in reversion " and at 20 years' purchase for those " in possession ". The succeeding journal entry records the profit " beinge by valuation of the reversions from the time of the disburse of my mony til now "; that is to say, no profit on sales or on capital appreciation had been calculated for a period exceeding 14 years. The next revaluation (of the rents in reversion) took place three years after the next balancing date. And more than two years later, another balancing date having been skipped, there was a final revaluation of the two classes of fee farm rents, at 18 and 21 years' purchase, respectively. The journal entry for the profit on the revaluation of the rents in reversion runs: " beinge soe much as now worth, advanced by them for my forbearance as I compute at present."

Bad and Doubtful Debts

The accounting treatment of bad and doubtful debts is a particular aspect of the valuation of assets. The early treatises suggest two approaches which were to some extent alternatives. First, when a debt is thought to be irrecoverable, it is written off to profit-and-loss account. However, there is often a possibility that the debtor's circumstances might improve and that he might be able to pay his old debts. Hence in the second method the account is not written off, but is transferred (with other similar debtors' balances) to a suitably-titled account which serves as a reminder to the merchant of his dubious debts; the grouping of the several doubtful balances in one account disencumbers the ledger of some unnecessary and space-filling accounts, and reduces the work involved in transferring balances from one ledger to its successor. (*Cf.* extracts 81 and 82.) [22]

Both methods are to be seen in our group of account-books. The first method is best exemplified in Braund's ledger G. Here, it may be recalled, a balance account was made up at the end of 1770. At this time debts to the total of £789 were written off against profit-and-loss account. A loose sheet of paper headed " Account of Debts wch carried to Profit & Loss 1770 " lists nine debtors' accounts with entries such as " I suppose worth nothing ", or " he failed, have not proved the debt ". The Peers journal has several entries for the elimination of bad debts. One example reads:

> . . . Richard Overman £10 to ballance his acc^{tt} to this day wch I looke upon to be a bad debt if anything ever can be recovered of him must be creditted agayne to proffitt & losse.

(For another example, see Plate XI.)

The second and less familiar method was adopted by Banks and Peter Du Cane. In the Banks ledger C on the final balancing date, the balances on 23 debtors' accounts were transferred to " doubtfull Debts ", and the total of this account (£1,001) appears in the balance account among the asset balances. (The journal entry is shown on Plate X.) In the next ledger there are further transfers from other personal accounts with entries such as " owinge by them, w^h place heer til be receaved " or " brought here til payd ". (The account also includes the losses on East India and Royal Fishery stock already referred to.) The new balance of over £7,000 is carried through the ledger unchanged. The

---

[22] The segregation of doubtful debtors' balances in a collective asset account seems to have been a widespread practice; see, for example, J. Heers, *Le Livre de Comptes de Giovanni Piccamiglio homme d'affaires Génois*, Paris, 1959, p. 96; J. Denucé, *Inventaire des Affaitadi Banquiers Italiens a Anvers de l'Année 1568*, Antwerp, 1934, pp. 119, 144 and 149; O. ten Have, *De Leer van het Boekhouden tijdens de Zeventiende en Achttiende Eeuw*, Delft, 1933, p. 279; and Stuart W. Bruchey, *Robert Oliver and Mercantile Book-keeping in the Early Nineteenth Century*, unpublished thesis, Johns Hopkins University, Baltimore, p. 86.

Peter Du Cane ledger C has an account "Doubtfull and Bad Debts" which opens with a debit balance of £200 brought forward. During the first year, 1754, a small sum was received from one of the doubtful debtors, and the proceeds were properly credited. In 1755 three Lisbon debts were added: "I suppose to be bad since the destruction of Lisbon by an Earthquake the 1 Novr last." At the end of the year £499. 12. 2 was written off to profit-and-loss account, and the debit balance of £50 carried forward unchanged through 1756 and the succeeding ledger D.

The treatment in both the Banks and the Peter Du Cane ledgers does not tell us how the owners would have been able to know which debtors' accounts had been brought into the omnibus account, since the details of the debts were not carried forward on the periodic closing and re-opening of the account. Presumably a separate memorandum was kept outside the ledger; but if this was done, there was little point in not writing them off completely, assuming that the main purpose of the procedure, as some of the treatises imply, was to reduce the number of dead accounts cluttering up the ledger and adding to the labour of balancing.[23] Whatever the answer may be, the procedure suggests, particularly in the Banks ledgers, an attitude to profit calculation and asset statement quite different from that now governing accounting practice.

[23] The segregation of records of doubtful debtors outside the ledger is illustrated in James Peele's *Pathewaye to Perfectnes*, 1569. In the illustrative example, six "doutfull detters" are listed at the end of the opening inventory; but the amounts owing by them are not included in the arithmetic of the inventory, nor are accounts opened for them in the ensuing ledger—according to the text, they are "set aparte, to be kept in minde, but reserved out of thaccompte." When some of the debtors make payments, the entries in the inventory are suitably annotated; in the ledger, the profit-and-loss account is credited in the absence of the personal accounts.

The celebrated Datini archives, mainly of late fourteenth-century records and account-books of Francesco di Marco Datini, merchant of Prato, include some *libri dei ma' debitori* (books of bad debtors). Doubtful debts, written off in the ledger, were entered in separate personal accounts in these books, kept outside the accounting system, to serve as reminders of the existence of the debts. See F. Melis, *Aspetti della Vita Economica Medievale (Studi nell'Archivio Datini di Prato)*, Siena, 1962, vol. 1, p. 379.

BIBLIOGRAPHY: BOOKS ON ACCOUNTING IN ENGLISH, 1543–1800

Books are listed by authors, arranged chronologically according to the date of the first entry for each author listed. In this respect it follows similar lines to Cosmo Gordon, *Bibliography of Bookkeeping*, vol. II of the catalogue published in 1937 by the Institute of Chartered Accountants in England and Wales, and H. W. Thomson and B. S. Yamey, "Bibliography of Bookkeeping and Accounts—1494 to 1650", *Accounting Research*, October 1958.

The bibliography is compiled on the basis of the collections of the Institute of Chartered Accountants in England and Wales and of the Institute of Chartered Accountants of Scotland, augmented by information from a number of sources, notably Arthur H. Woolf, *A Short History of Accountants and Accountancy*, 1912, and David Murray, *Chapters in the History of Bookkeeping, Accountancy and Commercial Arithmetic*, 1930. All the bibliographies and the two sources referred to above are now out of print.

Abbreviations:

E: In the collection of the Institute of Chartered Accountants in England and Wales.

S: In the collection of the Institute of Chartered Accountants of Scotland.

*:   Photo-copy only.

Ext: Numbered extracts from the work of the author included in Part One of this book.

Ref: Books or articles (identified by numbers) on the history of accounting listed on pages 225, 226, below, containing some discussion of the author or his book(s).

OLDCASTLE (HUGH)

A Profitable Treatyce called the Instrument or Boke to learne to knowe the good order of the kepyng of the famouse reconynge called in Latyn, Dare and Habere, and in Englyshe, Debitor and Creditor.

4to. John Gough, 1543

Ref: 1, 2, 3, 10, 12, 13, 18, 19, 20, 21, 22.

YMPYN CHRISTOFFELS (JAN)

A Notable and very excellente woorke, expressyng and declaryng the maner and forme how to kepe a boke of accõptes or reconynges . . . Translated . . . out of Frenche into Englishe.

4to. 19 ll. (Richard Grafton), 1547. E*

Ext: 2, 15, 33, 98, 99.
Ref: 1, 2, 4, 5, 6, 7, 9, 10, 12, 14, 16, 18, 20, 22.

PEELE (JAMES)

The Maner and fourme how to kepe a perfecte reconyng, after the order of the moste worthie and notable accompte, of debitour and creditour . . .

Fo. 87 ll. Richard Grafton, 1553. E

The Pathwaye to perfectnes, in th'accomptes of Debitour and Creditour . . .

Fo. 213 ll. T.Purfoot, 1569. E*

Ext: 13, 14, 20, 26, 28, 41, 45, 83.
Ref: 2, 10, 11, 12, 15, 19, 20, 22, 26, 27.

WEDDINGTON (JOHN)

A Breffe Instruction, and manner, howe to kepe, merchantes bokes, of accomptes . . .

4to. 129 ll. Antwerp, Peter van Keerberghen, 1567. E*

Ext: 16, 19, 27, 37, 78, 91.
Ref: 20, 27.

MELLIS (JOHN)

A Briefe Instruction and maner how to keepe bookes of Accompts after the order of debitor and creditor . . .

8vo. 140 ll. John Windet, 1588. E

Ext: 18, 40, 56, 64.
Ref: 1, 2, 3, 12, 13, 18, 19, 20, 21, 22, 26.

BROWN (JOHN)

The Marchants Avizo very necessarie for their sonnes and servants, when they first send them . . . to Spaine and Portingale . . .

4to. 64 ll. Richard Field for William Norton, 1589

—— another edition

Thomas Orwin, 1590

—— another edition

Thomas Orwin, 1591

—— another edition

4to. John Norton, 1607

—— another edition

4to. 70 pp. John Bill, 1616. E

—— another edition

4to. E.G. for Richard Whitaker, 1640

Ref: 17, 20.

[PETRI (NICOLAUS)]

The Pathway to Knowledge . . . of keeping of a marchants booke, after the Italian manner . . . written in Dutch, and translated into English. (Translated by W.P.).

4to. 129 ll. William Barley, 1596. E

Ref: 2, 12, 19, 20.

TAP (JOHN)

The Path-way to Knowledge; containing the whole Art of Arithmeticke . . . wherewith is also adjoyned a briefe order for the keeping of marchants bookes of accompts, by way of debitor and creditor.

8vo. 216 ll. Th. Purfoot, 1613. E

Ref: 12, 19.

MALYNES (GERARD)

Consuetudo, vel Lex Mercatoria, or the ancient law-merchant . . .

Fo. 501 pp. Adam Islip, 1622. E.

—— another edition

Fo. 501 pp. Adam Islip, 1629. E

—— another edition

Fo. 333 pp. Adam Islip, 1636. E.

—— another edition

Fo. 333 pp. William Hunt, 1656. E

—— third edition

Fo. 340 pp. For T.Basset, 1686. E

Ext: 38.
Ref: 2, 12, 19, 22.

CARPENTER (JOHN)

A Most Excellent Instruction for the exact and perfect keeping Merchants Bookes of accounts, . . .

Fo. 141 pp. I.B. for James Boler, 1632. E.

Ext: 23, 51, 65, 66.
Ref: 2, 12, 19, 22, 25, 26.

HANDSON (RALPH)

Analysis or resolution of Merchants Accompts.

[Broadside] 3rd edition. Nicholas Bourne, 1633

—— fourth edition

33 × 43 cm. I ll. W.G. for Robert Horne, 1669. E

—— fifth edition

35 × 45 cm. I ll. Thomas Horne, 1700. E

Ext: 49, 50.
Ref: 12, 25.

DAFFORNE (RICHARD)

The Merchants Mirrour: or, directions for the perfect ordering and keeping of his accounts; . . .

Fo. 163 ll. R.Young for Nicolas Bourne, 1635. E.

—— second edition

Fo. 160 ll. J.L. for Nicolas Bourn, 1651. E

—— third edition

Fo. 206 ll. R.H. and J.G. for Nicolas Bourn, 1660. E

—— another edition

Fo. 161 ll. Miles Flesher for Robert Horne, 1684. E.

The Apprentices time-entertainer accomptantly; or a methodical meanes to obtain the exquisite art of accomptantship . . .

4to. 124 ll. R.Young for Nicolas Bourne, 1640. E

—— third edition by John Dafforne . . .

4to. 123 ll. W.Godbid, 1670. E.

The English Merchants Companion: or, an Entertainment for the Young Merchants, . . . the perfect method of merchants book-keeping . . . 4th edition.

4to. 118 ll. For Tho. Horne, 1700. E

Ext: 7, 29, 43, 60, 67, 72, 94.
Ref: 2, 9, 11, 12, 19, 22, 26.

Collins (John)

An Introduction to merchants accounts.

Fo. 46 ll. James Flesher, 1653. E

—— another edition

1664

—— another edition

1665

—— another edition

Fo. William Godbid, 1674. S

—— another edition

Fo. 62 ll. William Godbid, 1675. E

Several points very necessary to be known by a merchant, . . .

13 ll. [1660]. E*

The Perfect Method of merchants-accompts demonstrated.

Fo. 62 ll. For Thomas Horne, 1697. E

Ref: 8, 19.

Marius (John)

Advice concerning Bills of Exchange . . . with (short instructions how to keep merchants books of account . . .). Fourth edition.

Fo. 24 ll. Robert Horne, 1684. E

Liset (Abraham)

Amphithalami, or, The Accomptants Closet, being an abbridgment of Merchants-Accounts kept by debitors and creditors . . .

Fo. 58 ll. James Flesher, 1660. E

—— another edition

Fo. 56 ll. Miles Flesher, 1684. E.S.

Ref: 19.

Willsford (Thomas)

The Scales of commerce and trade . . . with . . . merchants accounts by debitor and creditor . . .

8vo. 168 ll. J.G. for N.Brook, 1660. E

Browne (Thomas)

Merchants' Accompts epitomized, illustrated by two demonstrations . . .

Fo. I ll. 1666

—— another edition

Fo. I ll. 1674

The Accurate-Accomptant: or, London-Merchant: containing an analysis for instructions and directions for . . . Merchants Accompts, . . .

Fo. 1668

—— another edition

Fo. 15 ll. Will. Godbid, 1669. E

—— another edition

Fo. W.Godbid, 1670

—— another edition

Fo. 1673

—— another edition

Fo. 1674

—— another edition

Fo. 1678

The Infallible, most accurate . . . Method of Merchants' Accounts . . .

1680

Ref: 11, 19.

Every (John)

Speculum Mercativum. Or The Young Merchants . . . Accompts, after the Italian way of Debitor and Creditor . . .

Fo. 1673

Monteage (Stephen)

Debtor and Creditor made easie: or, a short instruction for the attaining the right use of Accounts . . . :

4to. 86 ll. John Richardson, 1675. E

—— second edition

4to. 105 ll. John Richardson, 1682. E.

—— third edition

4to. 105 ll. John Richardson, 1690. E

—— another edition

4to. 120 ll. T.W. for Benj. Billingsley, 1708. E.

Advice to the women and maidens of London.

4to. 16 ll. (c. 1677). E

Instructions for Rent-Gatherers Accompts, &c. made easie.

4to. 18 ll. J.Richardson, 1683. E

—— another edition

4to. 16 ll. For Benj. Billingsley, 1708. E

Ext: 6.
Ref: 19, 22, 28.

Vernon (John)

The Compleat Comptinghouse: or, The young lad taken from the writing school, and fully instructed . . . in keeping accompts . . .

8vo. 132 ll. J.D. for Benj. Billingsley, 1678. E.

—— third edition

12mo. 108 ll. For Benj. Billingsley, 1698. E

206

—— fifth edition

12mo. 192 ll. For T.Payne, 1722. E.S.

—— seventh edition

8vo. 126 ll. Dublin, G.Grierson, 1734

—— eighth edition

8vo. 126 ll. Dublin, George Grierson, 1741. E

Ext: 68.
Ref: 19.

CHAMBERLAIN (R.)

The Accomptants Guide or Merchants Book-Keeper, . . .

4to. 136 ll. For John Clark, 1679. E

Ref: 19.

COLINSON (ROBERT)

Idea Rationaria, or the perfect accomptant, . . . containing the true
forme of book-keeping, according to the Italian methode . . .

Fo. 144 ll. Edinburgh, David Lindsay and others, 1683. E.S.

Ext: 3, 30, 76.
Ref: 2, 19.

HALE (SIR MATTHEW)

A Short Treatise touching Sheriffs Accompts . . . to which is added,
A tryal of witches . . .

8vo. 1683. E

—— another edition

8vo. 143 pp. For D.Brown and others, 1716. E

H. (N.)

The Compleat Tradesman . . . second edition.

14 cm. 180 pp. For John Dinton, 1684. S

—— another edition

14 cm. 191 pp. Thomas Norris, 1720. S

AYRES (JOHN)

Trades-man's Copy-Book, or Apprentices Companion.

1688

HAWKINS (JOHN)

Clavis Commercii: or, the key of commerce: shewing the true
method of keeping Merchants Books . . .

20 cm. 190 pp. Sarah Passinger, 1689. S

—— second edition: by John Raynor.

4to. 121 ll. For Eben. Tracey, 1704. E

Ref: 19.

HATTON (EDWARD)

The Merchant's Magazine: or, trades-man's treasury. containing
. . . merchants accompts . . .

4to. 178 pp. For Chr. Coningsby, 1695. E.S.

—— second edition

4to. 258 pp. J.Heptinstall for Chr. Coningsby, 1697. E

—— third edition

                 4to. 258 pp. J.H. For Chr. Coningsby, 1699. E

—— fifth edition

          4to. 264 pp. E.M. for Chr. Coningsby and Dan Midwinter, 1707. E.S.

—— sixth edition

                J.H. for Christopher Coningsby, 4to. 1712. S

—— seventh (edition)

                4to. 260 pp. For Chr. Coningsby, 1719. E

—— eighth (edition)

                4to. 276 pp. J.Knapton and others, 1726. E

—— ninth (edition)

                4to. 276 pp. J.Knapton and others, 1734. E

     Ext: 106.
     Ref: 19.

MATHER (WILLIAM)

The Young Man's Companion, Or Arithmetic made easie . . . [with] Rules and Directions for Book-keeping, or Merchants Accompts. Fourth edition.

                12mo. 1695

—— eighth edition

                12mo. 1710

—— seventeenth edition

                1741

—— another seventeenth edition

          12mo. 231 ll. For R.Ware, 1747

—— twentieth edition

        17 cm. 445 pp. For R.Ware and others, 1755. S

—— twenty-fourth edition

                18mo. 1755

     Ref: 19.

AMMONET (S.)

The Key of Knowledge for all Merchants, shewing . . . Debtor and Creditor . . .

                Dublin. 1696

WEIR (JAMES)

Ready Accomptant, or Book-Keeping reform'd . . .

                4to. 1700

A New Remembrancer for young Accomptants . . .

                4to. 1706

Italian Book-Keeping, reduced into an Art . . . : second edition.

                1720

—— another second edition

        4to. 164 ll. For J.Hodges &c., (c. 1740). E

SNELL (CHARLES)

Rules for Book-keeping, according to the Italian manner: now in general use . . .

28 cm. 8 ll. John Place, 1701. E

The Elements of Italian Book-keeping or, Merchants Accompts

17 cm. 24 pp. (c. 1710). S

Accompts for Landed-Men: or; a plain and easie form which they may observe, in keeping accompts of their Estates.

29 cm. 16 ll. For Thomas Baker, (1711). E

A Short and easy Method after which Shop-keepers may state, post and balance their books of accompts.

15 cm. 35 pp. For Tho. Norris, (1714). E

—— another edition

14 cm. 35 pp. For Tho. Norris, (1718). E

The Merchants Counting-House: or, waste-book instances . . .

29 cm. 22 pp. For Jonas Brown, 1718. E

Book-keeping, in a Method proper to be observ'd by super-cargos and Factors . . . second edition.

29 cm. 6 ll. For John Bateman, 1719. E

(Charles Snell in his examination of the books of Turner and company . . . Anonymous.) 39 cm. I ll. (1721). E

Charles Snell, writing master and accomptant, his answer to a paper without a name, relating to his examination of the books of Sawbridge and Company.

31 cm. I ll. (1721). E

Observations made upon examining the books of Sawbridge and company.

31 cm. 2 ll. (1721). E

Ref: 19.

FORBES (WILLIAM)

A Methodical Treatise concerning Bills of Exchange.

16 cm. 178 pp. Edinburgh, Andrew Anderson, 1703. S

RICHARDS (THOMAS)

The Gentlemans Auditor: or a new and easie method for keeping accompts of Gentlemens Estates . . .

4to. 14 ll. For Jno. Chantry, 1707. E

—— third edition

4to. 15 ll. For John Chantry, 1707. E

The Young accomptant's Tutor: or, brief rules for the most exact keeping of shop-books . . .

4to. 20 ll. W.P., 1710. E

ALLEINE (JOSEPH)

An Introduction to Bookkeeping, or Rules to find Debtors and Creditors . . .

8vo. 1711

—— another edition

1731. E

NICHOLAS (ABRAHAM)

The Young Accomptant's Debtor and Creditor.

1711

—— second edition

8vo. For D.Browne, 1713. S

NORTH (ROGER)

The Gentleman Accomptant: or, an Essay to unfold the Mystery of Accompts. By way of Debtor and Creditor, . . . by a Person of honour.

8vo. 154 ll. For E.Curll, 1714. E.

—— second edition

12mo. 126 ll. For E.Curll, 1715. E.

—— third edition

12mo. 124 ll. For E.Curll, 1721. E

Ext: 1, 12, 44, 97, 103.
Ref: 8, 19.

WATTS (THOMAS)

An Essay on the Proper Method for Forming the Man of Business.

20 cm. 43 pp. George Strahan and others, 1716. S

KING (THOMAS)

A Exact guide to Book-keeping by way of debtor and creditor: done after the Italian Method . . .

4to. 88 ll. For S.Cruttenden (and others), 1717. E

DRUMMOND (JOHN)

The Accomptant's Pocket Companion: a Manual instructing merchants . . . : to which is added the method of catching and curing cod fish . . .

4to. Edinburgh. 1718. S

MACGHIE (ALEXANDER)

The Principles of Book-keeping explain'd . . .

4to. 88 ll. Edinburgh, James Watson, 1718. E

Ext: 42, 54, 74.

MALCOLM (ALEXANDER)

A New Treatise of arithmetick and book-keeping . . .

4to. 200 ll. Edinburgh, For J.P., 1718. E.

A Treatise of book-keeping, or, merchants accounts; in the Italian method of debtor and creditor.

4to. 136 ll. For J.Osborn and T.Longman, 1731. E.

—— second edition

8vo. 168 ll. Dan. Browne, 1743. E

Ext: 35, 36, 53, 58, 62, 71, 73, 77, 80, 86.
Ref: 19.

LUNDIN (ROBERT)
The Reason for accompting by Debtor and Creditor . . .
4to. Edinburgh, 1718
Ref: 19.

WEBSTER (WILLIAM)
An Essay on Book-keeping, according to the true Italian method of
debtor and creditor, by double entry . . .
12mo. 39 ll. H.Meere, 1719. E
—— second edition
12mo. 48 ll. H.Meere, 1721. E
—— third edition
12mo. 48 ll. For C.King, 1726. E
—— another edition
17 cm. 38 pp. A.Bettesworth and others, 1731. S
—— sixth edition
12mo. 48 ll. For A.Bettesworth & C.Hitch, 1738. E
—— seventh edition
12mo. 48 ll. For D.Brown, 1740. E
—— eighth edition
12mo. 48 ll. For D.Browne, 1744. E
—— ninth edition: by Ellis Webster.
12mo. 48 ll. For D.Browne, 1747. E
—— tenth edition: by Ellis Webster.
12mo. 48 ll. For D.Browne, 1749. E
—— twelfth edition: by Ellis Webster.
12mo. 48 ll. For D.Browne, 1755. E
—— fourteenth edition: by Ellis Webster.
12mo. 48 ll. For H.Woodfall, etc., 1765. E
—— fifteenth edition: by Ellis Webster.
12mo. 48 ll. For J.Rivington and others, 1772. E
—— revised edition: by S.Thomas.
12mo. 52 ll. Newcastle. For T.Slack, 1779. E
Essays on Book-keeping . . . to which is added . . . a variety of
specimens in company accounts . . .
12mo. 116 ll. Glasgow. For John Orr, 1758. E
Short Notes on Mr. Webster's set of books annexed to the compleat
compting-house . . .
12mo. 16 ll. Dublin. S.Powell, 1747. E
Ref: 19.

BRODIE (ALEXANDER)
A New and Easy Method of Book-keeping . . . by way of Debtor
and Creditor . . .
Fo. 1722. S
Ref: 19.

DEFOE (DANIEL)
The Mercantile Library or, complete English tradesman . . .
containing (Supplement . . . Ch. 3 . . . of bookkeeping).
For Charles Rivington, 1726. S

—— second edition
> 8vo. For Charles Rivington, 1727. S

—— another edition
> 12mo. 189 ll. Dublin. For A.Kelburn, 1766. E

—— another edition: 2 vols.
> Oxford. D.A.Talboys, 1841. S

Ref: 19.

LAURENCE (E.)

The Duty of a steward to his lord . . . to which is added . . . (a plain and easy method to be practised . . . in keeping his accompts . . .).
> 4to. 212 pp. For John Shuckburgh, 1727. E

The Duty and Office of a Land Steward . . .: second edition.
> 8vo. 296 pp. For J. & J.Knapton, 1731. E

ANONYMOUS

Advice to a young student. with a method of study for the four first years.
> 8vo. 32 pp. John Crownfield, 1730. E

F. (W.)

A Short Treatise of Book-keeping: second edition.
> 12mo. 1730

HAYES (RICHARD)

The Ship and Supercargo Book-keeper . . .
> 20 cm. 72 ll. J.Brotherton and W.Meadows, 1731. S

Modern Book-keeping: or, the Italian method improved . . .
> 8vo. 95 pp. John Noon, 1739. E

The Gentleman's Complete Book-keeper . . .
> 8vo. 268 pp. J.Noon, 1741. E

Ext: 31, 46, 69, 70, 92, 100.
Ref: 22.

CLARK (JOHN)

Lectures on Accompts, or book-keeping; after the Italian manner . . .
> 1732

—— second edition
> 4to. 28 pp. For J.Brotherton, 1738. E

STEVENSON (WILLIAM)

A General Discourse shewing the usefulness of the Italian method of Book-keeping . . .
> 8vo. Edinburgh. 1732

An Advice to Tradesmen to learn book-keeping . . .
> 8vo. Edinburgh. 1756

A Serious advice to tradesmen shewing them the inconveniences they lye under . . . by not learning book-keeping . . .
> 12mo. Edinburgh. R.Fleming, 1756. S

Book-keeping by Double Entry . . .
> Fo. Edinburgh. R.Stirling, 1762. S

Ref: 19.

FORD (J.)
> A serious Address to men in business, . . . with advice in the case
> of those who have unhappily mismanaged: . . .
>> 12mo. 22 ll. For R.Ford, 1733. E

HAMILTON (W.)
> Book-keeping new modelled: or, a Treatise of merchants accounts
> . . .
>> 4to. 90 ll. Edinburgh. R.Fleming, 1735. E
>
> Ref: 19.

STEPHENS (HUSTCRAFT)
> Italian Book-keeping, reduced into an art . . .
>> 4to. 161 ll. W.Mears, 1735. E
>
> —— another edition
>> 8vo. 160 ll. Dublin. G.Grierson, 1737. E
>
> —— second edition: by James Weir.
>> 4to. 167 ll. For J.Hodges, (c. 1740). E
>
> —— another edition
>> 8vo. 160 ll. Dublin. For P.Wilson, etc., 1754. E
>
> Ext: 32, 82, 109.
> Ref: 11, 19.

FISHER (GEORGE)
> The Instructor: or, young man's best companion. Containing . . .
> merchants accompts, and a short and easy method of shop and
> book-keeping . . .
>> 15 cm. 244 pp. Dublin. James Hoey, 1736. S
>
> —— tenth edition
>> 12mo. 199 ll. For C.Hitch, 1750. E
>
> —— another edition
>> 17 cm. 384 pp. Edinburgh. Gavin Alston, 1772. S
>
> —— twenty-third edition
>> 12mo. 210 ll. For W.Strahan and others, 1779. E
>
> —— thirtieth edition
>> 12mo. 169 ll. For F. & C.Rivington, 1810. E.S.
>
> —— another edition
>> 12mo. 144 ll. J.Bailey, 1813. E

MAIR (JOHN)
> Book-keeping Methodiz'd: or, a methodical treatise of
> Merchant-Accompts, according to the Italian Form, . . .
>> 8vo. 132 ll. Edinburgh. T. & W.Ruddimans, 1736. E
>
> —— another edition
>> 8vo. 132 ll. Dublin. Mary Fuller, 1737. E
>
> —— second edition
>> 8vo. 133 ll. Edinburgh. W.Sands, 1741. E
>
> —— another edition
>> 8vo. 132 ll. Dublin. I.Jackson, 1748. E
>
> —— third edition
>> 8vo. 152 ll. Edinburgh. W.Sands and others, 1749. E

—— another edition

        8vo. 148 ll. Dublin. I.Jackson, 1750. E
—— fourth edition

        8vo. 152 ll. Edinburgh. W.Sands and others, 1752. E.
—— fifth edition

        8vo. 148 ll. Dublin. I.Jackson, 1754. E
—— another fifth edition

        8vo. 216 ll. Edinburgh. Sands and others, 1757. E
—— sixth edition

        8vo. 216 ll. Edinburgh. Sands and others, 1760. E
—— seventh edition

        8vo. 216 ll. Edinburgh. W.Sands and others, 1763. E
—— another edition

        8vo. 139 ll. Dublin. I.Jackson, 1764. E
—— eighth edition

        8vo. 216 ll. Edinburgh. W.Sands and others, 1765. E.S
—— another eighth edition

        8vo. 201 ll. Dublin. H.Saunders, 1767. E
Book-keeping moderniz'd: or, Merchant-accounts by double entry,
according to the Italian form . . .

        8vo. 317 ll. Edinburgh. A.Kincaid and others, 1773. E
—— second edition

        8vo. 316 ll. Edinburgh. J.Bell and W.Creech, 1778. E.S
—— third edition

        8vo. 316 ll. Edinburgh. J.Bell and W.Creech, 1784. E
—— fifth edition

        8vo. 316 ll. Edinburgh. For Bell & Bradfute and W.Creech, 1789. E
—— sixth edition

        8vo. 316 ll. Edinburgh. Bell & Bradfute and W.Creech, 1793. E
—— seventh edition

        8vo. 316 ll. Edinburgh. Bell & Bradfute and W.Creech, 1797. E
—— eighth edition

        8vo. 316 ll. Edinburgh. Bell & Bradfute and W.Creech, 1800. E.S
—— ninth edition

        8vo. 318 ll. Edinburgh. Bell & Bradfute and W.Creech, 1807. E.S
Ext: 22, 52, 84, 87, 93.
Ref: 19, 22.

MARKHAM (W.)

A General Introduction to Trade and Business: or, the young
merchant's and tradesman's Magazine . . . IX. Merchant's
Accompts . . . second edition.

        12mo. 192 ll. For A.Bettesworth and C.Hitch, 1739. E

ANONYMOUS

A Present for an Apprentice: or, a Sure Guide to gain both esteem
and an estate . . . : second edition.

        8vo. 76 pp. For T.Cooper, 1740. E

ANONYMOUS

The Gentleman's and Lady's Accomptant: or, an essay toward rendering the most approved method of keeping accompts very plain, pleasing, and useful to the nobility and gentry . . .

25 cm. 45 ll. For the author, 1744. E

ANONYMOUS

The Universal Library of trade and commerce . . . containing . . . a series of merchants accounts . . .

4to. 134 ll. For J.Robinson, 1747. E

LONDON (JOHN)

A Compleat system of Book-keeping after the Italian method . . .

22 cm. 110 ll. For the author, 1748

—— another edition

1752. E

An Abridgement of Mr. London's Complete System of Book-keeping.

25 cm. 42 pp. 1757. S

CROSBY (THOMAS)

Book-keeping after the modern way of debtor and creditor.

1749

DODSON (JAMES)

The Accountant, or, the method of Book-keeping, deduced from clear principles . . .

4to. 118 ll. For J.Nourse, 1750. E.S.

Ext: 24, 57.
Ref: 8.

CLARE (M.)

Youth's Introduction to trade and business . . . seventh edition.

8vo. 94 ll. For S.Birt and others, 1751. E.S.

—— to which is added:
A Short and familiar sketch of Book-keeping per double entry, in the Italian manner.

8vo. 19 ll. For S.Birt and others, 1751. E.S.

—— eighth edition: to which is added by way of appendix a short sketch of book-keeping by double-entry, in the Italian manner.

8vo. 104 ll. For J.Fuller and others, 1758. E

POSTLETHWAYT (MALACHY)

The Universal Dictionary of Trade and Commerce translated from the French of the Celebrated Monsieur Savary . . . 2 vols.

41 cm. 1017 pp. For John & Paul Knapton, 1751. E.S.

—— second edition. 2 vols.

41 cm. 856 pp. For John Knapton, 1757. E.S.

WESTON (WILLIAM)

The Complete Merchant's Clerk: or, British and American compting-house . . .

8vo. 162 ll. Charles Rivington, 1754. E

SHEPHERD (R.)

. . . Book-keeping.
[*Title-page incomplete*]

20 cm. 76 ll. Preston. 1755. S

WISE (THOMAS)

Arithmetic made easy . . . to which is added A Short and Easy Method of Book-keeping after the Italian Method . . . second edition.

17 cm. 152 pp. Berwick. R.Taylor, 1755. S

ANONYMOUS

The Tradesman's Director . . . shewing a most easy and useful method of keeping books of accompts . . .

12mo. 91 ll. For W.Owen, 1756. E

DONN (BENJAMIN)

The Accountant: containing essays on book-keeping . . .

1758

—— second edition

8vo. 114 ll. For J.Johnson, 1775. E

—— another second edition

8vo. 114 ll. For J.Johnson, 1778. E

—— another edition

8vo. For J.Johnson, 1788

The Accountant and Geometrician: containing the doctrine of circulating decimals, logarithms, book-keeping . . .

8vo. 202 ll. For J.Johnson, 1765. E

The Young Shopkeeper's, Steward's, and Factor's, Companion . . . Second edition.

8vo. 63 pp. J.Johnson, 1773. E

Ext: 48, 55.

MORRIS (CORBYN)

A Plan for arranging the Accounts of a Landed Estate.

Fo. 1759

DUNN (J.)

The New method of book-keeping, showing how merchants may keep their books . . .

1760

ROOSE (RICHARD)

An Essay to make a compleat accomptant . . .

8vo. 110 ll. For Hannah Roose, (1760). E.S

Ext: 25, 34.

COOKE (JOHN)

The Compting-House Assistant; or, book-keeping made easy . . .

17 cm. 108 ll. For S.Hooper, 1761. S

—— second edition

12mo. 110 ll. For J.Nourse and S.Hooper, 1764. E

Practical book-keeping, or the merchant & tradesmans Assistant being a compleat treatise on Merchants Accompts . . .

12mo. 120 ll. S.Hooper, 1788. E

ANONYMOUS

The Compleat compting-house Companion: or, young merchant and tradesman's Sure Guide . . .

8vo. 324 ll. For William Johnston, 1763. E

CHAPMAN (THOMAS)

The Merchant's and Tradesman's universal Director and Assistant: being a new and accurate system of merchants accompts . . .

8vo. 96 ll. Thomas Bailey, 1764. E

Chapman's Introduction to Business . . . containing . . . sketch of Book-keeping.

12mo. 68 ll. J.Dixwell, (1774). E.S.

EVERARD (W.)

Mercantile Book-keeping; or A Treatise on merchants' accounts . . .

20 cm. 371 pp. 1764. S

HARRIS (JOHN)

A Complete system of Book-keeping . . .

8vo. Isaac Jackson, 1764

DOWLING (DANIEL)

A Complete system of Italian Book-keeping, according to the Modern Method, practised by Merchants and others.

8vo. 124 ll. Dublin. For John Mitchell, 1765. E

—— second edition

8vo. 124 ll. Dublin. For James Williams, 1770. E

—— third edition

8vo. Dublin. For the United Company of Booksellers, 1775. E

Ext: 39, 47, 85, 89.
Ref: 19.

FENNING (DANIEL)

The Schoolmaster's most useful Companion . . . a short and simple sketch of book-keeping.

1765

—— third edition

8vo. 1775

The Youth's guide to trade . . .

1772

The British youth's Instructor: . . . to which is added, a compendious method of book-keeping. Thirteenth edition: by Thomas Smith.

17 cm. 150 ll. For J.Johnson and others, 1806. E

Ref: 19.

GORDON (WILLIAM)

    The Universal Accountant and Complete Merchant . . . Second edition. 2 vols.

        8vo. 240: 237 ll. Edinburgh. For A.Donaldson and J.Reid, 1765. E
  —— third edition: 2 vols.

        Edinburgh. For Alexander Donaldson, 1770. S
  —— fourth edition: 2 vols.

        8vo. 238: 237 ll. Edinburgh. For A.Donaldson, 1777. E
  —— fifth edition: 2 vols.

        8vo. 556: 489 pp. Edinburgh. For A. & J.Donaldson, 1787
    The General Counting-House, and Man of Business . . .

        20 cm. 487 pp. Edinburgh. For A.Donaldson, 1766. S
  —— second edition

        8vo. 250 ll. Edinburgh. A.Donaldson and S.Crowder, 1770. E
    Ext: 4, 17, 21, 63, 79, 88, 101.
    Ref: 19.

WOOLGAR (WILLIAM)

    Youth's faithful Monitor . . .

        17 cm. 372 pp. D.Steel and others, 1766. S

ANONYMOUS

    Lecture upon partnership accounts, foreign and domestic, by a merchant. Second edition.

        1768

SQUIRE (WILLIAM)

    The Modern Book-keeper; or, Book-keeping made perfectly easy . . .
        17 cm. 63 ll. For J.Cooke, 1769. E

SEALLY (J.)

    The Accountant's Companion; or, schoolmaster's new assistant . . . to which is added, a course of book-keeping by single entry . . .

        17 cm. 152 pp. J.Rosen, 1770. S
  —— another edition

        12mo. 192 pp. For William Goldsmith, 1773. E

FITZGERALD (E.)

    An Epitome of the elements of Italian Book-keeping . . .
        Whitehaven. A.Foster, 1771. E

HUTTON (CHARLES)

    The School-master's Guide: or, a complete system of practical arithmetic and Book-keeping . . . Third edition.

        17 cm. 228 pp. T.Saint, 1771. E
    A Complete Treatise on Practical Arithmetic and Book-keeping . . . Seventh edition.

        19 cm. 240 pp. For C.G.J. & J.Robinson, 1785. E
  —— ninth edition

        17 cm. 236 pp. For C.G.J. & J.Robinson, 1792. E
  —— another edition

        1796. S

—— eleventh edition
> 17 cm. 236 pp. For C.G. & J.Robinson, 1801. E

—— new edition by A.Ingram.
> 18 cm. 259 pp. Edinburgh. G. & J.Ross, 1804. E

—— new edition by A.Ingram.
> 17 cm. 259 pp. Edinburgh. G. & J.Ross, 1805. E

—— twelfth edition
> 17 cm. 236 pp. For J.Johnson and others, 1806. E

—— another edition by A.Ingram.
> 17 cm. 259 pp. Hawick. R.Armstrong, 1811. E

—— new edition by J.Trotter.
> 17 cm. 60 ll. Edinburgh. Oliver and Boyd, 1840. E

—— another edition
> 17 cm. 60 ll. Edinburgh. Oliver and Boyd, 1856. E

—— another edition
> 17 cm. 252 pp. Edinburgh. Oliver and Boyd, 1858. E

—— another edition
> 17 cm. 60 ll. Edinburgh. Oliver and Boyd, 1863. E

—— another edition
> 17 cm. 60 ll. Edinburgh. Oliver and Boyd, (1871). E

A Complete course of book-keeping both by single and double entry.
> Dumfries. James Thorburn Creighton, 1838. S

Ref: 19.

JACKSON (W.)

Book-keeping in the True Italian Form . . .
[Title-page missing]
> 20 cm. 296 pp. (c. 1771). E

—— another edition . . . (from D.Dowling) . . .
> 21 cm. 296 pp. Dublin. R.Jackson, 1785. E

—— another edition
> 21 cm. 296 pp. Dublin. R.Jackson, 1792. E

KELLY (WILLIAM)

The Merchant's Companion; being a complete system of book-keeping . . .
> 20 cm. 183 ll. Cork. P.Donnoghue, 1774. E

PERRY (WILLIAM)

The Man of Business, and gentleman's assistant: . . . containing . . . book-keeping by single and double entry . . .
> 8vo. 152 ll. Edinburgh. David Willison, 1774. E

—— third edition
> 8vo. 214 ll. Edinburgh. For the Author, 1777. E

ANONYMOUS

An Easy introduction to Book-keeping . . . particularly calculated for the improvement of young accountants.
> 8vo. 38 ll. For F.Newbery, 1776. E

QUIN (MATTHEW)

Quin's rudiments of book-keeping . . .

12mo. 62 ll. J.Bew, 1776. E.S

—— third edition

12mo. 84 ll. J.Bew, 1779. E

Ext: 5.
Ref: 19.

ROSE (JOHN)

The Transactions of the British Farmer Accomptant . . .

Fo. 1776

DILWORTH (THOMAS)

The Young Book-keeper's Assistant: shewing . . . the Italian way of stating debtor and creditor . . . seventh edition.

20 cm. 82 ll. Richard and Henry Causton, 1777. E

—— eighth edition

21 cm. 82 ll. R. & H.Causton, 1781. E

—— ninth edition

21 cm. 82 ll. R. & H.Causton, 1784. E

—— eleventh edition

20 cm. 81 ll. R. & H.Causton, 1790. E

—— twelfth edition

21 cm. 82 ll. R. & H.Causton, 1793. E

—— thirteenth edition

20 cm. 82 ll. R. & H.Causton, 1798. E

—— sixteenth edition

20 cm. 82 ll. T.Wilson and R.Spence, 1800. E

—— another edition

20 cm. 80 ll. Henry Mozley, 1801. S

—— another edition

21 cm. 81 ll. T.Wilson and Son, 1810. E

—— another edition

21 cm. 81 ll. T.Wilson and Sons, 1815. E

—— another edition

21 cm. 82 ll. York. T.Wilson & Sons, 1828. E

—— another edition

17 cm. 84 ll. Thomas Allman, 1853. E

—— another edition

17 cm. 84 ll. Thomas Allman and Son, 1856. E

—— another edition

18 cm. 84 ll. T.J.Allman, 1870. E

SCRUTON (JAMES)

Practical Counting-House; or, Calculation and Accountantship illustrated.

8vo. Glasgow. For James Duncan, 1777. S

Ref: 19.

SEDGER (JOHN)

Sedger's Rudiments of Book-keeping . . .

17 cm. 37 ll. Fielding & Walker, 1777. S

—— another edition
> 21 cm. 55 ll. For Fielding & Walker, 1779. E

An Introduction to Merchants' Accounts . . .
> 17 cm. 89 ll. For the author, 1807. E

THOMPSON (WARDHAUGH)

The Accomptant's Oracle . . . Vol. 1: common arithmetic . . . Vol. 11: . . . practical system of Book-keeping . . .
> 8vo. 184: 142 ll. York. N.Nickson, 1777. E

Ext: 108.
Ref: 8.

WOOD (WILLIAM)

Book-keeping familiarised: or, the young clerk's, manufacturer's and shop-keeper's Directory.
> 8vo. 140 ll. Birmingham. Pearson and Rollason, (c. 1778). E

THOMAS (S.)

The Economist: or, housekeeper's accompts made easy, after the Italian method . . .
> (Newcastle. T.Slack, 1779). E

EDWARDS (SAMUEL)

A Complete system of book-keeping according to the modern method practised by merchants . . .
> Dublin. 1781

DICKINSON (ROBERT)

Universal Mercantile Tables . . . to which is added, a Treatise on Book-keeping . . .
> 4to. 94 ll. Dublin. D.Graisberry, 1783. E

TAYLOR (WILLIAM)

A Complete system of Practical Arithmetic with . . . book-keeping, by Single and Double Entry . . .
> 8vo. 304 ll. Birmingham. For the author, 1783. E

—— second edition
> Birmingham. 1800. E

HAMILTON (ROBERT)

An Introduction to Merchandise containing . . . book-keeping in various forms. Second edition.
> 8vo. 276 ll. Edinburgh. For C.Elliot, 1788. E.S.

—— third edition
> 8vo. 280 ll. Edinburgh. For Tho. Kay, 1797. E

—— fourth edition
> 8vo. 298 ll. Edinburgh. J.Hunter, 1799. E

—— fifth edition
> 21 cm. 290 ll. Edinburgh. Murray & Cochrane, 1802. S

A Short system of arithmetic and book-keeping . . . Fifth edition.
> 18 cm. 143 ll. Edinburgh. J.Fairbairn and others, 1802. E

An Introduction to merchandize: containing . . . book-keeping . . . by Elias Johnston.

22 cm. 563 pp. Edinburgh. Archibald Constable & Co. and others, 1820. E.S
Ext: 10, 11, 61, 75, 81, 90, 95, 101, 105, 107.
Ref: 8, 11, 19.

Booth (Benjamin)

A Complete system of Book-keeping, by an improved mode of double-entry . . .

4to. 248 pp. Couchman & Fry, 1789. E.S
Ext: 59.
Ref: 22.

Young (David)

The Farmer's Account-Book . . .

Edinburgh. (c. 1790)

Hudson (Peter)

A New Introduction to Trade and Business. . . . Seventh edition.

17 cm. 116 pp. J.Johnson, 1791. S

Anonymous

The Ship-Master's Assistant and Owner's Manual: containing . . . disbursements and other ship-accounts . . . fourth edition.

8vo. 224 ll. For David Steel, 1792. E

Reina (P.A.)

A Remarkable and important commercial . . . rule in balancing partnership effects . . .

Fo. 1794

Shaw (John)

Book-keeping epitomized: or, a compendium of Mair's methodical treatise of merchants-accompts . . .

12mo. 66 ll. Leeds. For J.Binns, 1794. E

Jones (Edward Thomas)

An Address to bankers, merchants, tradesmen, &c. intended as an introduction to a new system of Book-keeping . . .

21 cm. 12 ll. Bristol. R.Edwards, 1795. E

Jones's English System of Book-keeping, by single or double entry . . .

27 cm. 38 ll. Bristol. R.Edwards, 1796. E.S

—— second edition

27 cm. 37 ll. Bristol. R.Edwards, 1796. E

—— second American edition

25 cm. 28 ll. New York. G.Forman, 1797. E

A Defence of the English System of Book-keeping . . .

Bristol. 1797. E

The Science of Book-Keeping, exemplified in Jones's English Systems [1] . . .

    31 cm. 129 ll. T.C.Hansard, 1831. E

—— second edition

    32 cm. 129 ll. T.C.Hansard, 1831. E

—— fourth edition

    31 cm. 130 ll. T.C.Hansard, 1834. E

—— fifth edition, Part I

    28 cm. 50 ll. W.Tyler, 1837. E

—— sixth edition: ed. by his sons.

    25 cm. 107 ll. W.Tyler, 1839. E

—— seventh edition, Part II

    25 cm. 55 ll. W.Tyler, 1840. E

—— ninth edition: ed. by the author's son.

    25 cm. 106 ll. James Nichols, 1847. E

—— eleventh edition: ed. by Theodore Jones.

    27 cm. 109 ll. Theodore Jones & Co. and others, [c. 1857]. E

—— fifteenth edition: ed. by Theodore Jones.

    26 cm. 100 ll. Theodore Jones & Co. and others, [c. 1867]. E

—— sixteenth edition: ed. by Theodore Jones.

    25 cm. 101 ll. Theodore Jones & Co. and others, [c. 1877]. E

—— twenty-first edition: ed. by Theodore Jones.

    25 cm. 100 ll. Wertheimer, Lea & Co. and others, [c. 1880]. E

Jones's English system of bookkeeping for schools.

    18 cm. 79 pp. [? 1882]. E

Jones's English system of book-keeping for the million . . . second edition.

    18 cm. 80 + xxiv pp. [? 1882]

  Ext: 9, 96, 104.
  Ref: 2, 18, 22, 23, 24.

ANONYMOUS

A Letter to Mr. T. Edward Jones . . . , by a Merchant.

                1796

COLLIER (JOSEPH)

A defence of double entry, with a new arrangement of the Journal and objections to Jones' English system.

                1796

GOSNELL (THOMAS KNOLLES)

An elucidation of the Italian method of book-keeping, with free observations on Jones' English system.

                1796

---

[1] In the fifteenth and later editions the title appears as " Jones's English systems of Book-keeping . . .".

MATTHEWS (JOHN)

 A New and perfect model of a set of books for the shopkeeper or retail trader.

           Bristol. 1796

MILL (JAMES)

 An examination of Jones' English system of book-keeping.

              1796

MITCHELL (WILLIAM)

 A New and complete system of Book-keeping, by . . . Double Entry . . .

   21 cm. 454 pp. Philadelphia. Bioren & Madam, 1796. E

WICKS (J.H.)

 Book-keeping Reformed or the method by double-entry so simplified, elucidated and improved, as to render the practice easy, expeditious and accurate.

       4to. 80 ll. Egham. C.Boult, 1797. E

BUCHANAN (COLIN)

 The Writing-master and accountant's assistant . . .

      27 cm. 60 ll. Glasgow. R.Chapman, 1798. S

 Practical book-keeping . . .

      21 cm. 210 pp. Edinburgh. 1806. S

LIDDEL (R.)

 The Seaman's New Vade Mecum; containing a practical essay on Naval Book-keeping . . . third edition.

    21 cm. 354 pp. G.G. & J.Robinson, 1798. S

 —— fourth edition

    21 cm. 236 ll. G.G. & J.Robinson, 1803. E

SHIRES (JOHN)

 An Improved Method of Book-keeping . . .

    28 cm. 42 ll. W. & C.Spilsbury, 1799. E

FULTON (J.W.)

 British-Indian Book-keeping. A new system of Double Entry.

          Bengal. 1799. E

 —— another edition

    23 cm. 152 pp. G.Auld, 1800. E.S.

  Ext: 8, 110.
  Ref: 11, 24.

References

BESTA, F.   [1] *La Ragioneria*, vol. III, Milan, 1932 (2nd edition).

BROWN, R.   [2] *A History of Accounting and Accountants*, Edinburgh, 1905.

COOMBER, R.R.   [3] "Hugh Oldcastle and John Mellis", in Littleton, A.C. and Yamey, B.S. (eds.), *Studies in the History of Accounting*, London, 1956, pp. 206–14.

DE ROOVER, R.   [4] *Jan Ympyn*, Antwerp, 1928.
     [5] "Een en ander over Jan Ympyn Christoffels", *Tijdschrift voor Geschiedenis*, vol. LII, 1937, pp. 163–79; summarised in *The Accountant*, vol. XCVII, 1937, pp. 657–8.

DE WAAL, P.G.A.   [6] *De Leer van het Boekhouden in de Nederlanden tijdens de zestiende eeuwe*, Roermond, 1927.

     [7] "De Engelsche vertaling van Jan Impyn's Nieuwe Instructie", *Economisch-Historisch Jaarboek*, vol. XVIII, 1934, pp. 1–58.

EDWARDS, R.S.   [8] "Some Notes on the Early Literature and Development of Cost Accounting in Great Britain", *The Accountant*, vol. XLVII, 1937, pp. 193–5, 225–31, 253–5, 283–7, 313–6, 343–4.

GEIJSBEEK, J.B.   [9] *Ancient Double-Entry Bookkeeping*, Denver, 1914.

GORDON, C.   [10] "The First English Books on Book-keeping", in Littleton and Yamey, *op. cit.*, pp. 202–5.

JACKSON, J.G.C.   [11] "The History of Methods of Exposition of Double-Entry Book-keeping in England", in Littleton and Yamey, *op. cit.*, pp. 288–312.

KATS, P.   [12] "De Invloed der Nederlanders de 16e en 17e eeuw op de Engelsche literatuur van het Boekhouden", *Maandblad voor het Boekhouden*, vol. 32, 1925, pp. 168–75.

     [13] "Hugh Oldcastle and John Mellis", *The Accountant*, vol. LXXIV, 1926, pp. 483, 641.

     [14] "The 'Nouvelle Instruction' of Jehan Ympyn Christophle", *The Accountant*, vol. LXXVII, 1927, pp. 261–9, 287–96.

     [15] "James Peele's 'Maner and Fourme'", *The Accountant*, vol. LXXXII, 1930, pp. 41–4, 88–91, 119–22.

225

KHEIL, K.P.   [16]   *Über einige Bearbeitungen des Buchhaltungs Tractates von Luca Pacioli*, Prague, 1896.

McGRATH, P.   [17]   *The Marchants Avizo*, Soldiers Field, Boston, 1957.

MELIS, F.   [18]   *Storia della Ragioneria*, Bologna, 1950.

MURRAY, D.   [19]   *Chapters in the History of Bookkeeping, Accountancy and Commercial Arithmetic*, Glasgow, 1930.

STEVELINCK, E., and HAULOTTE, R.   [20]   " Galerie des Grands Auteurs Comptables "— a series of articles in *Documentation Commerciale & Comptable*, 1956–59.

SUTHERLAND, P. [GORDON, C. and COOMBER, R.R.]   [21]   " Hugh Oldcastle and the ' Profitable Treatyce ' of 1543 ", *The Accountant*, vol. CII, 1940, pp. 334–6.

WOOLF, A.H.   [22]   *A Short History of Accountants and Accountancy*, London, 1912.

YAMEY, B.S.   [23]   " Edward Jones's ' English System of Bookkeeping ' ", *Accounting Review*, vol. XIX, 1944, pp. 407–16.

[24]   " Edward Jones and the Reform of Book-Keeping, 1795–1810 ", in Littleton and Yamey, *op. cit.*, pp. 313–24.

[25]   " Handson's ' Analysis of Merchants Accounts '," *Accounting Research*, vol. 8, 1957, pp. 299–304, and vol. 9, 1958, pp. 61–2.

[26]   " Carpenter's ' Most Excellent Instruction ' ", *The Accountant*, vol. CXXXVII, 1957, pp. 683–4.

[27]   " Weddington's ' Breffe Instruction ' ", *Accounting Research*, vol. 9, 1958, pp. 124–33.

[28]   " Stephen Monteage, A Seventeenth Century Accountant," *Accountancy*, November 1959, pp. 594–5.

INDEX

Index

Manzoni, D., 162, 164
Marius, J., *205*
Markham, W., *214*
Mather, W., *208*
Matthews, J., *223*
Mellis, J., 26–27, 50–51, 67–68, 76–77, 155–159, 168, *203*
Mennher, V., 163, 164–165
Mill, J., *223*
Mitchell, W., 177, *224*
Monteage, S., 12–15, 173, *206*
Morris, C., *216*

Nicholas, A., *210*
North, R., 5–6, 19, 56, 124–125, 131, 174, *210*

Oldcastle, H., 51, 155–159, *202*

P., W., 166, *203*
Pacioli, L., 155–159, 160, 161, 162, 165
Peele, J., 19–20, 20–22, 29–31, 35, 37, 40, 51–52, 54, 55, 56–57, 108, 156, 161, 162–166, 168, 170, 184, 192, 201, *203*
Perry, W., *219*
Pietersz, C. (Petri, N.), 166, 170, *203*
Porte, de la, 174
Postlethwayt, M., 169, *215*

Quin, M., 11, *220*

Reina, P. A., *222*
Richards, T., *209*
Roose, R., 34, 45–46, *216*
Rose, J., *220*

Scruton, J., *220*

Seally, J., *218*
Sedger, J., *220*
Shaw, J., *222*
Shepherd, R., *216*
Shires, J., *224*
Snell, C., *209*
Squire, W., *218*
Stephens, H., 43–44, 106–107, 135–142, 178, *213*
Stevenson, W., *212*
Stevin, S., 72, 170

Tagliente, G. A., 160
Tap, J., 166, *203*
Taylor, W., *221*
Thomas, S., *221*
Thompson, W., 134–135, 171, *221*

Vernon, J., 79, *206*

Waninghen, H., 38, 167–168, 170
Watts, T., *210*
Webster, W., 46, 173, *211*
Weddington, J., 24–25, 27–29, 36–37, 48–49, 97–98, 114–115, 156, 162–165, 174, 184, 192, *203*
Weir, J., *208*
Weston, W., *215*
Wicks, J. H., *224*
Willemsz, J., 170
Willsford, T., *205*
Wise, T., *216*
Wood, W., *221*
Woolgar, W., *218*

Ympyn, J., 6–7, 22–24, 44–45, 126, 127–128, 156, 159–162, 163, *202*
Young, D., *222*